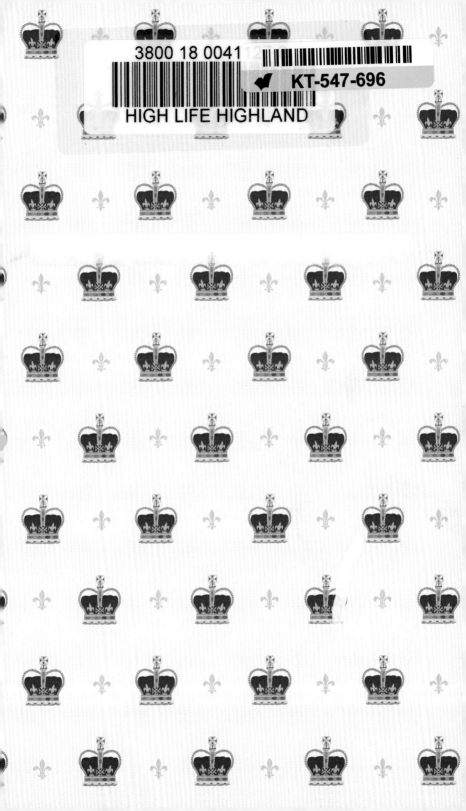

3800 18 0041

KT-547-696

HIGH LIFE HIGHLAND

BOGNOR
and other
REGISES

Published by AA Publishing, a trading name of AA Media Limited,
Fanum House, Basing View, Basingstoke, Hampshire, RG21 4EA, UK.

theAA.com

First published in 2018

Text © Caroline Taggart 2018
The right of Caroline Taggart to be identified as author of this work has
been asserted by her in accordance with the Copyright, Designs and
Patents Act 1988.

A CIP catalogue record for this book is available from the British Library.

ISBN: 978-0-7495-7921-0

All rights reserved. This publication or any part of it may not be copied
or reproduced by any means without the prior permission of the publisher.
All inquiries should be directed to the publisher.

Editor: Donna Wood
Art Director: James Tims
Designer: Liz Baldin
Illustrations: David J Plant

Printed and bound by CPI Group (UK) Ltd, Croydon CR0 4YY

A05563

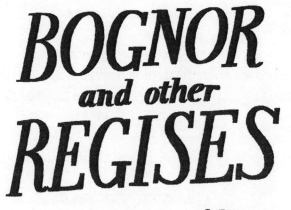

BOGNOR
and other
REGISES

A potted history of Britain in 100 royal places

HIGH LIFE HIGHLAND LIBRARIES	
38001800411278	
BERTRAMS	09/10/2018
941	£14.99
ANF	

Contents

Introduction

Most of us are fascinated by royalty, past and present. Whether glamorous or sordid, merrie or morose, our monarchs and their families have led lives very different from ours – and all too often they've held the Fate of the Nation in the palms of their hands. They've married for diplomatic reasons and created diplomatic incidents when they divorced. They've refused to marry and endangered the succession; they've borne a dozen children and still left no one to succeed them. They've got themselves excommunicated and created their own religions. They've waged war against their neighbours and their cousins; built frivolous summer palaces and formidable fortresses (and imprisoned their cousins in them). In so doing, they've left their mark all over Great Britain, in castles and churches, on battlefields and stained-glass windows. Their stories are written all across our landscape, if we know where to look for them.

So I went looking. From Tintagel in Cornwall, where King Arthur may or may not have been

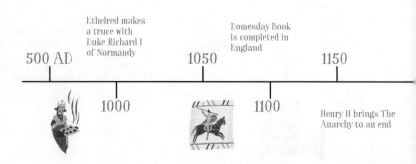

Ethelred makes
a truce with
Duke Richard I
of Normandy

Domesday Book
is completed in
England

500 AD

1050

1150

1000

1100

Henry II brings The
Anarchy to an end

conceived, to Birnam Wood, which may or may not have uprooted itself and come to Dunsinane to destroy Macbeth, I've sought out places that are associated with kings, queens, princes, princesses, dukes and duchesses. While legend and rumour abound (and Shakespeare has been guilty of the odd inaccuracy), there is, of course, lots that is factual: Caernarfon Castle, birthplace of the first English Prince of Wales; Leicester, where Richard III no longer lies beneath the car park; Kenilworth Castle, where 13th-century barons held out for six months in the longest siege in English history and Elizabeth I all but bankrupted the Earl of Leicester by bringing her vast entourage to stay for nearly three weeks. From Katherine Howard entertaining a lover in Pontefract Castle to Charles II trysting with Nell Gwynne in Newmarket and Winchester, there is plenty of food for gossip, too.

Selecting the places, now, that was another matter. The list of one hundred could easily have been twice that, and 'assigning' each one to a single royal personage involved some tricky decisions. The Tower of London – begun by William the Conqueror, expanded by Edward I and Henry III. Edward V possibly murdered there; Anne Boleyn, Katherine Howard and Lady Jane

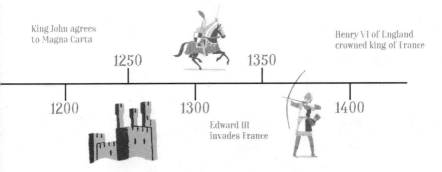

King John agrees
to Magna Carta

1250

Henry VI of England
crowned king of France

1200

1300

1350

Edward III
invades France

1400

Grey all certainly beheaded there. Hmm. I 'plumped' for Edward V, the Prince in the Tower whose life was (allegedly) so short he had little time to be associated with anywhere else. Windsor Castle and Hampton Court simply broke the rules I'd set myself by ending up with two entries each. As for the royals themselves, Queens Consort, Princes of Wales who never became king and powerful Regents who were king in all but name made their way in if they were important to the story, or if they were associated with a place (such as Castle Rising or Dunstanburgh Castle) that just begged to be included.

Some of the places I've included are more obscure or less obviously royal than the Tower of London and Hampton Court – Corpus Christi College Oxford, where much of the work was done on translating James I's 'Authorised Version' of the Bible; the statue of George I on St George's Church, Bloomsbury; the kitchens at Kew where they prepared George III's first decent meal for weeks after his initial bout of 'madness'. They're scattered all over the country: battlefields from Culloden in the Scottish Highlands to Battle on the Sussex coast; castles from Beaumaris on Anglesey to

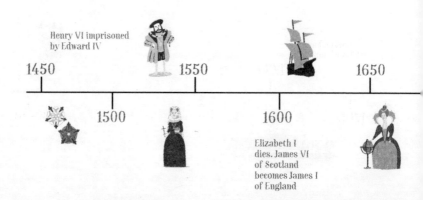

Henry VI imprisoned
by Edward IV

1450

1550

1500

1600

1650

Elizabeth I
dies. James VI
of Scotland
becomes James I
of England

Framlingham in Suffolk; cathedrals and abbeys from Canterbury to Dunfermline. And of course there's Bognor, of which George V famously said 'Bugger' – when the town petitioned him to grant it royal status, according to one version of the story. It all proves that you don't have to live in London or Edinburgh to have royal history at your fingertips and on your doorstep – and also that you don't have to believe all that you hear.

What I've tried to do with this book is tell a story, working through the history of our royals through the last 1,500 years or so and linking the people not only to the places but to each other. I've tried to unearth little-known facts and shed fresh light on famous ones. Most of all, I've tried to have fun, on the basis that if I think something is weird or wonderful, you might think so too. Because, with the greatest possible respect to our royals past and present, there are quite a few weird and wonderful people – and places – in our heritage, and it's easy to get out there and celebrate them. Just two things, though: if you plan to visit Culloden, take your warmest waterproof; and if you're going to Runnymede, wear your most mud-proof boots.

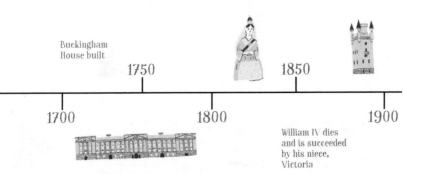

Buckingham House built

1750

1850

1700

1800

1900

William IV dies and is succeeded by his niece, Victoria

1066 AND BEFORE

1

TINTAGEL CASTLE
Arthur

'DRAMATIC' IS THE WORD for the location of Tintagel on the west Cornish coast. It's a hard-hearted visitor who will claim that King Arthur didn't exist, because as you stand among the ruins you feel that he darned well ought to have done and, if he did, he ought to have been born somewhere like this.

That said, you'd be forgiven for thinking this was a daft place to build a castle. Part on the mainland, part on a peninsula and part on the neck of land that linked the two, you might have guessed that centuries of landslips and erosion would result in great chunks of it falling into the sea. Which is exactly what has happened. Lovers of Arthurian legend will be pleased to know that the blame doesn't lie with their hero, though. The man responsible for the castle over whose ruins you clamber today was not Arthur, but Richard, the wealthy 13th-century Earl of Cornwall and brother of Henry III.

Underneath Richard's ruins are the remains of an extensive Dark Age settlement. Legend has it that Arthur lived in the late 5th and early 6th centuries; archaeology confirms that quite a lot of people were living in and near Tintagel at that time. The discovery of remnants of pottery, metalwork and glass shows that some of them were prosperous and were trading with cultures as far afield as Byzantium (modern Istanbul) and North Africa. Arthurians became very excited in 1998 when a piece of slate whose inscription included the name 'Artognou' was discovered, but calmer analysis points out that the resemblance between Artognou and Arthur is inconclusive and that the inscription looks more like graffiti than the sort of lettering that would be used to engrave a king's name.

Legend persists, however, and if the tides are kind a visit to Tintagel includes an exploration of Merlin's Cave. You approach it via a beach known as the Haven, which for centuries provided an excellent and safe harbour for (real) ships. The story goes that Arthur's father, Uther Pendragon, made himself unpopular with the local lords by using trickery to gain the favours of the Lady Ygraine; these same lords would have killed the infant Arthur rather than see his father's son inherit the throne. When Uther died on the day of Arthur's birth, the wizard Merlin took the baby into his care. At the risk of making another unromantic observation, I should mention that the name Merlin's Cave dates from only the late 19th century, and that Tennyson's epic

WHILE YOU'RE HERE
Spare a thought for the medieval castle, which served the aforementioned Richard of Cornwall as a source of revenue and status rather than a residence. For half a century after Richard's death it was neglected; then Edward III's son, the Black Prince, became the first Duke of Cornwall and set about having it put to rights. That didn't last long and we next hear of the castle being used to house state prisoners. Even that role was obsolete by the end of the 16th century and the castle was left to fall into ruins (and the sea), with only the Arthurian legend to save it from total oblivion.

poem *Idylls of the King*, which
relates the story of Merlin
plucking the baby from the
waves and crying out, 'The
King! Here is an heir for
Uther!', was published in…
the late 19th century.

In fact, even if you believe that
there was a Cornish king called Arthur around this time,
there is no contemporary evidence to connect him with
Tintagel: the first mentions come in the *History of the
Britons*, probably written by the Welsh monk Nennius
around 830 AD, and Arthur's legend really takes off after
the publication of Geoffrey of Monmouth's fanciful
History of the Kings of Britain in the 12th century.
Geoffrey is the source of many Arthurian legends, and
he was the first to link the King with what he describes
as the 'island fortress' of Tintagel. The Round Table is a
later invention and the stories have been expanded and
adapted by many subsequent writers, both historians and
poets. But there is something about Tintagel that makes
you want to believe at least some of them.

2

GLASTONBURY
Arthur

THERE WAS A CHURCH in Glastonbury at least as far
back as the 7th century, though the place had Christian
significance long before that. Joseph of Arimathea, a
disciple and possibly a relative of Christ's, is said to
have brought the Holy Grail (the cup used at the Last
Supper) to Glastonbury in the 1st century AD; in the
5th century, the belief that St Patrick died here was
sufficiently widespread for his shrine to become a place
of pilgrimage for the Irish faithful.

The church became an abbey around 700 AD and
by the time of the Domesday Book (1086) it was the
richest in the country. A suitable place for a powerful
Saxon king and his queen to be buried, you might
think. And so legend – there is no shortage of that in
Glastonbury – would have us believe. After a fire
destroyed most of the abbey in the 12th century, the
monks, possibly digging foundations for replacement
buildings, found two bodies in a deep grave. Alongside
them was a lead cross inscribed 'Here lies buried the
famous King Arthur with Guinevere his second wife in
the isle of Avalon.' Almost a hundred years later the
bodies were reburied in a black marble tomb inside the
church, in a grand ceremony graced by the presence of
Edward I. No one seems to know why it took them so

long, but holy relics were big business in the Middle Ages and Arthur and Guinevere, although they had no claims to sainthood, might well have been money-making attractions.

Geoffrey of Monmouth, whom we met in Tintagel (see previous entry), mentions the Isle of Avalon: he tells us that Arthur's sword – which he calls Caliburn but which became better known as Excalibur – was made there, and also that, when Arthur was mortally wounded in battle against his nephew Mordred, he was carried there to have his wounds treated. Geoffrey doesn't tell us in so many words that Arthur died at Avalon, but he does say that he gave up his throne to his kinsman Constantine, so we draw our own conclusions.

It was the discovery of the bones mentioned above that led people to connect Avalon with Glastonbury. Like Athelney (see page 23), Glastonbury sits on a highish spot in the low-lying Somerset Levels, an island of dryness in what was once surrounding marsh. The name Avalon means 'isle of apples', and even today Glastonbury is in cider-making country: another piece of evidence for anyone looking for it.

The abbey continued to thrive until the Dissolution of the Monasteries, when it was despoiled, flogged off and otherwise humiliated (in common with the other 850 monasteries that existed in England in the 1530s). So the black marble tomb is no more; Arthurian pilgrims today have to be content with ruins and a grave-like rectangle that is said to lie in the position of the tomb, beneath the (long vanished) high altar. But the ruins, particularly those of the Lady Chapel, are as romantic as anyone could wish for, and the energetic can either climb the famous Tor and admire the roofless St Michael's Tower, on the site of a church that was here in Arthur's time; or, at the other end of the town, trudge up the well-named Wearyall Hill, where a fatigued Joseph of Arimathea struck his staff into the ground and gave rise to the first Glastonbury Thorn.

Some of this may be true. Or none of it. You pays your money, as they say...

WHAT ABOUT CAMELOT?

We've looked at Arthur's birthplace and his burial place, but what about his life in between? Both Geoffrey of Monmouth and Chrétien de Troyes, the 12th-century French poet who is credited with inventing the character of Sir Lancelot, place Arthur's capital at Caerleon in South Wales, where an Iron Age fort known as Belinstocke may well have been a suitable stronghold for a Briton holding out against the invading Anglo-Saxons. Thomas Malory's 15th-century compilation of tales, *La Morte d'Arthur*, says that Arthur was crowned at Caerleon but places Camelot itself in Winchester Castle, where a replica of the Round Table has been displayed in the Great Hall since 1540. Other sources claim that Camelot was based at Cadbury Castle, which is rather closer to Glastonbury; archaeological excavation shows that Cadbury was massively refortified around 500 AD, the time when Arthur might have been at the height of his warlike powers. More choices to be made for those who care to make them.

3

OFFA'S DYKE
Offa of Mercia

WE DON'T KNOW A GREAT DEAL about Offa, except that he was King of Mercia at the end of the 8th century, and he almost certainly built the dyke along the border between England and Wales which bears his name. He was obviously a powerful ruler: the monk Asser, writing about a hundred years after Offa's death, describes him as 'vigorous'; his realm, at its peak, extended across all of England south of the Humber (there were other kingdoms, including Wessex, but they were at the time subservient to him). But Mercia's heartland was the Midlands: Offa's capital was at Tamworth and he had a cathedral at Lichfield. Here he created a short-lived archbishopric, much to the disgust of the Archbishop of Canterbury, who rightly saw it as an attempt to diminish his own power and status. But Offa's appointing of an archbishop is an early indication of the King getting involved with the Church – a theme that will crop up more than once in the course of this book.

Offa's Dyke is a massive earthwork-and-ditch frontier, built almost certainly for defensive reasons: the ditch is on the Welsh side, which would have made it more difficult for anyone coming from the west to storm it. Asser describes it as running 'from sea to sea' – an exaggeration, but building the dyke was nevertheless an extraordinary achievement that would have required hundreds if not thousands of men. The modern Offa's Dyke footpath is closer to Asser's description: it extends from the Severn Estuary in the south to Prestatyn on the North Wales coast, crossing the Black Hills and the Shropshire Hills en route. Both path and dyke run fairly close to the modern border, switching back and forth between England and Wales as they do so. The highlight of the walk is towards the southern end: the glorious view over Tintern Abbey from the Devil's Pulpit, so called because the devil apparently tried unsuccessfully to lure the Cistercian monks of the abbey into sin. The details, although doubtless lurid, have sadly been lost in the mists of time. Equally sadly, the abbey's only royal connection (before it was dissolved by order of Henry VIII) seems to be that Edward II stayed there for two nights in 1326.

Offa was a great trader. The penny coins he issued bear the inscription *Rex Anglorum* – 'King of the English' – and he's the first king for whom that title was more or less accurate. Enough of these coins have been found to indicate that they were in wide circulation: money rather than barter was becoming the order of the day. But the gold coin known as the Offa Dinar – in the collection of the British Museum but not currently on display – shows his broader ambitions. Although the words *Offa Rex* appear in the centre of the coin, the rest of the inscription is in Arabic and refers to Allah sending Mohammed out into the world to proclaim the true religion. There is no suggestion that Offa converted to Islam; rather that he copied the coinage of the empire

WHILE YOU'RE HERE

If you are walking along Offa's Dyke near Welshpool, you'll come upon a celebration of a more recent monarch. Beacon Ring, an Iron Age hill fort, contains a substantial copse of beech and conifers. It's a lot of trees for one hill fort, but this was a deliberate planting, in 1953, to commemorate the coronation of Elizabeth II. From the air, the monogram E II R is still visible, although the trees have matured and spread somewhat in the intervening years.

with which he wished to trade. Any trader of the period would have been happy to have a foot in the door of the vast Islamic Empire: it stretched all the way from Portugal to Pakistan and gave access to spices, silk and other exotic goods.

Tamworth Castle, by the way, looks like a lot of the other Norman castles scattered about the country, but it existed as a *burh* or fortified settlement in the 8th century and was a favoured royal residence: it is almost certainly where Offa chose to spend Christmas. After his time, Mercia's influence and extent declined and a hundred years later it was ruled by a mere lord, who paid homage to Alfred the Great. Today, the royal who is commemorated here is Athelflaed, Alfred's daughter, who was married to the then Lord of the Mercians and was responsible for extending the fortifications of a number of Midland towns, including Tamworth. A statue of her can be seen at the foot of the hill on which the castle stands.

4

ATHELNEY
Alfred the Great

THERE ISN'T MUCH TO SEE of the place where Alfred the Great is said to have burned the cakes, but the incident almost certainly never happened, so the lack of evidence may not matter much. There is a monument, though, which commemorates the Benedictine abbey that Alfred founded in 878 AD on the Isle of Athelney, a slightly raised piece of land in the marshy Somerset Levels. Most of the area's 160,000 acres lie below high-tide level, so a 'natural island' that stood 30ft above the rest was one of the few safe places to build.

Alfred was only 22 when, in 871, he succeeded his brother Aethelred as King of Wessex and took over the responsibility of resisting the invading Danes. Earlier that year he'd been instrumental in a great victory at Ashdown, on the Berkshire Downs, but the early part of his own reign was occupied with indecisive battles and peace treaties that remained in force for no time at all. Then in January 878 the Danes unexpectedly attacked and overran Alfred's stronghold at Chippenham, slaughtering most of the inhabitants. With a small band of survivors the King took refuge in the nearby Levels and this is where the cake legend comes from. A 12th-century account tells that a local peasant woman took him in and, unaware of his identity, left him to keep an

23

eye on the cakes (they were probably more like rolls or scones) that were cooking over her fire. Alfred, perhaps with other things on his mind, neglected his duties and had his ears boxed as a result. Where the rest of his retinue was during this time is not recorded.

Anyway, over the next four months Alfred rallied a substantial force from the surrounding area and built a fortress at Athelney before overwhelming the Danes at the Battle of Edington. He didn't become King of All England at this stage, but he forced the Danish leader, Guthrum, to convert to Christianity and to retreat to East Anglia, leaving Alfred in control of the lands to the south and west.

It was in thanks for this victory that Alfred had the abbey built at Athelney; it survived, without ever being particularly affluent, until the Dissolution of the Monasteries, when the church was destroyed and the rest of the buildings allowed to fall into disrepair. Over the years the site has yielded rich pickings for archaeologists: fragments of painted masonry, the remnants of a medieval chapel, even graves and human remains. Today, however, the obelisk, erected in 1801 by the then lord of the manor, is all that the visitor can see. Surrounded by railings, it is somewhat squat as monuments go: a two-tier base bears a cameo-like bust of Alfred, topped with a rather chunky pyramid.

Considerably more impressive is the 160ft-high King Alfred's Tower situated on the edge of the Stourhead Estate in Wiltshire, an hour's drive east of Athelney. Generally described as a folly, its only apparent purpose is to allow visitors to climb it and be rewarded with spectacular views over the surrounding countryside. It was conceived as a celebration of the end of the Seven Years' War against France and the accession of George III in 1760. But it's said to stand near the Egbert Stone where Alfred rallied his troops before Edington, and a plaque above the door describes the King as 'The Light of a Benighted Age…a Philosopher and a Christian, The Father of his People, The Founder of the English MONARCHY and LIBERTY'. Clearly Alfred, rather than the young and as yet untried George, is the inspiration here.

MORE ABOUT ALFRED

The Ashmolean Museum in Oxford has, among its many treasures, a jewel found near Athelney in the late 17th century, but dating from the late 9th. It's a teardrop shape, with finely wrought gold framing a portrait, in cloisonné enamel, of a man holding two plant stems, thought to represent the sense of sight. Experts believe the jewel once held an ivory pointer that allowed the bearer to follow the text as he read the Bible. And it bears the inscription *Aelfred mec heht gewyrcan* ('Alfred ordered me to be made'). Alfred was a scholar as well as a warrior and leader; one of his greatest achievements was to commission translations of religious texts into the English of the day, and he is said to have sent out an *aestel* or pointer with each copy he dispatched to monasteries round the country. The Ashmolean's 'Alfred Jewel' is almost certainly one of them.

5

Hyde Abbey, Winchester
Alfred the Great

The people of Winchester are proud of their connection with Alfred the Great. A huge Victorian statue of him stands in the Broadway, near the even huger Victorian Guildhall. There's no evidence that he spent much time here (he was mostly away dealing with the Danes), but it was his nominated capital, and he was certainly buried here. Three times.

The first time was the conventional one – just after he died, in 899. Winchester's Old Minster was then an important destination for pilgrims and a royal burial place; it was the obvious resting place for the great King of Wessex. But only two years later, Alfred's son Edward the Elder founded a New Minster, in the precinct of the present cathedral, and had his father's remains moved to a position of honour in it.

By 1110 the city-centre site was too small for all the monks, pilgrims and others it had to accommodate, so Henry I had a new abbey built at Hyde, on the north side of town. In due course the monks from the New Minster moved there, processing with great pomp and bearing whatever valuable relics they had accumulated over the last couple of hundred years. Macabre though it sounds to the modern ear, these included the remains of Alfred the Great, his wife Alswitha and their son Edward.

Today, only the arch and gatehouse of Hyde Abbey survive, but in the Hyde Abbey Garden, a short walk away, a tablet in the ground marks Alfred's gravesite, with those of Alswitha and Edward on either side of him. In front of them stands the highlight of the visit – a glass panel etched by local artist Tracey Sheppard, depicting the pillars, the arches, the altar, the cross above it and the three graves below: a truly beautiful reconstruction, based on archaeological evidence, of what the abbey church was like. The effect is stunningly 3D – you feel as if you could just walk through the glass and stroll around the building. Well beyond the gravesite, where you might expect an ordinary park bench to be, sits an intricately carved choir bench. It's positioned where it would have been all those years ago – inside the church, with another altar beyond. The place must have been vast.

Along with most others of its kind, the abbey was destroyed in the 1530s, but the royal remains weren't disturbed until 1788, when the local authorities decided to build a prison on the site. Convicts digging the foundations for their future home came across a number of graves and, because these were in their way, they broke up the three stone coffins they found, sold off the lead lining and reburied the bones – somewhere. No one seems to have bothered to note where, despite the fact that the expensive nature of the coffins, and their location, makes it overwhelmingly likely that they belonged to Alfred and his family.

Renewed interest in Alfred in the 19th century led to an antiquarian/charlatan called John Mellor discovering a number of skeletal remains, including five skulls, which he was adamant were those of members of the Royal House of Wessex. The remains were buried in the churchyard of nearby St Bartholomew's, then later dug up and re-examined. It was established that they belonged to people who had died between the 12th and 15th centuries, perhaps in the abbey infirmary, and their gravestone now acknowledges this. But more recent discoveries include a male pelvis that has been dated to the end of the 10th century. It may well be that, after all these centuries and all this upheaval, we have discovered a substantial part of Alfred. Or his son.

Don't miss the cathedral itself, where ornate mortuary chests probably contain the remains of King Cnut. It was also here that Mary Tudor married Philip II of Spain in 1554. Winchester was strongly pro-Catholic and the controversial marriage ran less risk of provoking public protests here than if it had taken place in London. Staging the celebrations apparently cost the city so much that Mary gave them the local mill in payment.

WHILE YOU'RE HERE

Take a closer look at the statue of Alfred in the Broadway. Erected to mark the thousandth anniversary of his death, it's a fine example of Victorian / Edwardian romanticism. The only brief to the sculptor, Hamo Thornycroft, was that it should be 'colossal', and it is certainly that: from the base to the top of Alfred's raised arm it is 17ft high and it stands on two pieces of Cornish granite which together weigh over 100 tons. It portrays Alfred as a Christian soldier-king: he wears a crown and carries a shield, but his sword, held out in front of him like a cross, is the most eye-catching feature of the composition and an unmistakable piece of Christian symbolism.

6

MALMESBURY ABBEY
Athelstan

THE PRESENT ABBEY at Malmesbury dates only from the 12th century: still pretty old, you might have thought, but by the time it was built its most famous resident had been dead for over 300 years. Athelstan, a grandson of Alfred the Great and known in some quarters as 'the Glorious', was the first King of All England and his memorial in Malmesbury is, if not exactly glorious, at least substantial. He is shown as having long, flowing ringlets; a watchful lion lies at his feet, keeping guard over his remains. Not very successfully, it would appear: the 15th-century memorial is empty, Athelstan's bones having disappeared sometime when the lion's attention had wandered.

The medieval abbey was substantial, too, with a spire reaching a height of 430ft – 26ft taller than Salisbury's, which is today the tallest in England. The current building replaced a much earlier one: there was a Christian community here in the 7th century, when it, its buildings and its wealth flourished under the influence of a man later canonised as St Aldhelm.

Athelstan became King of All England by capturing York from the Danes in 927 and demanding homage from all the northern kings, including the King of Scotland. Ten years later he defeated a combined force

of Danes, Scots and Irish at the Battle of Brunanburh.
England was thus united for the first time, with borders
much as they are today. This surely makes Brunanburh
one of the most important battles ever fought on British
soil, a defining point in our history. Yet only keen
historians have heard of it and, intriguingly, no one
knows where it was. There's an argument for saying that
it was near Malmesbury, though, as Athelstan had some
of his fallen comrades buried there.

Athelstan lived only another two years after the
battle, but he found time to expand shrewdly on his
grandfather's system of central government. He issued a
series of charters on subjects such as the suppression of
thieves, the regulation of the weight of coins and the
codes of conduct for markets and merchants – all fairly
commonplace now, but only because Athelstan thought
of instigating them a thousand years ago.

Much of what we know about Athelstan comes
from the 12th-century chronicler William of
Malmesbury, who claimed that 'no one more just or
more learned ever governed the kingdom'. According
to William, Athelstan was renowned for his piety and
founded a number of churches; like Alfred he also
encouraged learning and may even have sponsored a
translation of the Bible into Anglo-Saxon. It was by his
own choice that he was buried in Malmesbury rather
than in Winchester near his father and grandfather:
William tells us that he was devoted to the abbey and to
the memory of St Aldhelm. According to one 20th-
century record, 'He loaded the abbey with gifts which
included a gold cross with a relic of the True Cross,

which he used to wear in his battles, and numerous relics of saints purchased from abroad.'

None of these glories is available to the modern visitor (presumably Henry VIII pocketed them), but we can still see a 15th-century illuminated Bible, a Norman porch and a memorial to a local woman called Hannah Twynnoy, who was killed by a tiger in 1703 – an incident that took place (and you couldn't make this up) at the White Lion Inn. Sadly, the stained-glass window that commemorates an 11th-century monk who designed a pair of wings and tried to fly from the top of the spire is in a room not open to the public. Despite the loss of the tower and the spire, services are still held in the nave, the only part of the abbey that remains standing. Athelstan may never have seen it, but its sheer magnificence makes you glad that he encouraged the early monks to settle here.

WHILE YOU'RE HERE
Look into the Athelstan Museum and read up about Malmesbury Castle. Although its physical remains are long gone, the castle played an important role in the wars between Stephen and Matilda (see page 60), being besieged three times without being captured. Once that war was over, the castle was both surplus to requirements and in the way of the abbey's plans to expand. The monks petitioned King John to sell the castle to them; he agreed in 1216 and they promptly knocked it down, reusing some of the stone for their own building works.

7

CORONATION STONE, KINGSTON
Ethelred the Unready

AT FIRST GLANCE, Kingston-upon-Thames seems to be
little more than a pleasant pedestrianised shopping
centre, but if you persist you discover a small but
significant piece of royal history. You also realise why the
place is called Kingston. It was the site of the coronation
of seven Anglo-Saxon kings, from Edward the Elder in
900 to Ethelred the Unready in 979, with Athelstan (see
page 29) in between. Its royal associations go back even
further: a document of 838 refers to 'a great Council
presided over by King Egbert held in Cyningestun, that
famous place in Surrey' – and that strange-looking word
translates as Kingston, 'the king's estate'.

As at Scone in Scotland (see page 91), Anglo-Saxon
kings were crowned on a ceremonial stone – the
precursor of the throne-like Coronation Chair used
more recently. Their Coronation Stone, a chunk of
sandstone about 30in high, today sits in the garden of
Kingston's Guildhall, surrounded by railings with
Saxon-style spearheads. The names of the seven kings
and the dates of their coronations are inscribed around
its seven-sided plinth, and alongside each name is
embedded a coin from that king's reign, donated by the

British Museum. The British Museum didn't, of course, exist in the 10th century – coins, plinth and railings alike are Victorian contributions, added when the stone was installed, amid the sort of pomp the Victorians loved, on a site near its current one. It has been moved a number of times since it was used for coronations in the Saxon chapel of St Mary, and has been in its latest location only since the Guildhall was built in the 1930s. (A much older Guildhall in the Market Place, restored during the time of Queen Anne, was replaced in the 19th century by what is now known as the Market House. On the parapet, a gilded statue of Anne, wearing a crown and carrying orb and sceptre, gives us no opportunity to forget Kingston's royal connections.)

As for the kings who were crowned here, the best known is probably Ethelred the Unready. A direct descendant of both Alfred and Athelstan, he didn't live up to his pedigree: although his name means 'good counsel', his nickname suggests either that he was badly advised or that he didn't listen to advice at all. Danish raids during his reign meant that he lost control of much of the kingdom his ancestors had accumulated. He was succeeded not by his own son – who turns up later as Edward the Confessor (see page 37) – but by the Danish Cnut (see page 34). Cnut chose to be crowned in London and, with all respect to the statue of Queen Anne, Kingston was never again a royal centre.

It remained a commercial hub, though; the 16th-century historian John Leland described it as 'the best market town in all Surrey'. Perhaps its current emphasis on shopping is merely following a venerable tradition.

8

BOSHAM
Cnut

Let all men know how empty and worthless is the power of kings.

CNUT

THE POINT ABOUT THE STORY of King Cnut and the waves is not so much that he failed to stop them but that when he failed to stop them he was able to say, 'I told you so.' Contrary to what many people believe, he was trying to demonstrate his own lack of omnipotence to his sycophantic courtiers.

There are several places in England where this performance may have taken place, but Bosham seems as likely as any. It's a pretty little village on Chichester Harbour where you are warned to be careful where you park at low tide, lest you return a few hours later to find your car has been flooded. At high tide – even on a calm and sunny day – the water reaches no more than about 3ft below a retaining wall that wouldn't have been there in Cnut's day, and sneaks up an unprotected road towards an antique shop on the corner. A very good place for a wily king to prove a point.

Bosham's claim to fame is more than a tidal accident, though: Cnut is known to have had a palace here, and a daughter of his is believed to have drowned in the local Mill Stream – there is a memorial to her in the church.

All this may be mere folklore (except the bit about being careful where you park – that's true enough), but it's stood the test of time.

Whatever the truth of it, Cnut was clearly no fool. Born in Denmark in about 995, he was the son of the wonderfully named Sweyn Forkbeard and grandson of Harald Bluetooth, both powerful Viking leaders. Said by a 13th-century chronicler to have been exceptionally tall and strong, he accompanied his father on an invasion of England before he was out of his teens. They took control of the northern part of England – an area that became known as Danelaw, which proclaimed Cnut king when Sweyn died in 1014. The rest of the country, however, stayed loyal to Ethelred the Unready, who had taken refuge in Normandy. The English nobles called him back and there ensued two years of conflict and changing loyalties. Two premature deaths in 1016 resolved the situation: Ethelred died in April and, in the aftermath of a comprehensive defeat at Danish hands, his son Edmund Ironside agreed to divide the kingdom with Cnut. Then Edmund himself died in November, leaving Cnut King of All England and conspiracy theorists with food for thought.

> **AN ALTERNATIVE LEGEND**
> *If Bosham doesn't appeal to you, try catching a glimpse of the Trent Aegir, a tidal bore on the River Trent. It occurs at various points in and just north of Gainsborough, Lincolnshire, and relies on a high spring tide meeting the downstream flow of the river. This is another spot that lays claim to the wave-stopping story and there is no denying that the bore in full spate would be even harder to subdue than the tide at Bosham.*

Cnut promptly consolidated his position by having himself crowned in London and, within a year and despite the fact that he had a wife already, marrying Ethelred's widow Emma, daughter of the Duke of Normandy. He also executed or exiled many of his enemies and possible rivals for the throne. He then reigned for almost 20 years, acquiring the kingdom of Denmark when his brother died and much of Norway and Sweden when he defeated an incursion those realms made into Denmark. By 1026 Cnut was effectively king not only of England but of most of Scandinavia, too.

It's almost inevitable that the death of such a man should create an opportunity for mayhem. Cnut left two sons, one by each of his wives, to squabble over his kingdoms; both died without legitimate heirs, so that a mere seven years after Cnut's death the throne of England reverted to a son of Ethelred the Unready. This is the man who became known as Edward the Confessor (see page 37), which means we are racing towards the most famous date in English history, 1066. And that brings us neatly back to Bosham, whose other claim to fame is that it features on the Bayeux Tapestry. A replica

of part of the tapestry is on display in the church, showing Harold Godwinson and his soldiers riding towards Bosham in 1064 before setting sail for Normandy and launching a chain of events that changed English history like no other before or since.

9

WESTMINSTER ABBEY
Edward the Confessor

THERE'S A CLUE IN THE NAME by which he is always
known: this was the most genuinely pious monarch
we have ever had and he founded one of our greatest
churches. The epithet 'Confessor' was bestowed on
him when he was declared a saint a century after his
death: it means that he led a saintly life but didn't
suffer martyrdom.

The son of Ethelred the Unready and Emma of
Normandy, Edward became king in 1042. He was in his
late thirties, had spent much of his youth in exile in his
mother's homeland, and now came home to face the
daunting prospect of keeping the peace between a
number of powerful barons. With this in mind he
married Edith, daughter of the most important of them,
Godwin, despite the fact that Godwin had been
responsible for the death of Edward's brother. Modern
historians dismiss the earlier (and surely daft) suggestion
that, having entered into this political alliance, Edward
then refused to consummate the marriage either because
of his aversion to the Godwin family or because, in his
piety, he had taken a vow of chastity. But for whatever
reason the marriage produced no children, a fact that,
as we shall see, caused a certain amount of strife when
Edward died at the beginning of 1066.

Tradition has it that, during his period of exile, Edward had promised that if he could return safely to England he would make a pilgrimage to St Peter's in Rome, the forerunner of the present basilica there. Established as king, he found it impossible to take the time off, so instead set about founding a monastery in London dedicated to St Peter, replacing an existing Saxon church at Westminster. His Norman upbringing had, of course, exposed him to Norman architecture and explains why the original church was of Norman design, despite having been built before the Conquest. Work on the most ambitious building project yet seen in England began shortly after Edward's accession to the throne. The unfinished Westminster Abbey was consecrated on 28 December 1065, possibly because it was apparent that the King would not live to see it completed. He was too ill to attend the ceremony and died only a week later; the building work continued for another quarter of a century.

What we see today isn't Edward's Norman church – it's Henry III's Gothic one. When he wasn't fighting barons (see page 82), Henry was a notorious spendthrift and was responsible for major extensions to Windsor Castle, the Palace of Westminster and the Tower of London, among others. He also made the interiors more comfortable and decorative. Edward's abbey had been state of the art, more awe-inspiring than anything on the Continent, but by Henry's time (close to 200 years later), Notre-Dame de Paris and great cathedrals in Chartres, Cologne, Burgos and elsewhere were under construction and it seemed important to emulate them.

At Westminster he emulated them to the tune of about £15 million in today's money.

In addition to building a grand new church, Henry indulged his flair for expensive decoration. He created a magnificent new shrine to Edward the Confessor, of whom he was a fervent admirer; it can be seen to this day. He also commissioned the Italianate Cosmati pavement in front of the High Altar. Measuring about 25ft square and composed of pieces of stone of different colours and shapes arranged in a complex geometric pattern, it is the finest surviving example of its kind and must have taken a large chunk out of that £15 million.

Although Edward the Confessor's building no longer stands, his original dream to make Westminster Abbey a royal mausoleum has been fulfilled: 17 of the 40 or so monarchs who have succeeded him are buried here, along with a number of their consorts and, thanks to filial devotion on the part of her son, Mary, Queen of Scots. Edward's own shrine became a place of pilgrimage where invalids came to pray for a cure – and wore away the steps at the base of the shrine with their knees. In addition, all the English/British monarchs since 1066 have been crowned here (though with some it has been a second, just-to-make-it-clear ceremony) and there have been 16 royal weddings, the most recent watched on television by an estimated 2 billion people worldwide. Henry III, eager to make rivals on the Continent eat their hearts out, would have been ecstatic. The unworldly Edward the Confessor, on the other hand, probably turned in his expensive grave.

10

DUNSINANE HILL/ BIRNAM WOOD
Macbeth

About the time that building work was starting on Westminster Abbey (see page 37), up in Scotland the King was being told:

Macbeth shall never vanquish'd be, until
Great Birnam wood to high Dunsinane hill
Shall come against him.

According to Shakespeare, that is. And, again according to Shakespeare, Macbeth laughed off the prophecy. No one was going to 'bid the tree unfix his earth-bound root' – nothing to worry about there. Little did he know that Malcolm, son of King Duncan, whom Macbeth had murdered, would instruct each of his 10,000-plus men to hew down a bough and use it to camouflage their numbers. No wonder the usurper wasn't best pleased when a messenger told him, 'I look'd toward Birnam, and anon, methought/The wood began to move.'

It must have been quite a sight. It's not known how big 'great Birnam wood' was, but, given that it lay at the southern limits of the Great Wood of Caledon that once covered most of northern Scotland, the chances are it was pretty big. Big enough to spare 10,000 boughs and live to tell the tale.

What remains of Birnam Wood lies along the south bank of the Tay, some of the loveliest country in Scotland. If you park in Birnam itself, signs point you along the appropriately named Oak Road and very quickly take you to an enormous tree. In front of it is a gravestone-shaped slab on which are carved the words, 'It's not me – I'm a sycamore.' Not 20 yards further along, another gravestone smirks, 'Not me either. Keep going.' So you do, and there it is – the Birnam Oak, some 23ft in girth and reaching skywards as far as the eye can see. It's at least 500 years old, so if it wasn't there in Macbeth's day it certainly was in Shakespeare's. Next to it is the even more impressive Birnam Sycamore, with vast buttress roots, a girth of 26ft and massive horizontal branches not much above head height. You *really* want this tree to be a thousand years old, but it's a disappointingly youthful 300 or so, and an introduced species at that. But let's not be greedy. Like most ancient woodland, the remains of Birnam are breathtaking and somehow magical.

Access to 'high Dunsinane' is harder to find. It's marked on the map as King's Seat, on a twisting back road between Perth and Dundee, and its stark, glowering peak is visible enough, but the signboard is well hidden. In fact, if you're coming from the wrong direction (east), you glimpse it only in the rear-view mirror as you are about to give up hope.

Once found, though, it is full of useful information. 'Dunsinnan Hill Fort – Macbeth's Castle?' it begins, before going on to describe the two separate forts that were once found here, one probably still occupied in the 11th century, when Macbeth was around. It's not certain that this was his stronghold, but it is a hilltop site with evidence of a powerfully defended citadel that would have commanded views over the surrounding countryside (including, some 15 miles away, Birnam Wood). It was *someone's* stronghold and it is – at worst – plausible to suppose that that someone was Macbeth.

Historical records suggest that Shakespeare maligned Macbeth. The truth is that 11th-century Scotland was rife with conflict between rival chieftains. Duncan, despite being described by Shakespeare as meek and virtuous, invaded Macbeth's territory and was killed in battle, not treasonably murdered in his bed. Macbeth subsequently ruled for 17 largely peaceful years, resisting an invasion instigated by, of all people, Edward the Confessor (another notably meek man, you'd have thought) and eventually dying in battle against Malcolm's forces. That Macbeth was buried on the sacred island of Iona, alongside other early Scottish kings, scarcely suggests a bloody tyrant whose sins are best written out of history.

Macbeth's reputation may not be the only thing that Shakespeare adapted. That helpful signboard says that the spelling Dunsinnan is supported by documentary evidence and local pronunciation, which stresses the second syllable. It's possible that the Bard invented Dunsinane, with the stress on the first or third syllable, for the convenience of his verse.

11

BATTLE ABBEY
Harold

ONLY THREE TIMES in the last millennium has England
had three kings in the space of a year. In 1483, Edward
V was allegedly murdered, having been on the throne
only three months; in 1936 Edward VIII succeeded in
January and abdicated in December. But before that, it
happened in 1066.

It was Edward the Confessor dying on 5 January
that started the trouble. He had no children and left
three strong claimants to his throne: his brother-in-law,
a powerful Saxon earl called Harold Godwinson; the
Norwegian Harald Hardrada; and William, known as 'the
Bastard', Duke of Normandy. There was also a young
prince, Edgar, a great-nephew of Edward's, but he was
no more than 15 and there was little enthusiasm for
putting a lad of his age on the throne. Harald, as King of
Norway, felt he had a right to the rest of Cnut's empire,
including England. William's father had been Edward's
cousin and William always maintained that Edward had
promised the throne to him. But Harold claimed the
same thing – and he was the man on the spot.

He was in for a busy few months. The Witan –
the council whose job it was to decide such things
– convened on 6 January, appointed Harold king and
had him crowned that very day. William promptly made

plans to invade; Harold, hearing the news, assembled
an army on the Isle of Wight. And then he waited. For
months. Unfavourable winds prevented William from
sailing across the Channel and in September Harold
disbanded his army, only to hear that Harald Hardrada
had invaded Northumbria. To add to the complications,
Hardrada was supported by Harold's brother Tostig, who
had been ousted as Earl of Northumbria the previous
year. Harold now had to hasten north to repel the force
that was marching south. The two armies met at
Stamford Bridge, just outside York, on 25 September;
the Norwegians were defeated and both Hardrada and
Tostig were killed.

But by now the winds had changed – literally and
perhaps metaphorically, too. William's forces landed in
Pevensey in Sussex on 28 September, with William
stumbling to his knees as he disembarked. It could have
been a disastrous omen in that superstitious age, but
William was no fool. Grabbing handfuls of pebbles from
the beach, he cried, 'By the grace of God I have taken
hold of my kingdom. England is in my hands.' In
Yorkshire, Harold's exhausted army had to turn straight
round and hasten 300 miles south.

For a while it looked as if Harold was going to repel
two invasions within three weeks. On the morning of
14 October, having taken up a strong position on the
crest of a hill and deployed his troops in a tight
defensive formation, he was able to fend off the two
great Norman strengths – archers and cavalry. But then
it seems that William's forces pretended to retreat,
enticing the English to break ranks and pursue them.

The Normans were able to cut off and crush different flanks of the English army, and when Harold himself was killed – possibly shot through the eye with an arrow – it was all over. William lost no time in sending to Winchester to secure the Royal Treasury, then proceeded to London, where he was crowned on Christmas Day.

The battle had been a gruesome one. Out of total forces estimated at around 15,000, at least 6,000 and perhaps as many as 10,000 men were killed. William built Battle Abbey as a penance and ordered that the high altar should be placed on the spot where Harold had fallen: a stone slab still marks the place. He granted the abbey all the land that could be seen for half a league round – roughly a mile and a half. It became immensely wealthy and the town now known as Battle, which grew up to service it, was in the 15th century the largest in Sussex (today, with a population of 6,000, it is about 35th).

Substantial parts of the abbey church walls still stand, with behind them a south-facing slope said to be part of the very one defended by Harold's army. On a sunny day it takes quite a leap of the imagination to take yourself back to that bloody October 950 years ago, but the excellent visitor centre will get you in the mood, talking you through events and allowing you to assess whether you would have been strong enough to carry a Norman shield into battle. The energetic can also climb to the top of the gatehouse and view what were once the abbey's vast holdings and the battlefield that turned William the Bastard into William the Conqueror.

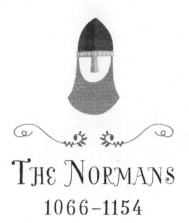

THE NORMANS
1066–1154

12

PRUDHOE CASTLE/ RICHMOND CASTLE
William I

HAVING DEFEATED HAROLD at Hastings, William needed to establish himself in the eyes of his new subjects. He quickly had himself crowned at Westminster Abbey then set about reinforcing his position by building a series of formidable castles.

Norman castles were unlike anything the British had seen before. Beginning with timber motte and bailey constructions that were quick to put up and gave an immediate power base and shelter for his forces, William soon diverged into stone. Choosing imposing and strategically useful sites on high ground, overlooking rivers, harbours or towns, he produced permanent buildings centred on a tower-like keep, with substantial curtain walls capable of withstanding a siege.

His two greatest monuments are the Tower of London and Windsor Castle (see pages 149 and 114), but in the North of England – and in Yorkshire in particular – you seem to find a Norman castle in almost every town. This is largely because, having subdued the South, William faced resistance in other parts of his kingdom and embarked on a particularly brutal campaign known as the Harrying of the North.

It may have been effective but, in terms of going down in history as a decent human being, this was not William's finest hour. Over the winter of 1069–70, he had crops destroyed, villages burned, people starved and enemies slaughtered, all apparently without mercy. When, some 16 years later, he ordered a stock-take of everything in his kingdom – the vast survey that became known as the Domesday Book – it was recorded that over half the manors in Yorkshire were 'waste'. Historians continue to argue over just how much damage William's small army could have done, but 'quite a lot' seems a reasonable answer.

Having made his point, William established a Norman aristocracy in the North, to replace the Anglo-Scandinavian one he had just crushed. He granted land to his loyal supporters and encouraged them – you guessed it – to build castles. A breathtaking number of these sprang up over the next generation or so, with spectacular ruins still to be seen at Knaresborough, Pickering, Tickhill and, a bit further north, Prudhoe, to pick a few names almost at random.

Prudhoe was established to guard a ford across the River Tyne and soon found itself in the thick of things. In the 12th century it resisted two Scottish sieges; then in the 14th it was acquired by the Percy family, of whom we shall hear more (see page 129), and became the home of the Earls (and later the Dukes) of Northumberland. Because it was constantly occupied it never fell into disrepair, as so many other castles did when they ceased to be needed as fortresses; instead it was subjected to a Gothic Revival makeover in

Victorian times. For a Norman castle in the 21st century it's in remarkably good nick, though some would say that the Regency style and Egyptian motifs sit slightly oddly alongside the 12th-century gatehouse, the towering keep and the chapel with its projecting oriel windows, among the earliest in England.

For a more authentic experience you might head south, to Richmond, Yorkshire, which offers perhaps the best preserved 11th-century castle in Europe. Its keep dominates the town and the massive walls still surround two sides of a huge hilltop triangle that once contained a market place and a number of houses, as well as the castle itself. On the third side, cliffs dropping steeply down to the River Swale defied anyone to scale them.

Visitors to Richmond Castle are attracted to the Robin Hood Tower, although there is no suggestion that the famous outlaw had anything to do with it – the guidebook suggests 'Victorian romanticism' as the source of the name. But it does house the chapel, one of the finest survivors of its kind, where you can see such intriguing features as niches that probably once held candles, and traces of the original paintwork. It doesn't take much imagination to conjure up the Percys celebrating mass here, just as it's easy to fancy yourself joining in the meals and festivities in the – now roofless, but once obviously very grand – Scolland's Hall.

All these remains tell us clearly what William wanted us to know. We're in charge, these Norman castles said to their Anglo-Saxon underlings, and we are here to stay. Nearly 10 centuries on, it's hard to argue.

13

THE RUFUS STONE, NEW FOREST
William II

THE SUDDEN DEATH IN 1100 of William II, nicknamed Rufus (perhaps for his red hair, perhaps for his ruddy complexion) is the best-known event of his career and has given conspiracy theorists plenty to chew over for almost a millennium.

One of three sons of William the Conqueror to survive their father, this William had had a rocky reign. Acceding to the throne instead of his elder brother Robert, Duke of Normandy (see page 57), he found that his barons faced a dilemma: they owned lands in both England and Normandy, and as such owed allegiance to two lords. Tricky, particularly when the two lords were at each other's throats. It was fortunate that Robert decided to embark on a Crusade and, in return for a substantial sum of money, leave his brother in charge of his dukedom.

But that provided William with only a brief respite. In the course of his 13 years on the throne, he quashed two rebellions, invaded Normandy and restored order there, resisted an invasion by the Scots and attempted without much success to extend his influence in Wales. He also had to deal with a recalcitrant Archbishop of

Canterbury who, like Thomas Becket 80 years later (see page 67), insisted that his loyalty was to God rather than to the king.

No wonder William occasionally wanted to take the day off and go hunting. As it happens, his father had commandeered a substantial chunk of Hampshire to be his new hunting ground or 'forest', and that is where William went on a fateful day in August 1100. Precisely what happened in the New Forest that day isn't known, except that William was killed by an arrow. The man accused of the deed was Walter Tyrrell, one of the royal entourage. He was a good archer and unlikely to have fired off a careless shot that hit an oak tree and accidentally rebounded into William's chest – but could he have done it on purpose? Rather than offer any explanation, he galloped away in panic and fled into exile in France; one contemporary record says that he denied any involvement in the King's death, though it is tempting to add, 'Well, he would, wouldn't he?'

In fact, the chroniclers don't seem to have been too bothered about the facts. William, although a good administrator and successful general, was one of the most unpopular monarchs we have ever had. Given that he had plenty of enemies within the Church and that most of the chroniclers were clerics, it's not surprising that they recorded the opinion that his death, however it happened, was a just end to a bad man.

William's brother Henry, another of the hunting party that day, is said to have dashed straight to Winchester to secure the Royal Treasury, leaving William's body to be dealt with by – well, by someone who didn't need to make a dash for the Treasury. He had himself crowned in London just three days later. No contemporary account actually accuses Henry of plotting William's death (while his other brother was conveniently somewhere in Europe, on his way back from the Holy Land), but there is plenty of scope for those who don't believe in coincidence.

The metallic monument in the New Forest that marks the spot is an understated one: about 5ft high, it describes the circumstances of William's death and explains that, the original stone having been badly mutilated and defaced, 'this more durable memorial' was erected in 1841. (The fact that such a monument should have been mutilated and defaced shows how unpopular the man was, even in death.) It seems a shame that they covered the entire original, however mutilated it might have been, but it's in a lovely part of the forest, worth a visit anyway. There are plenty of ancient oaks around – not to mention birch and beech – and on a fine day there can be few prettier sights in southern England. None of the trees is old enough to have been involved in William's death, though there is one only 10 paces away from the memorial that may – just may – be a descendant of it. William himself left no descendants: uniquely among English kings since 1066 who grew to adulthood, he never married, which, considering how important having legitimate male heirs was, is odd. But then he was an odd man.

14

READING ABBEY
Henry I

A short stroll from Reading Station brings you to
Forbury Gardens, a Victorian park built on what has
always been open ground – for centuries the Forbury
was part of the outer court of Reading Abbey, bridging
the gap between it and the town. Queen Elfrida, widow
of Edgar the Peaceful and mother of Ethelred the
Unready, founded a nunnery hereabouts in 979,
apparently as a penance for killing her stepson, known
as Edward the Martyr. Edgar had several sons by various
wives, none of them grown up at the time of their
father's death, so Elfrida – who has gone down in
history as a stereotypical wicked stepmother – may have
taken drastic steps to ensure that it was her son who
became king.

So there was already a Christian foundation on the
site by the time Henry I came along in 1121 and
established an abbey for the salvation of his own soul
and those of his predecessors and successors. His vision
was that it would be a royal mausoleum to rival
Westminster Abbey, though to this day he remains the
only monarch to have been buried here. But Reading
Abbey, like many of the period, became very wealthy
and influential, and remained so until the Dissolution of
the Monasteries in the 1530s.

Henry spent much of his reign fighting for supremacy: his elder brother, Robert, who had become Duke of Normandy on the death of their father, William the Conqueror, staked a claim to the throne that ended with Henry imprisoning him in Cardiff Castle (see page 57). Battles against various French nobles continued, meaning that Henry was absent from his kingdom more often than not. He was a capable administrator, however, extending the fiscal system known as the Exchequer and ruling by proxy in a way that laid the foundations for today's Civil Service. He also took care to keep the English aristocracy on his side by treating them, as one chronicler put it, 'with honour and generosity, according to their wealth and estates' – which meant, of course, that they carried on funding his wars.

But Henry's real problem was with the succession.

WHILE YOU'RE HERE

Reading had a fit of royalist enthusiasm in the late 19th and early 20th centuries. A statue of Queen Victoria was erected outside the magnificently High Gothic Town Hall to mark Her Majesty's Golden Jubilee in 1887; red wrought-iron gates at the southwest corner of Forbury Gardens bear the legend 'Queen Victoria 1897', commemorating her Diamond Jubilee; and down towards the station a statue of Victoria's son Edward VII celebrates his coronation in 1902. A long-standing rumour that Victoria disliked Reading and that her statue (with its back to the Town Hall) indicates her attitude to the town seems to have no foundation: she's not known ever to have visited. In fact, the Great Western Railway arrived here in 1840, only three years into her reign, and for about a hundred years, until 1980s buildings obscured it, her statue would have been visible (face on) from the train. She would also have been well placed to greet any visitor walking up from the station to the Town Hall. As, when his turn came, would Edward VII.

Despite an array of mistresses and a plethora of illegitimate children, he lost his only legitimate son to drowning and was left with just one daughter, Matilda or Maud. He was determined that she should succeed him, but the country's loyalties were divided and, as we shall see (page 60), Henry's death plunged the country into civil war. The contemporary chronicler Henry of Huntingdon produced the sorrowful epitaph 'Each of his triumphs only made him worry lest he lose what he had gained; therefore though he seemed to be the most fortunate of kings, he was in truth the most miserable.'

On a happier note, it is known that Henry was buried under the high altar of Reading Abbey, long since vanished and probably now covered by the playground of the adjacent primary school. There is every chance that current excavations will bring his sarcophagus to light with as much fanfare as that which accompanied Richard III's appearance in a Leicester car park (see page 156). The Reading Abbey Revealed project is working on it.

15

CARDIFF CASTLE
Robert of Normandy

As THE ELDEST SON of William the Conqueror, Robert could expect to inherit his father's homeland, the Duchy of Normandy. It was not an unusual arrangement for the eldest son to inherit the property his father himself had inherited, while younger sons got any lands acquired during their father's lifetime. But in this case the acquisition – England – was much larger and richer than the patrimony, and it was to go to Robert's younger brother, the future William II (see page 51). Of course, this rankled, as did the fact that, in order to inherit either money or power, Robert had to wait for his father's death. By the late 1070s he was in open rebellion and, when in 1087 the Conqueror was fatally wounded in battle, the younger William was dutifully at his father's bedside; Robert was not.

The bad blood between the brothers lasted throughout William II's reign. Robert joined the English barons in a rebellion against the new king in 1088, but then he seems to have abandoned the fight and, mortgaging his duchy to William to raise the money, set off for the Holy Land. If he couldn't have power, he might have reasoned, at least he could have the prestige won by taking part in a Crusade. It was while he was on his way back, in August 1100, that William was killed in

the New Forest (see page 51), which meant that for the
second time in his life Robert missed a deathbed scene
and saw the kingdom of England pass to a younger
brother. It has to be said, however, that there was
nothing in Robert's character or track record to suggest
that he would have been a good choice of king.

That younger brother, now Henry I, prepared for the
inevitable backlash from Robert, which duly came in
July 1101; some powerful English barons rushed to
Robert's support, but enough remained loyal for Henry to
be able to negotiate a truce and buy his brother off.
Trusting Robert and his powerful allies in England and
Wales would have been a mistake, however, so Henry
decided to invade Normandy and destroy his brother's
power once and for all. He defeated and captured
Robert at the Battle of Tinchebray in 1106, brought
him back to England and imprisoned him first in
Devizes and latterly in Cardiff Castle.

If you visit Cardiff Castle today you are most likely
to be struck by the Victorian Gothic interiors, designed
by the architect William Burges for the fabulously
wealthy Third Marquess of Bute in the late 19th century.
No other surviving Norman castle is decorated in such

> **WHILE YOU'RE HERE**
> *Check out Burges' stained glass
> in the entrance hall to the castle
> apartments. In the 15th century,
> Cardiff Castle belonged to George,
> Duke of Clarence (see page 146),
> through his marriage to Isabel
> Neville, and then to Isabel's sister
> Anne, future wife of Richard III.
> All four, along with Henry VII
> and his wife Elizabeth, Henry
> VIII, Katherine of Aragon and
> other notables of the period, are
> commemorated in glass.*

an over-the-top style; it's worth a trip even for those with no interest in Britain's royal heritage. But it is the keep that interests us here: an impressive 12-sided structure probably built by an illegitimate son of Henry I. This man, another Robert, had married the daughter of the Lord of Glamorgan and through her acquired the wooden castle and garrison that previously stood on the site. It's likely that he built the stone keep just in time to find room for the royal prisoner. Moved here in 1126, when he was already in his seventies, Robert of Normandy remained for the rest of his life – and he lived to the quite remarkable age of 83. His only legitimate son had predeceased him and left no children of his own, so for the last years of his reign Henry I was untroubled by rebellious relatives across the Channel. It wasn't often, between about 1066 and 1483, that any King of England could make that claim.

William Burges paid due homage to both Roberts in his decoration of Cardiff 's Banqueting Hall. The mantelpiece shows Robert of Glamorgan armed and on horseback setting off on a journey, against a repeating pattern of the letter R adorned by a crown, while in a lowly corner, Robert of Normandy, wearing a crown, can be seen behind bars. Did Burges or his wealthy patron have some sneaking sympathy for this hard-done-by prince?

16

OXFORD CASTLE
Stephen

Henry I may have wanted his daughter Matilda to succeed him, but this was 1135, several hundred years before many people thought that having a woman on the throne could possibly be a good idea. Particularly when she had a male cousin, Stephen, the son of William the Conqueror's daughter Adela, ready and willing to take her place. They were both of mature years – Stephen in his forties, Matilda 33 – but gender was what counted.

Matilda was married to Geoffrey, Count of Anjou, and at the time of her father's death was living with her husband in France. Stephen, although born in France, had been brought up at the English court and was known there; conveniently, his brother was Bishop of Winchester, so he could command the support of the Church. He, too, was in France when Henry died, but only in Boulogne: he was able to cross the Channel swiftly and was crowned king within days.

Of course, in the 12th century it was never going to be that easy. Three years into Stephen's reign, one of Matilda's illegitimate half-brothers and staunchest supporters, Robert of Gloucester, rebelled against him. The following year Matilda invaded England, setting off a civil war that has rightly come to be known as The

Anarchy. It was, frankly, chaos, and it went on being chaos for some years. Stephen had the opportunity to imprison Matilda, but for some reason let her go; she defeated him in battle and took him prisoner, but was then forced to do an exchange, as Robert too had been captured. In the meantime, Stephen had offended his brother the bishop, who went over to Matilda's side, and various other nobles changed allegiance whenever it suited them.

By late 1142, things were going Stephen's way. Matilda, repulsed by both London and Windsor, took refuge in Oxford Castle, where Stephen promptly followed and besieged her. During a cold and snowy December, the story goes, she and a number of her companions camouflaged themselves in cloaks fashioned from undyed cloth – the colour of rather dirty snow – used ropes to lower themselves down the castle tower and made their escape along the frozen Thames.

A tour of Oxford Castle is fun (you can't visit except by guided tour). This is largely because the place was a prison for several centuries, so there is plenty of gallows (and pillory) humour. There's also a charming Norman crypt, an oasis of peace beneath the mayhem that went on above it over the years. The other principal remnant of Stephen and Matilda's time is St George's Tower, the top of which is accessed by the alarmingly narrow and twisting steps of the 12th-century stairway and offers a superb view across the castle's original mound and the city's more recent dreaming spires.

In Matilda's absence, Oxford Castle surrendered to Stephen and the war meandered on, with neither side making much headway, until Robert of Gloucester died in 1147. Matilda, having lost her most powerful ally, seems simply to have abandoned hope and retired to Rouen.

End of story? Far from it. 1150: Geoffrey of Anjou dies. His eldest son, Henry, inherits his father's substantial French domains – and wonders whether he shouldn't have another go at the English throne. 1152: despite the fact that he is at war with much of the rest of Europe, Henry invades England. 1153: Stephen's eldest son and heir conveniently (but not suspiciously) dies. Everyone in England is sick of the war, and Stephen negotiates a settlement with Henry. He, Stephen, will keep the throne, but on his death, it will pass to Henry. Stephen's surviving legitimate son, William, only a teenager, seems – in an odd piece of self-denial – to have been content with the Earldom of Surrey.

Again conveniently but (probably) not suspiciously, Stephen died only two years later. Henry of Anjou became Henry II without the need for any further blood to be spilled.

Stephen is a bit of a footnote in the chronology of English monarchs. Too chivalrous to imprison Matilda when he had the chance and put an end to the war; not determined enough to ensure that his own son succeeded him; not canny enough to keep his brother on his side. Historians have suggested that he was, unlike his three immediate predecessors, a reasonably kind and honourable man – certainly too nice to be a successful ruler in those ruthless times. If he'd lived at a time when it was easy for women to inherit their father's titles, we'd probably never have heard of him.

FOR MORE ABOUT STEPHEN

Take a trip to the pretty market town of Devizes in Wiltshire, where an 11th-century Norman castle played an important role in The Anarchy. At the time it belonged to Roger, Bishop of Salisbury, whose powerful family included the Bishops of Ely and Lincoln too. Stephen, convinced that these influential men were about to go over to Matilda's side, laid siege to Devizes Castle and forced them to surrender not only it but various other fortresses they owned around the country.

In addition to Robert of Normandy having been imprisoned here (see page 57), Devizes Castle boasted other royal connections: at one time it belonged to Katherine of Aragon and after that was besieged and destroyed during the Civil Wars. The present Victorian Gothic building dates only from the 1840s and is not open to the public, but you can admire its castellated towers and portcullis-like gateway from the road.

THE PLANTAGENET PERIOD
1154–1399

17

CANTERBURY CATHEDRAL
Henry II

*What a parcel of fools and dastards have I
nourished in my house, that not one of them will
avenge me of this one upstart clerk!*

HENRY II, ACCORDING TO THE *DICTIONARY OF NATIONAL BIOGRAPHY*

THESE FAMOUSLY EXASPERATED WORDS are more often
rendered as something along the lines of 'Who will rid
me of this turbulent priest?', but the impact is the same:
Henry had appointed his old friend Thomas Becket as
Archbishop of Canterbury. Thomas had previously been
his Chancellor, helping Henry to introduce reforms that
gave him direct control over much of his kingdom (and
thus alienated the hereditary nobility whom he was
bypassing), levied heavy taxes (alienating those who had
to pay them) and reducing the power of the Church and
its attachment to Rome (alienating the clergy). Pretty
comprehensive as alienation goes.

Henry had thought that having his friend as head of
the Church in England would bring at least that part of
his realm back on side. Thomas had done his best to
refuse the job, saying that as Archbishop he would have
to serve God and the Pope in preference to his King;
the King had insisted, the inevitable falling out had
occurred, and when various of his bishops had come to

report on Thomas's latest piece of insubordination, Henry had uttered the fatal cry. Four knights, taking him at his word, rushed to Canterbury and murdered Thomas in the cathedral on 29 December 1170.

What had happened was this. Henry, determined that there should be no argument over the succession when he died, had had his eldest surviving son, known as Henry the Young King, crowned earlier in the year. Permission for the ceremony, and the right to perform it, theoretically lay with the Archbishop of Canterbury, but Thomas was in exile in Europe and being difficult. So the older Henry called in the Archbishop of York. Both Thomas and the Pope were outraged. Thomas, home again, excommunicated the clergymen involved – and thus signed his own death warrant.

Henry, to give him his due, was horrified and did public penance for the sin for which he had inadvertently been responsible. Jean Anouilh's play *Becket* shows the King stripped and kneeling at Thomas's tomb, waiting for the monks to scourge him. And Thomas very quickly became a martyr and a saint – he was canonised in February 1173, little more than two years after his death (something of a record). Canterbury also became a place of pilgrimage – the pilgrims in Chaucer's *The Canterbury Tales*, written some two hundred years later, are heading to Thomas's grave.

Canterbury still attracts pilgrims, religious and secular alike. A plaque on the floor of the northwest transept, in a section of the church known as the Martyrdom, marks the spot where Thomas died, and a single candle burns in the Trinity Chapel, where his tomb used to be. It was destroyed and looted on the orders of Henry VIII, who maintained that Thomas 'had been a traitor to his king, and defied his honour' – a subject on which Henry VIII felt strongly. He probably also felt strongly about the 26 wagonloads of gold, jewels and other treasures he is alleged to have taken from the cathedral, including a large ruby that is now part of the Crown Jewels in the Tower of London.

Despite all that, Canterbury remains arguably the most magnificent and the most moving of all England's cathedrals. It's been here, in one form or another, since 597, when St Augustine first arrived on these shores with a mission to convert the local heathens to Christianity and it is the symbolic centre of the Anglican community throughout the world. Its 14th-century Gothic nave and its huge and remarkably well-preserved crypt are simply incomparable. As is its intricately carved Great Cloister – once you've admired everything at eye level, it's worth risking a serious crick in the neck to take in the faces, animals and heraldic shields above your head. And, back inside, it's difficult not to shiver – just a very little – as you stand on the site of Thomas's murder.

> **WHILE YOU'RE HERE**
> *Look in the Trinity Chapel for the tomb of Edward, the eldest son of Edward III. This Edward – known as the Black Prince because of the colour of his armour – had been a great general from the age of 16, winning many significant battles in France during the Hundred Years' War. Suffering probably from dysentery, which made him too weak to fight during the last years of his life, he died in London in his mid-forties and was buried in Canterbury at his own request.*

Ironically, crowning the young Henry did his father much more harm than good. He divided up his kingdom, giving Henry his own patrimony – England, Normandy, Anjou and Maine. His next son, Richard, became Duke of Aquitaine, Geoffrey had Brittany, and John had to wait until his father's invasion of Ireland made a new territory available. Needless to say, this pleased none of them, particularly as Henry, despite being nominally 'junior king' of a vast kingdom, was given little money and less power. The rest of Henry II's life was spent in dealing with rebellions from his sons and his wife (see page 73), and the ultimate blow came when young Henry contracted dysentery and died in 1183, aged only 28. He had been waging a campaign against his father at the time.

A GOOD TIME TO VISIT
A service of remembrance for Thomas Becket is held in the cathedral every 29 December.

18

DOVER CASTLE
Henry II

YOU CAN IMAGINE THAT the white cliffs of Dover, facing as they do the shortest passage across the Channel from France, have always been an important area to guard. We're often told that the first castle on any given spot was built by William the Conqueror (see pages 48, 114 and 149, to name but three), but Dover's defensive history goes back further than that. There may well have been an Iron Age fort here, and there was certainly a Roman lighthouse, guiding ships into the harbour – its four-storey remains are the only ones of their kind in Britain; having been built in the 2nd century AD, it was still in use in the 12th. You can also see the Saxon church, much restored but retaining original features. And although William the Conqueror did indeed strengthen the existing Saxon defences, it was Henry II in the 12th century who made Dover Castle what it is today.

What he did was extraordinary, simply in terms of scale. His most significant contribution was the Great Tower – and it is really worthy of those capital letters. Almost 100ft high and with walls over 20ft thick in places, it was the last and most elaborate of the great square keeps that the Normans had built all over the country. It's said that when William the Conqueror built the White Tower (the central keep of the Tower of

London), England had never seen anything like it before; a hundred years later Dover, drawing on the same architectural heritage, surpassed it in almost every way, including expense. Its concentric rings of stone walls dotted with rectangular towers made it virtually impregnable – it withstood a three-month siege during the reign of King John, eventually forcing the besiegers to give up and call a truce. It also boasted a well sunk to the astonishing depth of 400ft – that's deeper than St Paul's Cathedral is tall, an extraordinary feat of engineering in the 12th century and a useful thing to have on hand during a siege.

These were practical features, but Henry's works at Dover also included things designed to impress. A complex 'forebuilding' covers a staircase which, unusually, enters the building on the second floor and whose length allows visitors to be welcomed with great pomp. The galleried King's Hall was obviously designed for ceremonies, and the King's Chamber, almost as large, shows that the King received visitors and carried out affairs of state here. One of the most enjoyable things about Dover Castle is that the rooms of the Great Tower have been refurbished as if the court were in residence, with lavish wall hangings and colourful furniture based on contemporary illustrations and techniques. You can walk into the King's Chamber and imagine being told that His Highness – as he would have been called in Henry II's day – will be with you in a moment. Or, perhaps more likely, that you must await His Pleasure.

You can also take a walk through more recent history. Throughout the 18th century various wars with

France meant that England faced a fairly constant threat of invasion; in the early 19th, when the threat came from Napoleon, the government spent £80,000 strengthening the castle – upwards of £6 million in today's money. Some of that went on a complex of tunnels beneath the castle, which served as barracks and were extended and deepened during World War II. At that time, with the additional fear of aerial bombardment, they became a safe headquarters from which to plan the evacuation of Dunkirk and the defence of the south coast.

On the face of it, though, it's slightly odd that Henry II should have gone to so much trouble to make a palace out of Dover. A fortification, yes: strategic situation and all that. But when he went to France (as he very often did – some 28 times in the course of his reign), he tended to go through Portsmouth or Southampton. It's likely that the glamorisation of Dover Castle was a direct result of the death and canonisation of Thomas Becket (see page 66). Distinguished visitors – notably the King of France, hoping to restore an ailing son to health – started to pass through on their way to pray at Canterbury and Henry had to entertain them somewhere princely. He even installed a richly decorated Becket shrine in his new chapel. Was he taking his penance for Thomas's death to extremes, or accepting the consequences of his actions and cashing in on them? Who can tell?

19

QUEEN ELEANOR'S BOWER
Eleanor of Aquitaine

IT'S SAD THAT ONE OF OUR most formidable queens – a woman who was married to two kings, mother to two more and was Duchess of Aquitaine in her own right (as opposed to by marriage or any other subservient-to-a-man role) – should have left us with so few physical reminders of her life. But with Eleanor of Aquitaine, that's the way it is.

Aquitaine (a substantial chunk of southwest France centring on Bordeaux) was a wealthy and powerful dukedom; Eleanor inherited it at the age of 15 on the death of her father. A politically significant alliance was promptly arranged: she married the young and monkish heir to the French throne, who became Louis VII on the death of his own father a few days later. The marriage lasted 15 years and (being not entirely monkish) produced two daughters, but it wasn't a happy one and was eventually annulled. Only two months later, in May 1152, Eleanor married the Duke of Normandy and Count of Anjou, soon to become Henry II of England. Henry was 11 years her junior and their relationship was, to say the least, tumultuous, but she bore him eight children, including five sons.

It was disagreement between these sons and their father over who would rule which part of Henry II's vast domains (see page 69) that in 1173 led the eldest of them to revolt – with the support of two of his younger brothers, aged only 15 and 14, and the backing of his mother.

Contemporary sources give no clear explanation of Eleanor's motive. Was she trying to wrest back control of her own duchy, which was now under Henry's domaine? Or was she spurred on by jealousy of her husband's mistress, the famously beautiful 'Fair Rosamund'? Indeed, did Eleanor later have Rosamund poisoned? This seems improbable, given that royal mistresses were hardly unusual, and Eleanor – brought up in the court of her grandfather, a notorious womaniser – is unlikely to have been shocked. The fact remains that Henry's relationship with Rosamund became public in 1173,
just about the time of the revolt, and that she died in 1176, for unrecorded reasons, while still in her twenties. There may be no evidence, but there was no shortage of speculation.

Be that as it may, the revolt was eventually crushed and Eleanor was taken into custody, where she remained for 16 years, being released only after Henry had died. But we know frustratingly little of where she was imprisoned and how she spent her time. We know she was in England, because there are Exchequer records telling us that money was paid out for her keep. But beyond that... She may have been at some point in Winchester, though the Queen Eleanor's Garden behind the Great Hall there is named after another Eleanor, the wife of Henry III. She probably spent a while at Old

Sarum, the Iron Age hill fort that had been developed
into both a castle and a cathedral, just outside Salisbury;
she is known to have been released to spend the
Christmas of 1184 at Windsor with some of her family;
and in Shropshire the remains of a medieval fortress
perched on the side of Haughmond Hill are known as
Queen Eleanor's Bower.

This site is significant – to archaeologists, at least
– in that it is the remnant of a circular fortification
known as a ringwork, of which not many are known.
The fortress was built on a knoll that appears to have
been artificially steepened, making it easier to defend
(or harder to escape from…?). But for non-
archaeologists the main reason for making the climb
is the spectacular view over the Severn Valley and
Shrewsbury. Of Eleanor's presence there is no
clear proof.

She was a survivor, though: she made it to the then
remarkable age of 80, outliving all but two of her
children and serving as Regent for her son, by now
Richard I, during his lengthy absences on the Crusades.
When Richard was kidnapped on his way home from
the Holy Land it was Eleanor who raised the ransom
money. She travelled to Spain aged 77, being kidnapped
on the way but living to tell the tale. She died in France
and is buried alongside her husband and her son
Richard at Fontevraud Abbey, near Chinon. For all the
rumours associating her with various parts of England,
if you want to pay tribute to this extraordinary woman,
that's the best place to go.

20

Nottingham Castle
Richard I

RICHARD I – THE LIONHEART – is, of all our monarchs, the one who spent least time in England. He was born in Oxford, but was taken to Normandy at the age of eight. Through his mother (see page 73), he became Duke of Aquitaine while not much more than a boy, and thereafter spent most of his time either in France or on Crusade in the Holy Land.

He was in France in 1189 when his father, Henry II, died, but returned to be crowned in Westminster Abbey. He stayed in England only 17 weeks, collecting taxes and mortgaging lands to raise money for the Crusade he was determined to undertake. En route for the Holy Land he sorted out some problems his sister was having in Sicily, conquered Cyprus and married a Princess of Navarre while still officially betrothed to the woman who had probably been his father's mistress. He then fought in his Crusade, capturing the crucial port of Acre and negotiating with the Muslim leader Saladin to give Christians access to Jerusalem, and was returning triumphantly home when he was taken prisoner and held for ransom in Austria.

All of this – understandably – kept him out of the country for several years and enabled his younger brother John to attempt to usurp the throne. Nottingham was one of John's strongholds (this is Robin Hood time and the infamous Sheriff of Nottingham was one of John's supporters). Fortunately for Richard, his formidable mother Eleanor – by this time aged 69 but showing no signs of slowing down – was keeping an eye on his kingdom and on her youngest son. She forced John to surrender some of the fortresses he had seized, but he was still in control of Nottingham when his brother returned in 1194.

Richard was, with good reason, contemptuous of John. On hearing of his treachery, he is said to have remarked, 'My brother John is not the man to win lands by force if there is anyone at all to oppose him.' Richard's attack on Nottingham Castle bore out this observation: John's forces surrendered in a matter of days. Those of a

WHILE YOU'RE HERE

Beneath Nottingham Castle is a labyrinth of manmade caves, probably dating to the time of the castle's construction, around 1068. One is said to be haunted by the ghost of Roger Mortimer, the lover of Queen Isabella and almost certainly complicit with her in the murder of her husband, Edward II (see page 100). In 1330, three years after Edward's death, the lovers were captured in Nottingham by Isabella's son, now Edward III. Mortimer was taken to the Tower, convicted without trial and hanged at Tyburn.

Set against these caves is the pub believed to be the oldest in England. Ye Olde Trip to Jerusalem traces its history back to 1189, the year that Richard I came to the throne. His entourage met at Nottingham Castle before setting off for the Holy Land, so they may well have dropped in for a pint. The cave beneath the pub was once used as a brewery, and the ones on ground level are still very atmospheric places to go for a drink.

romantic turn of mind may like to know that tradition has it that Richard married Robin Hood to Maid Marian here; a plaque outside the castle commemorates the event.

John wasn't the only treacherous person in this story: Philip II of France had accompanied Richard on Crusade, but on returning to France took advantage of Richard's absence to win back large parts of Normandy, which had been under English control. After only three months in England, therefore, Richard was off back to France, recapturing his lost territory and dying of a wound received in battle in 1199. John – the youngest of Henry II and Eleanor's five sons – inherited the throne in the end.

That wasn't the end of Nottingham Castle's role in history-changing events, though. Richard III stayed here the night before the Battle of Bosworth (see page 153), and it was here that Charles I raised his standard to start the Civil War, rallying the Royalist troops (see page 239). Soon afterwards, the castle fell to the Parliamentarians and held out against several Royalist attacks but was destroyed in 1651. It was rebuilt as a palace for a 17th-century Duke of Newcastle, destroyed again, refurbished and reopened as a museum, but it had had its moments.

21

RUNNYMEDE
John

And still when Mob or Monarch lays
Too rude a hand on English ways
The whisper wakes, the shudder plays
Across the reeds at Runnymede.

RUDYARD KIPLING, 'THE REEDS OF RUNNYMEDE'

A A MILNE'S 'KING JOHN'S CHRISTMAS', published in 1927 and aimed at children, begins with the words 'King John was not a good man' and repeats them five times in the course of the poem: Milne was drawing on a popular prejudice that has not diminished with time. In 2015, the 800th anniversary of Magna Carta (of which more in a minute), two biographies with the title *King John* were published: the subtitle of one was *Treachery, Tyranny and the Road to Magna Carta* and of the other *England, Magna Carta and the Making of a Tyrant*. And the sad truth is King John was almost certainly not a good man. (Did he try to seize the throne while his elder brother was out of the country? Yes. Did he murder his young nephew Arthur, to rid himself of a rival? Probably. You get the picture.)

Certainly he was a sufficiently bad king for a number of his barons to get together in 1215, draw up what came to be called the Great Charter – Magna Carta in Latin – and force him to sign it. Or rather to put his seal, signifying royal agreement, to it. The Charter was an attempt to curtail the arbitrary way in which John exercised power, and included a definition of the barons' obligations to him, a confirmation of the freedom of the Church, the provision that a freeman should not be imprisoned or banished other than according to the law of the land (as opposed to on a whim of the King's) and the assertion of a widow's right not to remarry unless she chose to do so. It also covered a few surprisingly detailed matters such as a landowner's duty to maintain his fish preserves, ponds and mills, and the introduction of standard measures for wine, ale, corn and dyed cloth. This document was rescinded, revived and revised a number of times in the next few years; it is called the Great Charter simply because in 1217 a second charter, dealing with forest law, was issued – and it was smaller than its predecessor.

Despite its quirkiness – and despite the fact that few of its 63 clauses survive in law today – Magna Carta has come to be seen as a foundation stone of modern democracy; it was certainly one of the first attempts to limit the power of an absolute monarch. Four copies are still in existence, though there may once have been as many as 40. Two are in the British Library in London (where one is sometimes on display or readers can apply for permission to consult them) and the other two belong to the cathedrals of Salisbury and Lincoln. The one in Salisbury is the best preserved and is the centrepiece of an exhibition in the magnificent 13th-century Chapter House; the Lincoln copy is displayed in the castle, alongside a copy of the smaller Charter of the Forest, in a new, purpose-built vault.

The actual sealing of the Charter, however, took place not in any of these major centres, but at Runnymede, today a low-lying and muddy Thames-side meadow. It's not certain why this place was chosen: it's midway between John's residence at Windsor and the barons' headquarters at Staines and it had been used for council meetings of various kinds since as far back as Alfred the Great's time, so the answer may simply be 'Why not?' Whatever the reason, the Magna Carta memorial here has a Classical simplicity about it – it's an open-sided colonnade, a domed roof supported by a few columns. It feels, surprisingly and rather movingly, like a war memorial: despite all the mud on your boots, you instinctively sit quietly and talk in whispers.

The granite pillar at its centre is inscribed 'To commemorate Magna Carta, symbol of Freedom Under Law', and the whole thing was the gift, in 1957, of the American Bar Association. Representatives of the ABA have returned periodically in the intervening years to pledge their continuing support for the principles of Magna Carta.

It's strange, given this great and international legacy, that nobody seems to have taken much notice of the Charter once it was sealed. Within three months the country was engulfed in civil war; in not much over a year, John was dead and the whole business of persuading the king that his power was not absolute had to be started all over again.

22

GUILDFORD CASTLE
Henry III

HENRY'S REIGN BEGAN BADLY by any standards: he was
only nine years old and he inherited a war. The problem
was that his father, the deeply unpopular King John, had
put his seal on Magna Carta in 1215 (see page 79) and
then refused to abide by its provisions. Sparking what
became known as the First Barons' War, a group of
disaffected barons invited Louis, the Dauphin of France,
to invade – in order, according to a contemporary
document, to 'prevent the realm being pillaged by
aliens'. Louis was married to Eleanor of Brittany, the
daughter of a deceased elder brother of John's. As such,
should John and his children be ruled out of the
succession, Louis had an arguable claim to the throne;
the invitation wasn't as bizarre as it might at first appear.

Having sent a contingent of knights to help the
barons protect London in November 1215, Louis
invaded the following May. He had to besiege both
Dover and Windsor Castles, but many others, including
Guildford, simply opened their gates and welcomed him
in. He was proclaimed king (though not actually
crowned) in London, captured Winchester, the previous
capital, and controlled most of southern England.

It was at this inconvenient moment that John, who
had retreated north to Newark, contracted dysentery

and died. Forced to stop and think, the barons realised
that a powerful French prince was probably not the
ruler they wanted; a nine-year-old boy whom they
could mould to their interests might well be a better
bet. Many of them deserted the Dauphin to support
Henry, defeating Louis in battle at Lincoln and
Sandwich and withstanding his second attempt to
besiege Dover Castle. Louis, who had to all intents and
purposes been King of England for 18 months, accepted
a bribe of 10,000 marks to agree that he had never been
anything of the sort. He went home, to become King
Louis VIII seven years later.

Magna Carta, in a slightly revised form, came back
into circulation and in 1225, when Henry was 18, he
confirmed it again, in return for the barons' promise of
support and funding for wars in France. The wars proved
a disaster, however, and Henry's determination to rule
directly, rather than through his former regents and
senior ministers, alienated the barons all over again.

In 1236, Henry married Eleanor of Provence, who
was no more than 13 to his 29. She soon became widely
disliked, not least because she had brought with her to
England a retinue of relations who were deemed to have
undue influence over the King. So although no real
trouble broke out for a while, there was a lot of
festering going on.

It was during this period that Henry started
spending lavishly on his favourite castles. He expanded
both Winchester and Windsor, but the place that he
turned into one of the most luxurious royal residences
in England – and where he often chose to spend

Christmas – was Guildford. William the Conqueror is thought to have built a castle here, but the keep that still stands proudly on the hill looking down over the town is a 12th-century addition, dating from Henry II's time. Today it offers a 360-degree panoramic view that is well worth the entrance money and the climb.

But William the Conqueror and Henry II were concerned with fortifications; Henry III splashed out on decoration and buildings. None of the decoration remains, but there are ruins aplenty to wander through. Records show that he built a Great Hall, private chapels for himself and his Queen, and Great Chambers that served as their private quarters. The Queen's Chamber had a window made 'as large as possible' (not cheap); the wall paintings in the Great Hall recounted the New Testament parable of the beggar Lazarus and the rich man who neglected him, reminding the King to be charitable; and the garden was surrounded by a cloister with marble columns. To Henry's way of thinking, 'charitable' clearly did not equate with 'frugal'.

To be fair, he was equally lavish with his charitable donations and seems to have been genuinely devout, hearing mass at least once a day. He chose Edward the Confessor as his patron saint and role model, hoping to imitate both his piety and his ability to unite his kingdom. He even broke with family tradition and called his eldest son Edward in his patron's honour. But that unrest continued to fester and the very name of the First Barons' War gives a clue that there might be a second waiting to happen…

23

KENILWORTH CASTLE
Henry III

BARELY PAUSING FOR BREATH after the First Barons' War
(see page 82), we find Simon de Montfort, Earl of
Leicester, leading another revolt against Henry III.
Simon was married to Henry's sister Eleanor, and the
King had granted him the use of Kenilworth Castle,
a substantial pile that Henry's father, King John, had
expanded and refortified. John had even created a
lake around the castle to make it harder to attack –
a precaution that his son would come to regret.

The background to the Second Barons' War
(1264–7) is that in 1258 the barons had forced Henry
to submit to the so-called Provisions of Oxford. These
created an advisory council of 15 barons empowered
to reform the system of government, cut down on
corruption among local officials and curb the King's
habit of raising taxes on the slightest whim. It may not
sound much by today's standards of constitutional
monarchies, but for Henry's time it was revolutionary
– and he didn't like it. All those decorations to his
castles had to be paid for somehow.

The King's refusal to go along with the Provisions
led to armed conflict. Defeated at the Battle of Lewes
in 1264, Henry and his son, the future Edward I, were
imprisoned in Lewes Castle and Henry was forced to

sign over a lot of his powers. Simon de Montfort was now uncrowned king, though ruling ostensibly in the King's name. In 1265 he summoned the first Parliament in England to include representatives of cities and boroughs.

But it didn't last. A few months later Edward, having escaped from prison, routed the barons' forces at the Battle of Evesham; Simon was killed and Henry was able to take his kingdom back into his own hands. The death of their leader didn't quell the barons, however. They took refuge inside Kenilworth, which should in theory have been returned to the Crown on Simon's death. And they took with them a vast stock of provisions and a supply of siege engines to help them defend themselves should the need arise.

It's at about this time that Henry must have realised the folly of giving away one of England's strongest fortifications. The Kenilworth garrison, numbering perhaps 1,200 people, was able to counter his missiles, sent from a barrage of stone-throwing machines, with projectiles of their own: one contemporary chronicler described the two lots of stones 'clashing in the air'. The barons held out for almost six months, making Kenilworth the longest siege in English history. In the end, though, supplies ran out and they were forced to surrender. But the seeds of democracy had been sown and

Simon de Montfort's legacy lives on in the present House of Commons.

After the siege Henry gave Kenilworth to his second son, Edmund, later Duke of Lancaster; it remained in Lancastrian hands until the Lancastrian Henry IV came to the throne, when it reverted to the Crown. Subsequent kings were attracted to it by its excellent hunting and improved its leisure facilities – Henry V created a 'pleasance' or pleasure garden in which to relax on an island in the lake; Henry VII added a tennis court and Henry VIII extended the gardens. Then Edward VI granted it to the father of Elizabeth I's favourite Robert Dudley, Earl of Leicester (it was at Kenilworth that Dudley's wife conveniently fell – or was pushed – downstairs to her death).

Like many other castles, Kenilworth was 'slighted' – rendered indefensible – by the Parliamentarians in the 1650s. What remains is as romantic as any castle in England: the local red sandstone makes it stand out from other ruins you may be used to. You can admire the remains of the fine Great Hall built by John of Gaunt (see page 118); you can climb the tower that Dudley built in order to woo Elizabeth, or walk in the gardens she walked in. Or you can go outside the walls and consider the size of the meadow that the lake once occupied and how impressive the fortifications must once have been. It'll make you realise that Henry III must *really* have regretted handing the place over to a baron with unsettling ideas about democracy.

24

THE CASTLES OF NORTH WALES
Edward I

WITH ALL POSSIBLE RESPECT to William I (see page 48), no one in British history has built castles the way Edward I did. He had been on a Crusade in 1271, the year before he came to the throne, and had been inspired by the fortresses he'd seen in the Holy Land. Here, he thought, was a way to expand his kingdom and keep it expanded.

As king, the first part of his empire-building project was to subdue Wales. The border area known as the Marches was ruled by Marcher Lords who were supposed to be subservient to the English Crown but enjoyed considerable independence and were always fighting among themselves. Even more problematic was Llywelyn ap Gruffudd, who had been recognised as Prince of Wales by Edward's father Henry III in 1267, but in 1275 refused to pay homage to the new king. Edward gathered the largest army seen in Britain since 1066 and set out to subdue the lot of them.

The Welsh defeat at the Battle of Orewin Bridge in 1282, when Llywelyn was killed, effectively put an end to any question of Welsh independence, and Edward was free to embark on his building programme. Having already rebuilt and strengthened a number of fortresses further south, he now created a great 'iron ring' of castles across North Wales. Caernarfon has special significance in the history of Wales (see page 94), but among the rest Conwy, Harlech and Beaumaris stand out. Together, the four form the Castles and Town Walls of King Edward in Gwynedd World Heritage Site; individually they are all wonders in their own way.

The pretty little harbour town of Conwy is dominated by its castle. That's a remark that could be made about many places in North Wales, but in Conwy the effect is enhanced by the castle's location – on a rock that dominates the skyline for miles around – and by the spectacular chunks of defensive wall that are everywhere you look. From the castle's battlements, the views northwards, out to sea, and southwards, over Snowdonia, are breathtaking; look down and you can admire the roofless Great Hall: at almost 130ft long it was larger than the largest room in Buckingham Palace today. Nothing about Conwy Castle is subtle, but it was built to impress and intimidate and it still does plenty of both.

Further south, and also relying on its rocky location to aid its defences, Harlech Castle is the least well preserved of the four. By way of compensation, its position on Wales's west coast means it is easy to find a miserable day on which to visit, and in bad weather the substantial ruins are haunting. It's not surprising to feel a sensation of unrest here: Harlech endured a total of five sieges between the 1290s and 1640s, including one during the Wars of the Roses when the Lancastrian forces of Margaret of Anjou (see page 137) held out for seven years against the Yorkists – and, incidentally, inspired the anonymous composer of the Welsh anthem 'Men of Harlech'. Finally, in 1647, Harlech became the last Royalist stronghold to surrender to Oliver Cromwell, having withstood the Parliamentarian assault for five years.

Cromwell, ungracious even in victory, ordered the castle to be slighted – rendered unfit for use. So even in West Wales it is unfair to blame everything on the weather.

Beaumaris, on the island of Anglesey, is Edward's crowning glory. Everything his master architect, James of St George, had done before seems to have been in preparation for this. Designed as a castle within a castle, Beaumaris has a series of concentric walls: once an assailant was inside the first he was stuck, unable to retreat but with a massive fortification still to storm. If he made it over that, there was a third – and a fourth. And that's assuming he wasn't deterred by the arrows fired from hundreds of cleverly sited arrow slits or by the rocks or hot oil poured from the many 'murder holes' designed to defend the entrances.

Sadly, the effectiveness of all this was never put to the test. Beaumaris employed 400 highly skilled masons and 2,000 lesser workmen: after three years of work, the money simply ran out. Construction was halted in 1298 and Edward turned his attention to Scotland (see next entry) and took James of St George with him. A visitor to Beaumaris today can only marvel at what the two of them might have achieved if James's genius had been given free rein and an unlimited budget.

25

SCONE PALACE
Edward I

So, thanks to all at once, and to each one,
Whom we invite to see us crown'd at Scone.

WILLIAM SHAKESPEARE, *MACBETH*

SCONE – A FEW MILES FROM PERTH and just north of the
Antonine Wall, which marked the northern frontier of
the Roman Empire – was the Pictish capital in the 5th
century. The Picts were the hostile 'painted' or tattooed
tribes whom the Romans failed to subdue, and when
their 9th-century leader Kenneth MacAlpin united the
southern Scots he chose to be enthroned at Scone.
According to legend, he brought with him a 'king-
making seat', which he set up on Scone's Moot Hill.

It is this seat that came to be known as the Stone of
Scone or, to the more romantically inclined, the Stone
of Destiny. It's a rough-hewn slab of sandstone about
25in long, 16 wide and 11 deep, weighing over 300lb
and with two iron rings on its top to help you carry it.
Scottish kings – including Malcolm Canmore, who
spoke the closing words from *Macbeth* quoted above –
were enthroned (and later crowned as well) on it for
400 years. During this time an important Augustinian
Priory with a vast abbey church grew up around it
– indeed, the stone was housed in the abbey and

brought out on to the hill only for enthroning ceremonies. Then, in 1296, Edward I of England, determined to subdue the Scots as he had the Welsh (see page 88), captured it and took it to Westminster Abbey, where it formed part of the chair on which English and British monarchs were crowned until it was finally restored to Scotland in 1996.

Undaunted, Scottish kings continued to be crowned at Scone and to hold Parliaments here. The last coronation was that of Charles II in 1651, though he had to wait another 10 years before a second coronation, at Westminster Abbey, acknowledged him as King of England too. He would have been sitting on the Stone of Scone when that happened.

The stone that now sits on the Moot Hill is a replica; the one that used to be at Westminster is on display in Edinburgh Castle, alongside the Scottish Crown Jewels. But it is quite likely that that is a replica, too, and that Edward I never laid his hands on the original. No early documents describe the Stone as it looks today. One theory has it that the Abbot of the Priory, hearing that Edward was coming and knowing he was likely to ransack the place, quickly had a duplicate made and hid the original away. If that is true, then no one has the slightest idea where it is.

Today, you approach Scone Palace via an impressive driveway with oak trees on either side: it makes you realise where they got the wood they needed to make all those hammerbeam roofs. In the car park you are greeted by a condescending peacock or two, bred on the estate, and then you come to a wonderful four-square castle – everyone's idea of a castle, with lots of crenellated battlements. Rebuilt in the Gothic style in the 19th century, it's a sophisticated and beautiful version of the castle a six-year-old would draw.

To the right, the Moot Hill is tiny, little more than a mound, and the chapel is tiny too, smaller than the average village church. It stands on the site of the former abbey church and recent surveys have discovered large numbers of graves – including, probably, those of early Scottish kings – in the ground beneath it.

Inside the palace, the Long Gallery, at 150ft, is the longest room in Scotland. Charles II may well have walked along here in preparation for his coronation; certainly Victoria and Albert witnessed an indoor curling competition on the highly polished oak and bog oak parquetry floor. In today's terms, you could fit in two bowling alleys and still have room for a full-sized snooker table.

The palace has been in the hands of the Murray family, now the Earls of Mansfield, for generation upon generation, and the furniture and art on display are the result of years of careful and tasteful collecting. The arboretum – a tribute to the plant-hunter David Douglas, discoverer of the Douglas fir, who was born in the village – makes the grounds a particular delight. The maze is fun, too, planted in the shape of the five-pointed star that features in the Murray family crest. But it's Scone's status as 'the place of kings' that makes it special. For, as they say, 'As long as fate plays fair, where this stone lies, the Scots shall reign.'

26

CAERNARFON CASTLE
Edward II

And at the river mouth he could see a great castle,
the fairest that mortal had ever seen…

'THE DREAM OF MACSEN WLEDIG' IN *THE MABINOGION*

IF BEAUMARIS (SEE PAGE 90) IS AN unfinished masterpiece,
Caernarfon is, of all Edward I's castles, the most
overflowing with symbolism, the one that shows his
control of Wales as not only secure and settled, but
inevitable. A story from the collection of traditional
Welsh tales known as *The Mabinogion* associates
Caernarfon with the Roman Emperor Magnus
Maximus (or, to put him in Welsh, Macsen Wledig),
and it is widely believed that Edward built on this
connection by creating a fortress-palace inspired by
Constantinople, capital of the Eastern Roman Empire.
This may explain why Caernarfon is built in colour-
banded stone and has polygonal towers – those on
Edward's other Welsh castles are round. The grandest
of its towers is the Eagle Tower, the eagle being both
a Roman and a Welsh symbol: the remains of a stone-
carved eagle can still be seen on the battlements.

From the moment these distinctive features were
conceived, Caernarfon was going to be something
special. Those who refute the Magnus connection

suggest instead that Edward's inspiration was the legendary King Arthur. But wherever he was getting his ideas, he was using Caernarfon to stamp his authority on the Welsh – and to stamp it good and hard.

It wasn't all oppression, though: having been responsible for the death of the previous Prince of Wales, Llywelyn ap Gruffudd, Edward made a gesture of appeasement. He promised the Welsh a new prince, one who had been born in Wales and spoke no English. Although building work at Caernarfon had begun only in the summer of 1283 (and would continue for almost half a century), Edward brought his pregnant wife Eleanor here the following Easter so that, on 25 April 1284, she could give birth to her 16th child. That infant, speaking as yet no English, Welsh nor any other language, was presented to the Welsh as Prince of Wales. Or so the story, first recorded 300 years later, goes.

The title 'Prince of Wales' has, of course, been given to the heir apparent ever since. There have been only two of them in the last hundred years, and both have been ceremonially invested at Caernarfon. The first, in 1911, was the future Edward VIII, who became the centrepiece of a public pageant based on Welsh tradition. This was at the suggestion of the local MP, David Lloyd George, then Chancellor of the Exchequer and later to be Prime Minister. Given that Welsh Nationalism was worryingly on the rise at the time, it's likely that the wily 'Welsh Wizard' came up with the idea as a good piece of PR.

Edward VIII's successor George VI had no sons, so the title skipped a generation and the next investiture – that of Elizabeth II's son Charles – didn't take place till 1969. By then outside broadcasts and colour television were well established and the ceremony was witnessed by millions around the world (and can still be seen on YouTube). 'What a scene it was,' intoned the Pathé News commentator, 'the ancient castle providing an unequalled backcloth to an occasion of pomp and splendour which was yet also one of simplicity.' Not everyone would describe it as simple, as the young prince – in front of a packed house, both inside the castle and out – was invested by his mother with the sword, coronet, gold ring, gold rod and mantle that were his insignias of office. But it would be hard to take issue with his own diffident remark that 'the British, on the whole, tend to do this sort of ceremony rather well'.

As for the castle itself, its interiors were never completed and much of what you see today is 19th-century restoration. But the walls – of both castle and town – have survived unbroken, and overlook a pretty harbour where the materials for Edward's massive building project arrived by boat.

And that infant prince who spoke no English? Well, a much-weathered statue of him dating from 1320 can be seen above the King's Gate by which you enter the castle. He had survived four elder brothers to become King Edward II, but then his luck rather changed. Not to put too fine a point on it, he turned into a bit of a disaster, as we shall see later...

27

GEDDINGTON
Eleanor of Castile

YOU DON'T EXPECT MEDIEVAL royal marriages to be happy
ones, particularly when a 13-year-old princess is
married to a 15-year-old prince for overtly political
reasons. But Edward I and Eleanor of Castile were
devoted to each other. They were married in Burgos in
1254, 18 years before he became king. Once they
arrived in England, she played a significant role in the
Barons' War that was being waged against her father-in-
law, Henry III (see page 82). Having a French mother,
she was able to arrange for archers to be brought over
from France, and for a while she took charge of Windsor
Castle, where various of the rebel barons were
imprisoned. When the barons regained the upper hand,
Simon de Montfort thought Eleanor important enough
to be removed from Windsor and placed under house
arrest at Westminster Palace.

Once the war was over and, in 1272, Edward had
become king, Eleanor continued to accompany him
wherever he went, including on a Crusade. This was
despite the fact that she was pregnant at least 16 times
– she gave birth to her eighth child in the Holy Land.
It was during one of the last of these pregnancies that
she went along with his plans to placate the Welsh by
giving them a Welsh-born prince (see page 95). All very

well for Edward to make this grandiose gesture; for Eleanor, now aged 43 (well into late middle age by 13th-century standards), it meant having her baby in what was little more than a building site. This was devotion indeed.

Not long after this, Eleanor's health began to deteriorate and she died near Lincoln in 1290, aged 49. Edward's expression of grief has left us her most famous legacy. Her body was carried to London over a period of 12 days and, wherever it rested for the night, he had a cross erected in his wife's honour. The best known of these 'Eleanor Crosses' stands outside Charing Cross Station in London, but is a Victorian replica. The original was where the equestrian statue of Charles I now stands between Trafalgar Square and Whitehall: traditionally, distances from London are measured from this point. Along with many other royal monuments, the cross was destroyed on the orders of Parliament in 1647. But from surviving records we know that it was made of marble, built on a polygonal base and carved all over in the Decorative style that was fashionable at the time, with arches, delicate tracery and copious foliage motifs. The others were probably along similar lines, although the Charing Cross was the most lavish.

As for the real things, a chunk of the Stamford Cross can be seen in that town's museum and a 21st-century sculpture inspired by it (though the resemblance is token) stands in the Sheep Market. The one in Waltham Cross is in good condition, thanks to 19th- and 20th-century restoration. It has three statues of Eleanor, each in its own niche; these are Victorian, but

one of the originals can be seen in the V&A in London.
At Hardingstone, Northamptonshire, the cross stands
alongside the busy A508, on the edge of Delapre Wood,
where an abbey – dating from 1145 and, after recent
restoration, open to the public for the first time in 900
years – provided a suitable resting place. Its location is
now somewhat suburban and lacking in ambience, but
the cross is remarkably well preserved.

For the best experience you need to go to
Geddington, also in Northamptonshire. Here the
monument is slightly different from the others
– triangular in plan, taller and slimmer, with the base
decorated with rosettes rather than leaves. But the
statues of Eleanor are intact, the coats of arms on the
base clearly visible and, best of all, it stands in the
middle of a village street where it looks as if it belongs.
Not even the Geddington Cross, however, retains the
cross which was once the monument's crowning glory:
for that you have to go back to a London railway station
and a Victorian reconstruction.

If you prefer more conventional memorials, Eleanor
was buried in Westminster Abbey: her magnificent tomb,
topped with a gilt-bronze effigy, is in the St Edward the
Confessor Chapel, close to that of her devoted husband.
And, because it was the norm to embalm bodies and
take out the internal organs, a duplicate monument –
with Eleanor's viscera inside it – can be found in
Lincoln Cathedral. Its effigy was also destroyed in the
1640s and replaced in Victorian times.

28

BERKELEY CASTLE
Edward II

OF ALL THE PLACES CELEBRATED in this book, Berkeley Castle is perhaps the one with the starkest contrast between the old and the new. Today, it is an idyllic wedding venue; it's also a family home, inhabited by the same family for almost 900 years – longer than any other building in England. But back in 1327, it was the prison where the deposed Edward II died – murdered, if legend is to be believed, by the sadistic administration of a red-hot poker.

Edward's reign had been distinguished – if that is the word – by his ill-judged choice of favourites. As soon as he succeeded to the throne, he gave the prestigious and lucrative title of Earl of Cornwall to a young man named Piers Gaveston, who had been part of his household since both were in their teens. This at a stroke made Gaveston one of the most powerful men in the land and alienated the established nobility, who knew a money-grubbing upstart when they saw one. Within months, Edward went to France to marry the Princess Isabella (see page 103) and made Gaveston Regent in his absence. Long story short, after some years of toing and froing, with the barons demanding reforms and Edward ignoring them, some of them rebelled, took Gaveston prisoner and (depending on whose side you're on) either murdered or executed him in June 1312.

From that ill-omened start, Edward's reign continued to slither downhill. He constantly refused to accept the barons' attempts to restrict his powers, which meant that civil war was never far away; there were problems with France over who was to rule Gascony; then came the fiasco of Bannockburn (see page 106) and a famine. The fact that the barons were constantly falling out among themselves only made matters worse. And Edward acquired a new favourite, Hugh Despenser. Thanks to a propitious marriage, Despenser was already extremely wealthy; Edward appointed him Royal Chamberlain and he proceeded to line his pockets at every opportunity and to make an enemy of everyone else at court, including

WHILE YOU'RE IN THE AREA
About 20 miles north of Berkeley is Gloucester Cathedral, where Edward II is buried. In 1216, Gloucester's Romanesque abbey, as it then was, had been grand enough for Henry III's coronation, but a century later Edward's son, now Edward III, decreed that his father's burial place deserved something finer. Bizarrely, given his track record, Edward II's grave had become a place of pilgrimage – after the fall of Isabella and Mortimer (see page 105), his reputation improved and some even saw him as a martyr. Visitors donated huge sums to the abbey, allowing Edward III to commission experimental work in the French 'Rayonnant' style, which developed into English Perpendicular. The tall and flamboyant South Transept is the earliest surviving example of this style; the ceiling of the cloisters may boast the earliest fan vaulting. The tomb itself, recently restored, consists of an alabaster effigy on a limestone base, topped by an ornate limestone canopy. If you want to reflect on the irony of a disastrous king contributing to a ground-breaking piece of architecture, this is the place to do it.

Queen Isabella and her lover, the powerful Marcher Lord Roger Mortimer. When these two invaded England in 1326 (see page 104), there was suddenly an awful lot of writing on the wall. Edward was forced to abdicate, and Despenser, tried for treason and sundry other crimes, was executed with gruesome barbarity. Edward was imprisoned first in Kenilworth and then in the more secure Berkeley Castle, where he died – in what one historian has described as a 'suspiciously timely' manner – six months later.

Today visitors to Berkeley can admire the 30ft high Great Hall, built in the time of Edward III, a grand staircase, and a bedspread belonging to Elizabeth I. For the ghoulish, however, the real treat is the King's Gallery, which includes the cell and dungeon where Edward II was imprisoned and died. If you don't care for the poker story, Christopher Marlowe's play *Edward II*, first performed in 1592, contains the gruesome stage direction 'King Edward is murdered by holding him down on the bed with the table, and stamping on it.' We don't know for sure what happened to Edward, but it's probably safe to assume that it was unpleasant.

29

Castle Rising
Isabella of France

You have to be quite close to Castle Rising before you spot it, because the name doesn't mean what you probably think it means. The Norman keep, one of the finest survivors of its period, stands on banks which rise only some 60ft above the surrounding countryside, but the massive earthworks cover about 12 acres and the deep ditches made it well-nigh impregnable in its prime. This was a castle built by someone (in the reign of Stephen – see page 60 – when *lots* of people were building castles) who had a powerful point to make. Isabella of France – daughter of King Philip IV of France, wife of Edward II and mother of Edward III – owned, lost and regained many estates in her time, but this was one of the most formidable.

That is appropriate enough, because she was a formidable woman, often referred to as 'the She-Wolf of France'. Married to Edward II when she was only 12, she had to put up with his public infatuation with Piers Gaveston and the fact that he lavished jewels, lands and titles on his favourite while grudging her the money to maintain a household befitting her status. Isabella came into her own only after Gaveston's death and after she had given birth to an heir a few months later.

From that time on, although still in her teens, she was to all appearances not only a loyal wife but a canny politician, interceding with her less astute husband to calm various outbreaks of war with his own barons. Then in 1322 Isabella's brother Charles succeeded to the throne of France and demanded that Edward, as Duke of Aquitaine, come to pay homage to his new king. Edward had done this for Charles's predecessors, but now he had a new favourite, the ambitious and wildly avaricious Hugh Despenser (see page 101), and he knew that if he left Despenser in charge of his kingdom in his absence, the barons would rise in revolt – again. He sent Isabella to France in his place; when Charles made a fuss, Edward declared his 12-year-old son and heir Duke of Aquitaine and sent him too.

Isabella now issued an amazing proclamation, declaring herself a widow because 'someone has come between my husband and myself, trying to break [the marriage bond]. I protest that I will not return until this intruder is removed.' She meant, of course, Hugh Despenser. With her son at her side, she rallied troops to her cause. The exiled barons who joined her included Roger Mortimer, a sworn enemy of Despenser since the latter had grasped his lands in the Welsh Marches. He promptly became Isabella's lover and the two invaded England together. They were taking the unprecedented step of trying to depose an anointed king in favour of his young son, on the undeniable grounds that the King had been abusing his own power. Their arrival in England was greeted with relief as a sign that law and order might soon be restored.

The events that led to Despenser's execution and Edward's abdication and death are dealt with on page 100; let's move onwards to 1328. The young Edward III, now 16 and old enough to take the kingdom into his own hands, was unhappy about a humiliating truce Isabella and Mortimer had negotiated with the Scots. The Queen Mother and her lover had, moreover, lost the popular support they had once had by lining their own coffers in a way that would have made even Hugh Despenser sit up and take notice. Mortimer, as we have seen (see page 76), was arrested and executed in 1330; but Isabella suffered no such disgrace. Much of the rest of her life – which lasted until 1358, when she was into her sixties and had been a widow for 30 years – was spent in considerable luxury at Castle Rising.

Inside the inner bailey are the remains of a Norman church which is older than the castle itself. It's easy to imagine that Isabella, who turned pious as she grew older, spent her time in prayer here. She had plenty of time to repent the fact that she, a shrewd operator for most of her life, had been led, by the ambition of her lover, into putting personal interests before those of the kingdom she was supposed to be serving. Just as the husband she deposed had done.

30

BANNOCKBURN
Robert the Bruce

THE TOURIST DESTINATION known as the Battle of
Bannockburn isn't a museum, someone in the visitor
centre may tell you, because there are no artefacts.
Instead, it is a 3D experience which – thanks to
motion-capture technology, as used in the *Lord of the
Rings* films – immerses you in the battle. The guidebook
describes it as 'vicious, noisy and real'. It's a 21st-century,
high-tech version of the great defining moment in the
history of Scottish identity.

The question of who was to rule Scotland had been
a vexed one for many centuries, but by the early 14th
century the Scots had more or less decided. In 1306
Robert Bruce was crowned King of Scots. Not of
Scotland, you notice – that was still under discussion –
but of the Scottish people.

Unfortunately, south of the border, another king
had other ideas. Edward I of England, having filled
North Wales with as many castles as it could hold (see
page 88), had turned his attention to Scotland. Asked in
1290 to arbitrate on the question of who should take
over the vacant throne, he had established himself as
overlord and gained control of several castles. Of these,
the most important was Stirling (see page 167): not only
a royal residence, but an imposing fortress with views

east towards Edinburgh and north and west towards who knew where. Whoever held Stirling controlled access to the great majority of the country – and for the moment, that was Edward.

This fact had given rise to a powerful guerrilla movement, known more formally as the Wars of Scottish Independence. The crowning of Robert the Bruce was supposed to unite the Scottish forces, but only three months later Robert was defeated at the Battle of Methven and fled, possibly to Ireland, to reconsider his position. It was during this period of near despair that his celebrated encounter with the spider is said to have taken place. Watching it fail time after time to cast its web across a gap that seemed far too large for it, but persist until at length it succeeded, he was inspired by the similarity to his own circumstances and vowed to persevere in his battles against the English. Like many good stories in Scottish 'history', this was probably made up by the 19th-century Romantic novelist Walter Scott, but it has entered folklore.

Fast-forward to 1314. Edward I has died and his son, another Edward, lacking his father's genius for warfare, has suffered a number of losses. He still holds Stirling, but this is being besieged by Robert's brother and – as part of a strange piece of diplomacy – is to be handed over to the Bruces if it is not relieved by an English army by Midsummer Day, 24 June.

This gives Edward II a tight deadline; he musters a force at Berwick (one of his few remaining strongholds) and marches north. On 23 June he reaches a river known as the Bannock Burn (aha!), just south of

Stirling. He makes a bridge from local roofs and doorways, and crosses to the other side. Here, on the floodplain of the Bannock Burn, the English forces, some 20,000 strong, camp for the night.

Robert's force is appreciably smaller – about 8,000 men – but they have been in training, they are highly disciplined and they haven't had to march all the way from Berwick. They attack the English camp at dawn, catching the enemy unprepared and exhausted. In fierce hand-to-hand fighting, Scottish spearmen triumph over English archers. The Bannock Burn is soon full of the drowned bodies of men who have tried to flee, and by the end of the day it is all over. Edward escapes back to Berwick, minus his shield and his privy seal, and deeply humiliated.

Bannockburn was a battle, though, not a war. It cemented Robert's position, but it didn't force Edward to acknowledge him. It was not until 1328 that an English king – Edward III – recognised Scotland as an independent nation and Robert the Bruce and his successors as those entitled to rule it. And even that, as we shall see on page 110, didn't last long.

To calm yourself after taking in all this battle mayhem, try a gentle stroll towards the recently refurbished Rotunda. Here, a war memorial stands very close to the site of the battle and is complemented by a substantial statue of Robert the Bruce. Lit up at night, it is an impressive sight. But it can't compete with Stirling Castle itself, clearly visible across the valley and dominating the heart of Scotland today just as it did in 1314.

31

DUNFERMLINE ABBEY
Robert the Bruce

DUNFERMLINE ABBEY HAS BEEN connected with Scottish royalty since its foundation in the 11th century, when Queen (later Saint) Margaret established a priory here. Her son, David I, expanded the priory into an abbey and built the church whose soaring Romanesque nave is still remarkably intact. With three tiers of decorated archways and heavy pillars patterned with zigzags and spirals, it takes your breath away.

Over the centuries the Dunfermline Abbey guesthouse morphed into a favoured royal residence, and was much remodelled in the early 16th century. In 1589, James VI gave it as a wedding present to his bride, Anne of Denmark, who had further work done in time for her second son, the future Charles I, to be born here. After James became James I of England in 1603 the Royal Family spent much of their time in London; Dunfermline's buildings were abandoned and looted, leaving only the rather fine ruins that you see today.

But if an interest in royalty brings you to Dunfermline, chances are it's because of Robert the Bruce. He is known to have been buried here and experts are all but certain that the human remains discovered when the present abbey church (adjacent to the medieval nave) was built in the early 19th century are his. Those remains were carefully reinterred and today lie under the church's ornately carved pulpit, covered by a brass memorial. Before the reinterment took place, a cast was taken of the skull, enabling modern experts to produce a digital likeness of the man himself. It shows him as a bit of a bruiser, but that is entirely in keeping with his CV. To be fair, by the time of his death he was a battle-scarred old man of almost 55 and he is generally believed to have died from leprosy, which wouldn't have enhanced his looks.

Alongside the mortal remains were discovered fragments of carved and gilded marble and alabaster, remnants of the monument Robert the Bruce had commissioned for himself from Paris. These and written records have enabled experts to produce an extraordinary 3D and digital version of it. At the time of writing it is not on display, but there are moves afoot to get it to Dunfermline soon. In it, a crowned Bruce, holding a sceptre, lies peacefully with a lion at his feet atop multiple repeated images of himself, all of which would originally have been carved in marble. The surviving records give an indication of the cost, which, by the time he had paid for the materials, the mason and the shipping charges, was well over £100 – a king's ransom in modern terms.

And here's an irony: after all that trouble to establish the Bruce family as rulers of Scotland (see page 106), Robert's son David II died childless. He was succeeded by his sister's son, who became Robert II. Although he was the Bruce's grandson, he took his father's surname and became the first king of the House of Stuart.

32

BERWICK-UPON-TWEED
Edward III

WE'VE SEEN THAT EDWARD II was a bit of a disaster; his
son, coming to the throne in 1327 at the age of 14,
did much to restore both the power of the English
monarchy and the respect in which it was held. How?
By following the time-honoured path of waging war
against the Scots.

You'll remember (and if you don't, look back at
page 106) that Edward II had been routed at the Battle
of Bannockburn and had retreated to his stronghold at
Berwick-upon-Tweed. Berwick, positioned at the
mouth of the river that separated England from
Scotland, was of critical strategic importance in
skirmishes between the two countries and changed
hands many times over the centuries. It didn't just boast
a castle; it was an entirely fortified town, with its
fortifications rebuilt and strengthened every time
anyone felt the need to defend it.

The treaty of 1328 mentioned on page 108 had
been negotiated in the name of the young Edward III;
once he was old enough to reign for himself he
overthrew it. He had the support of many English
nobles who had previously owned land in Scotland and
who came to be known (among themselves, at least
– it's not recorded what the Scots called them) as the

'disinherited'. One of these was a man named Edward Balliol, whose father John had, for a few years in the 1290s, been King of the Scots.

When Robert the Bruce died in 1329, his son, who became David II, was only five – a perfect opportunity to try to put someone else on the throne. Edward III decided, covertly, that Edward Balliol was the man. More battles, collectively known as the Second War of Scottish Independence, ensued, with Balliol winning a decisive victory at Dupplin Moor in 1332, then being forced to flee the country three months later.

Edward III now decided to come into the open. His army met a Scottish one at the Battle of Halidon Hill, just outside Berwick, on 19 July 1333. Here, English archers made short and bloody work of the Scottish cavalry, who were forced to dismount and fight uphill. Archibald Douglas, Guardian of Scotland during David's minority, was killed, along with many, many other Scots. Berwick, which was in Scottish hands and which Balliol had been besieging, surrendered.

Putting Balliol on the Scottish throne, however, didn't solve anything. He wasn't an independent King of the Scots; he paid homage to Edward III, and the Scots simply didn't want him. Over the next few years, he was deposed, restored and deposed again. By 1341 David, now 18, was able to take control of his own kingdom, and the fact that he was married to Edward's sister didn't stop him attacking the North of England. Matters came to a head – again – at the Battle of Neville's Cross, near Durham, in 1346. The Scots were overwhelmed; David was captured and for most of the next 11 years kept prisoner in the Tower of London, where he proved a useful bargaining tool. Negotiations for his release, in exchange either for a large sum of money or for the promise that Edward III or one of his sons would be David's heir if he died without issue, went back and forth. Finally, a further outbreak of hostilities (during which Berwick briefly changed hands again) led, in 1357, to a truce known as the Treaty of Berwick. Conflicts between the English and the Scots didn't stop, but with the English engaged in fighting the French and, after David died in 1371, the Scots fighting among themselves, they became less important for a while.

This didn't put an end to the fortification of Berwick, however. The town changed hands twice during the Wars of the Roses and, when Calais, England's last remaining territory in France, was lost in the reign of Mary I, she ordered hugely expensive new bastions to be built in order to repel a possible Franco-Scottish attack. Although these were subsequently modified several times, you can still admire them (they're 20ft high, so hard to miss) if you walk round the fortifications. Which you should – it's one of the few places in England where you can do a complete circuit of the walls. Looking across the Tweed, you may like to consider that, although you are officially 4 miles south of the border, you are northeast of the river; logic and quite a few moments in history tell you (whisper it) that you're actually in Scotland.

33

WINDSOR CASTLE
Edward III

WINDSOR CASTLE IS ONE OF THE MOST iconic buildings in this book – instantly recognisable, with its Round Tower often bearing the Royal Standard, indicating that the monarch is in residence, and aerial views showing it covering more than 25 acres. It's been a royal home for over nine centuries, making it the oldest royal residence in Britain to have been in continuous use.

The reason Windsor Castle exists is that the hill on which it stands was a natural defensive site when William the Conqueror was building a ring of castles to protect London. In the 19th century George IV employed the foremost architects and interior designers of the day to make this out-of-town residence imposing from the outside and opulent within. In between whiles, various Tudors made additions and improvements, and Charles II created lavish state apartments and planted a 2½-mile avenue of elm trees in emulation of what Louis XIV was doing at Versailles. It seems as if almost every royal for nearly a millennium has had a hand in improving Windsor. But the man who first turned it from a fortress into a palace was Edward III.

Edward was born here in 1312 and in the 1350s he did something that no one in England had done before – he built a set of royal apartments in a coherent architectural style. These first-floor suites were arranged round a series of inner courtyards, supported by stone-vaulted undercrofts that can still be seen today. Going far beyond the merely defensive, Edward indulged in non-essential but decorative features such as tall arched windows for the chapel and a tiltyard where particularly magnificent tournaments were held. The cost was monumental – some £50,000, making it the most expensive secular building project in England during the Middle Ages. Two hundred years later, the chronicler Raphael Holinshed was still gushing: 'The King…caused diverse other fair and sumptuous works to be erected and set up in and about the same Castle, so that almost all the masons and carpenters that were of any account within this land were sent for.'

You might have thought Edward would have other things on his mind. What later became known as the Hundred Years' War (fought, to put it at its absolute simplest, between the French and English Royal Families over which of them should rule France) had begun in 1337 and dominated the second decade of his reign. He also had a major tragedy to contend with at home – the plague known as the Black Death had ravaged Europe and killed perhaps a third of the English population. Estimates vary hugely, from 20 per cent to over 50 per cent, but whatever the figure it was high enough to cause a massive shortage of labour and equally massive conflict over wages and food prices.

With all this going on, what was the King doing messing about with grand palaces and tournaments in which a single costume might contain 3,000 peacock feathers? Well, a lot of it was to do with his attitude to chivalry and nationalism, and a vague idea of setting up a court in the mould of King Arthur. That never came to fruition, but what Edward did do was establish the Order of the Garter, a chivalric order dedicated to St George, England's patron saint, to honour a select group of nobles. All very fine, but it didn't win any wars in France. These revived in 1369, after a lull of about a decade, and the next phase went very much the French way. Before long, Edward III and his son Edward the Black Prince, who had been instrumental in the earlier English victories, were on their deathbeds, and both England and France found themselves with kings not yet into their teens. A recipe, obviously, for further trouble (see page 121)…

Edward's state apartments at Windsor remained intact until the 17th century, and for a further 150 years a whole 110ft wall of the St George's Hall was dedicated to his memory: Charles II commissioned a mural from the Italian painter Antonio Verrio which showed Edward III greeting the Black Prince in a victory procession. It was dismantled by George IV when he extended the Hall to its present 180ft. Although the Hall had to be completely rebuilt after a catastrophic fire in 1992, it still harks back to Edward III every June, when the Knights of the Garter gather here with the monarch before their annual service in St George's Chapel (see page 141). Which is a place not to be missed.

LUXURY IN MINIATURE

Although the state apartments at Windsor are magnificent and contain a vast array of superb works of art, the same could be said of Buckingham Palace and one or two other royal residences. Surprisingly for such an ancient place, Windsor's unique attraction dates only from the 20th century.

This is Queen Mary's Dolls' House, created for the British Empire Exhibition at Wembley in 1924. It was designed by Edwin Lutyens, one of the foremost architects of the day; the garden was the work of Gertrude Jekyll, who frequently collaborated with Lutyens on projects on a larger scale; and literally hundreds of other distinguished craftspeople contributed furniture and decorations. The house, which represents an aristocratic residence of the day, boasts running water and electricity, a wind-up gramophone with functioning records, readable books and newspapers, a wine cellar and a garage full of limousines, all on a perfect 1:12 scale. It was designed as a present for George V's consort as a gesture of thanks for the charitable works she had performed during World War I, but it was the brainchild of George's cousin and Mary's childhood friend, Princess Marie Louise of Schleswig-Holstein. It was the Princess's idea to create a showcase of the best of British craftsmanship, and it was her contacts in the arts world that ensured the involvement of so many experts. You may think you can't get excited by a dolls' house, but trust me – you can.

34

DUNSTANBURGH CASTLE
John of Gaunt

JOHN OF GAUNT (so called because he was born in Ghent and the spelling and pronunciation were near enough) was the fourth son of Edward III. His three elder brothers all predeceased their father, leaving John to become Regent when his 10-year-old nephew came to the throne as Richard II in 1377.

As Duke of Lancaster, John was the most substantial landowner in the North of England and owned a fair bit of the South, too. He had a palace in Lincoln (no longer there, but its oriel window now adorns the castle); he owned Kenilworth Castle (see page 85), to which he added the splendid Great Hall, state apartments and grand reception rooms; he also owned Leicester Castle. In London, his Savoy Palace was the most magnificent nobleman's house in England; according to a contemporary chronicler, he kept there 'such quantities of vessels and silver plate, without counting the parcel-gilt and solid gold, that five carts would hardly suffice to carry them'. When the Savoy was burned down, John moved his London headquarters to Ely Palace, the property of the Bishops of Ely. This survives only in the form of the tiny St Etheldreda's Church, but once its gardens grew the finest strawberries in the capital.

This was a man who was bound to make enemies and, as the most influential of the King's counsellors, he took the blame for the hike in taxation, intended to help finance the war against France, which was one of the causes of the 1381 Peasants' Revolt. The burning of Savoy Palace and the wanton destruction of all its contents that occurred during this uprising were no accident – they were a personal attack on John of Gaunt and they rendered him particularly security conscious.

That may well be why he made the massive improvements he did at Dunstanburgh Castle. Another imposing item in John's bulging property portfolio, Dunstanburgh sits 30 miles south of the Scottish border, on a soaring bluff looking out over the North Sea. It had been built by an earlier Earl of Lancaster who forfeited it to the Crown after a failed rebellion against Edward II. If it had been a substantial fortress back then, that was nothing compared with what John made of it now. Deciding its defences were inadequate, he built an outer wall over 20ft high and 4ft thick to protect the keep. This was followed by a new

WHILE YOU'RE IN THE AREA
Alnwick, some 8 miles inland from Dunstanburgh, is another castle that inspired Turner. Less precariously situated, it is also in much better condition and has been the home of the Percy family, the Dukes of Northumberland, for over seven centuries: after Windsor, it is the second largest inhabited castle in England. Alnwick played its part in rebellions against Henry IV (see page 129), in the wars between the Scots and the English, and in the Wars of the Roses. Rather more recently (and possibly attracting rather more visitors) it featured in Downton Abbey *and appeared as Hogwarts in the first two* Harry Potter *films.*

tower and gateway separating his own
apartments from the rest of the castle
and making them less vulnerable
to attack.

Although all this is in ruins now,
enough remains to show an impregnable
(or paranoid) double keep, comprising the original and
John's reinforcement. The surviving parts of the curtain
wall also proclaim 'Keep out' as loudly as if the words
had been painted on them. This was a castle designed to
repel all possible marauders. OK, the modern visitor
thinks, I'll back off.

John's death in 1399 didn't stop Dunstanburgh
being important: it was besieged during the Wars of the
Roses, changing hands from Yorkists to Lancastrians and
back again. After that it became of less strategic value
and by the beginning of the 17th century was in
private hands, never again to be more than a romantic
ruin – romantic enough, though, to inspire the painter
J M W Turner, whose various portrayals of it are in the
Tate Britain collection.

The other notable thing about John of Gaunt is that
he sired an enormous number of children. His
legitimate heirs were the leaders of the House of
Lancaster; the children of his long-term mistress,
Katherine Swynford, were the Beaufort
family, whose descendants included both
Yorkist and Lancastrian kings. Never mind
blaming him for crippling taxation; if you
want to blame the entire Wars of the Roses
on a single individual, this is your man.

35

CHESTER CASTLE
Richard II

RICHARD II WAS ONE OF those sad monarchs who didn't really have a chance. He came to the throne when only 10, his father the Black Prince having predeceased his own father, Edward III. He grew up to be passionate about preserving the Royal Prerogative, so that he arrogantly dismissed any policy suggested by Parliament with which he happened to disagree. He is said once to have declared that 'he would not dismiss as much as a scullion from his kitchen at Parliament's request'. Even so, if you can sit through Shakespeare's play and not feel for him when, knowing he is about to be deposed, he says, 'For God's sake, let us sit upon the ground/And tell sad stories of the death of kings,' you have a heart of stone.

Still only 14 at the time of the Peasants' Revolt (see page 119), Richard displayed considerable personal courage in meeting the rebels and agreeing to many of their demands, but violence broke out, spread across the country and resulted in the peasant leaders (and many of their followers) being hounded down and executed. Richard backed down from the promises he had made and the revolt faded away with little but increased bad feeling to show for it.

The next few years were marked by religious upheavals and wars with France, Scotland and Ireland. Richard's foreign policy was at variance with that of Parliament; this fact, accompanied by continuing discord over taxes and perhaps a touch of paranoia, led him to embark on a tour of the country and establish a power base in Chester. Earl of Chester was one of his many titles (it is still one of the titles of the Prince of Wales) and Cheshire had the odd distinction of being a County Palatine, giving it special privileges, including the right to organise its own defences. It therefore boasted a uniquely talented group of archers, the longbowmen of the Hundred of Macclesfield and Cheshire, who served as the royal bodyguard. Richard used these men to enforce his will on a Parliament that met in 1397, which of course didn't go down well...

In the latter part of his reign Richard was frequently accused of tyranny and of being unfit to rule – rumblings about deposing him were never far away. A likely successor was his cousin, Henry of Bolingbroke, John of Gaunt's son (we'll look at the validity of his claim on page 126). In 1398, Henry reported to Richard what he thought were treasonable words spoken by the Duke of Norfolk; Richard, not always rational, thought it best to banish not only Norfolk but Henry too. Shortly afterwards, John of Gaunt died and Richard, instead of allowing Henry to inherit his father's (very considerable) property, made him petition for it. Henry, understandably incensed, took advantage of the fact that Richard was away fighting in Ireland and invaded England. Enough important people were disenchanted

for Henry quickly to gain sufficient support to depose
Richard and have himself declared king.

It's at this point that Chester Castle comes back into
Richard's life: he surrendered to Henry at Flint, but was
taken from there to Chester, from where he and his
predecessors had administered their earldom. He was
held in the Agricola Tower, the 12th-century stone
structure that had once been the gateway to the castle,
while Henry waited for a deputation from London that
would renounce the capital's allegiance to Richard.
Richard was then taken to London and subsequently
sent to Pontefract (see page 198), where he died in what
most historians describe as mysterious circumstances
– circumstances which were, at the very least,
convenient for Henry.

In Westminster Abbey, there's a portrait of Richard,
seated in the Coronation Chair, wearing a crown and
a crimson robe trimmed with ermine and bearing the
ceremonial orb and sceptre. Dating from the 1390s and
painted on a wooden panel, it's the earliest known
portrait of an English king. Richard's tomb is also there
– in another first, he is buried beside his wife, Anne of
Bohemia, in the first double royal tomb. The Latin
inscription on his tomb begins 'Sage and elegant,
lawfully Richard II, conquered by fate he lies here
depicted beneath this marble. He was truthful in
discourse and full of reason.' So Richard, arrogant
and misguided rather than evil, becomes something
of a martyr in death.

As for the Cheshire archers, we shall
be meeting them again (see page 129).

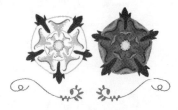

York and Lancaster
1399–1485

36

BOLINGBROKE CASTLE
Henry IV

AFTER ITS TURBULENT START (see page 122), Henry IV's reign was marked by… further turbulence. Whether or not he had had Richard II murdered, there were many who saw him as a usurper. Rumours (almost certainly false) circulated that Richard was still alive and could be restored to the throne; there was also another contender for the throne – Edmund Mortimer, the young Earl of March. He was descended from Edward III's third son; as such, he had seniority over Henry, whose father, John of Gaunt, was Edward's fourth son. On the other hand, Henry's descent from Edward ran entirely through the male line, whereas Edmund's involved a grandmother, which muddied the waters. A few months into Henry's reign the English nobles rose against him; then the Welsh prince Owain Glyndwr declared himself Prince of Wales, attacked various towns on the English/Welsh border and spearheaded guerrilla-style revolts throughout Wales. Henry's attempts at repression were complicated by the fact that the man he had put in charge, Harry Percy, son of the Earl of Northumberland, turned against him and instigated a rebellion of his own (see page 129). By the time this was subdued, Henry was nine years into his 14-year reign and it was the first time he'd experienced anything resembling peace.

It's perhaps surprising, then, that his life should have started in such a peaceful location. Today his Lincolnshire birthplace, Bolingbroke Castle (the reason he was known as Bolingbroke before he became king), is adjacent to the village of Old Bolingbroke, which boasts a mere 300 inhabitants in one of the most sparsely populated counties in England. Bolingbroke was one of the many castles belonging to John of Gaunt (see page 118); he used it as an administrative centre, which is why its towers have names such as Auditor's Tower and Receiver's Tower, reflecting the work done there.

Aerial photos of Bolingbroke Castle show the remains of the six towers that marked the corners of an impressive hexagonal site. They would once have enclosed a courtyard, a timber-framed Great Hall and all the other buildings required to keep a nobleman's household ticking over. Surrounded by a moat 100ft wide and situated atop what in Lincolnshire passes for a hill, it would have been hard to breach. But, like so many other castles, it was never the same after the Civil Wars: the Royalists survived a two-month siege in 1643, but after they surrendered much of the castle's stone was stripped and used for the buildings of Old Bolingbroke village. Clambering among the ruins today (and there are still plenty to clamber among), you can see where this has happened: most of what remains is the rough and unadorned aggregate that was once hidden by more expensive, finely carved stone.

As for Henry IV, he spent the last few years of his reign suffering from an unknown but debilitating illness. It had been predicted that he would die in Jerusalem, suggesting that, like many of his predecessors, he would go on a Crusade, to atone for past sins. Instead, he suffered what was probably a stroke while praying at Edward the Confessor's shrine in Westminster Abbey and was carried to the Jerusalem Chamber, then part of the abbot's house. According to Shakespeare, on being told where he was, he uttered these last words:

> *It hath been prophesied to me many years,*
> *I should not die but in Jerusalem;*
> *Which vainly I supposed the Holy Land:*
> *But bear me to that chamber; there I'll lie;*
> *In that Jerusalem shall Harry die.*

You can't visit the Jerusalem Chamber – nowadays it's one of the private rooms in the Deanery. To find Henry IV at rest you are better off heading back to his birthplace, or to his grave in Canterbury Cathedral, alongside that of Thomas Becket (see page 66). Born in peaceful Lincolnshire; died in peaceful Westminster Abbey; not much peace in between.

37

BATTLEFIELD, SHREWSBURY
Henry IV

WE MENTIONED ON PAGE 126 that Henry IV's reign wasn't noticeable for its peacefulness. Within months of becoming king in 1399, he survived a plot to assassinate him and his sons. Forewarned by one of the conspirators, he simply stayed away from Windsor, where the coup was to have taken place. He then raised an army and pursued, captured and executed the rebels. Job done, you might think, but it was only the first of many.

The real crunch came when, in 1403, he was deserted by the Percy family, previously his most powerful supporters. Fed up with Henry not giving them the rewards he had promised, the Percys now allied themselves with the Archbishop of York, uniting most of the North of England against the King. Also in their camp was Edmund Mortimer, uncle to that other Edmund, the young Earl of March, who was the obvious candidate for the throne if Henry could be disposed of (see page 126).

Harry Percy, son of the Earl of Northumberland and known as Hotspur, was marching to join the Welsh rebels he was supposed to be suppressing when he encountered Henry's army near Shrewsbury. And it is here that the Cheshire archers (see page 122) come back into the picture. Many of them had remained loyal to

Richard II and now flocked to support Hotspur against Henry. But Henry also had archers on his side. The Battle of Shrewsbury is renowned for being the first in England where longbowmen faced longbowmen; the battle formations used here were the ones that made Agincourt such a triumph for the archers only 12 years later.

In the end, Shrewsbury was a disaster for the rebels: Henry was in control of the town and Hotspur was based to the north of it, with both the King's army and the River Severn between him and any hope of Welsh reinforcements. When the two forces met, on 21 July, Hotspur and many of the other rebels were killed, marking the beginning of the end of resistance to Henry's rule. The Welsh revolt continued a little longer, but faded away after various military setbacks and broken alliances. The older Percy, Hotspur's father, rose against Henry one last time, in 1408, and was defeated and killed at the Battle of Bramham Moor, and after that Henry could enjoy a (very) few years of peace.

There's a church on the site of the Battle of Shrewsbury, in a village that is now called Battlefield. Tradition has it that it sits above a mass grave which may contain as many as 1,600 of the dead. It was built on Henry's orders 'for the souls of those who fell' and it's dedicated, slightly incongruously, to St Mary Magdalene, because the battle took place on the eve of her feast day. Most of the church's interior was restored in the 19th century, but the fabric of the building is original and the hammerbeam roof, although a reproduction, contains heraldic emblems of knights who fought in the battle. Panels depicting the main participants and a reconstruction of the battlefield talk you through what happened.

You can visit the battlefield, too – a 250-acre field on the Albrighton estate, where a (rather gorgeous) farm shop called Battlefield 1403 offers suggestions for walks and contains an exhibition describing the battle.

Shakespeare, as so often, gets some of the details wrong when depicting the Battle of Shrewsbury: he shows Henry IV's son Hal – the future Henry V – as being the same age as Hotspur, whereas the Prince was more than 20 years younger. Aged only about 17, he did fight at Shrewsbury, but there is no suggestion that he killed Hotspur in single combat. Shakespeare seems to have made this up for dramatic effect. And it's a great scene, so who can blame him?

As for young Edmund, Earl of March, he grew up to be a loyal supporter and counsellor of Henry V, refusing to take part in a later attempt to put him (Edmund) on the throne. All things considered, he caused remarkably little trouble for someone who could lay claim to being the rightful king. Unfortunately, the same couldn't be said of his nephew and heir, Richard, Duke of York, of whom we shall hear more…

38

MONMOUTH CASTLE
Henry V

WHETHER ALL THE YOUTHFUL shenanigans with Sir John
Falstaff described by Shakespeare are true or not, Henry
V matured into a pretty admirable ruler. He did his best
(and did it quite successfully) to unite the country after
the ructions of his father's reign. By the time he had
been on the throne two years he felt able to turn his
attention to the war with France that had never entirely
gone away since Edward III's time, and thereafter spent
most of his short life on the other side of the Channel.

He's best known for the successful siege of Harfleur
and his annihilating victory at Agincourt, the former of
which inspired Shakespeare to his rabble-rousing best:
'Once more unto the breach, dear friends, once more'
and 'Cry, "God for Harry, England and Saint George!"'
But to find somewhere in Britain that is closely
associated with Henry V, you have to go back to the
beginning, to Monmouth Castle, where he was born.

That was in about 1386, when Richard II was still
king and Henry's father was no more than Henry
Bolingbroke, heir to the Duchy of Lancaster. Monmouth
Castle had been built in Norman times; its location,
enabling its residents to keep a cautious eye on crossing
points on both the Wye and the Monnow Rivers, gave it
strategic importance during those long years when

control of the lands on the English/Welsh border was a continuing thorn in everyone's side. It passed into the possession of the House of Lancaster in the 13th century and was surrounded by good hunting territory, which is why Henry Bolingbroke took a fancy to it and spent time here, with his pregnant wife at his side.

Not a great deal is left of the castle, but the ruined Great Hall and Great Tower, the latter almost certainly where Henry V was born, are still impressive chunks of stone, with the walls standing almost to their full height. You can see the remains of carved 12th-century corbels projecting from the walls, and the frame of what was once a large decorative window. While you're here, spare a thought for Henry V's mother, Mary de Bohun. Forced into a politically motivated marriage when she was perhaps as young as 12, she then had seven children and died giving birth to the last of them, at the age of 26. She didn't even have the satisfaction of being queen – her husband didn't become Henry IV for another five years.

There's one other place in Britain where you can celebrate Henry V: the Globe Theatre, on London's South Bank. The prologue to Shakespeare's *Henry V* famously asks, 'May we cram within this wooden O the very casques [helmets] that did affright the air at Agincourt?' Tradition has it that *Henry V* was the first play staged at the original Globe, in 1599, so its prologue would have been the first speech ever uttered there. If you attend a performance at the Globe today, you are (possibly) sitting within a lovingly constructed replica of that same wooden O.

39

SOME ROYAL COLLEGES
Henry VI

IF HENRY VI HAD NEVER been king but just spent his time founding colleges, we'd have hailed him as one of the great architectural patrons of all time. Sadly, as a monarch he was a disaster. Henry V had died in 1422 aged only 36, so his son had inherited the throne when he was only nine months old. He grew up to have none of his father's skills as a general. The war against France took a calamitous downturn, culminating in the loss of Normandy in 1450 and of Bordeaux in 1453. This led Henry to suffer something like a nervous breakdown and to be oblivious to anything that was going on around him for over a year. Even when he regained his senses he seems to have been a passive observer of his own reign – a pious man who wanted peace when what was needed was a powerful figurehead and military tactician.

Discontent at home led to mini-wars between local nobles and encouraged Richard, Duke of York, to make a play for the throne (he's the one who inherited the claims of Edmund of March mentioned on page 126). Richard was killed at the Battle of Wakefield in 1460 (see page 137), but his son Edward won a decisive victory at Towton the following year, deposed Henry and had himself crowned King Edward IV. Henry then went into hiding in Scotland, was captured by Edward's forces and imprisoned in the Tower of London. He was freed and briefly restored to the throne in 1471, then defeated, deposed again and almost certainly murdered on Edward's orders. Even when he was in his right mind, he was out of his depth.

So let's focus on the good bits. In an attempt to promote learning, and Christian learning in particular, Henry founded All Souls College Oxford in 1438, Eton College in 1440 and King's College Cambridge in 1441. Significantly, in all three the most remarkable feature is the chapel.

The frontage, gate tower and quadrangle of All Souls are much as they have been for the last six centuries and all are lovely; but the chapel, with its glorious vaulted ceiling and complete set of 15th-century misericords, many of them carved with grotesque figures, is the highlight. The casual visitor isn't allowed into the choir area, so the statues in the medieval reredos – destroyed during the Reformation and replaced in the 19th century – are too far away for non-experts to identify. Which is a shame, as those portrayed include not Henry himself but two of his uncles: Thomas, Duke of Clarence, and Humphrey, Duke of Gloucester.

The idea with Eton was that 70 poor boys would be educated free of charge and then sent on to King's. Again, Eton's architectural highlight is the chapel (which, if you haven't had the foresight to send your son to the college, can be visited by pre-booked tour). It was designed to be a splendid place of pilgrimage and would have been even more splendid than it is – and twice the size – had Henry not been deposed (for the first time) before the work was completed. As it is, visitors can admire the 15th-century wall paintings which were hidden for almost 300 years: they were whitewashed over in 1560, when the prevailing Protestantism outlawed the portrayal of miracles, and rediscovered only in the 1840s. The glorious fan-vaulted ceiling is a 20th-century replacement of the original, which had succumbed to rot and deathwatch beetle; for the real thing, look in the side chapel known as Lupton's Chapel after an early 16th-century Provost of the College.

Eton Chapel's stained glass is modern, the originals having been bombed during World War II. For glass dating back to Henry VI's time, you need to visit his masterpiece, King's College Cambridge. Like St George's Windsor (see page 141), the chapel is built in the Perpendicular style – and soaringly so. It's some 80ft high and 289ft long, with the largest fan-vaulted ceiling in the world. Carvings or stained glass seem to cover every inch of the walls. You gasp as you enter it, and continue gasping until it's time to leave. The best time to go is when there is a concert in progress, though you'll be asked to keep your gasping to a minimum; it's from here that the famous Festival of Nine Lessons and Carols is broadcast all over the world on Christmas Eve – start queuing before dawn on the day and there's a good chance you'll get in.

While all this building was going on in Henry VI's lifetime, so were the Wars of the Roses. He may have chosen to ignore them, but his wife, the formidable Margaret of Anjou, did not...

40

SANDAL CASTLE
Richard, Duke of York/
Margaret of Anjou

BY 1460, MARGARET OF ANJOU and Richard of York were deadly enemies. A redoubtable French princess, she was married to the Lancastrian Henry VI and fought more strongly for his cause than he ever did. She didn't, Joan of Arc-like, lead her troops into battle, but she held councils, rallied troops and was a powerful figurehead. Richard, who had been Protector of the Realm during Henry's illness in the 1450s, had turned against him and taken the view that he, Richard, should be on the throne instead.

It all goes back to Edward III and the conflicting claims of his various descendants that had put Henry IV on the throne in 1399 (see page 126). Henry VI was Edward's great-great-grandson, descended in an entirely male line from Edward's third son, John of Gaunt. Richard of York was the great-great-grandson of Edward's second son, Lionel, but his line of descent included two women. You could argue till the cows come home over who should take precedence, but no one would deny that Henry was a hopeless king.

What we now call the Wars of the Roses, fought between the Houses of York and Lancaster, were initially known as the Cousins' War, because practically everyone involved was related (and they intermarried in the most confusing way). The roses were among the badges used by the various parties, and Shakespeare, writing over a hundred years later, created a back story: there's a scene in *Henry VI Part I* where Richard, Duke of York, and the Lancastrian Earl of Somerset are having an argument in a garden. Richard plucks a white rose and asks those who agree with him to do the same; Somerset picks a red rose, and Shakespeare has another good scene that owes little to historical accuracy.

In fact, it was the Lancastrian Henry VII who first laid emphasis on the 'roses' symbolism. Marrying the Yorkist Princess Elizabeth once the wars were over, he created a red and white Tudor rose, showing that England was united under the new, peaceful regime. The modern name didn't emerge until the 19th century – Walter Scott refers to 'the wars of the White and Red Roses' in his novel *Anne of Geierstein,* published in 1829, and he may have been the first, but the idea had been around for a while

Whatever you care to call it, in 1460 Richard of York's attempt to gain the throne led to a compromise: Parliament passed an Act of Accord making him Henry's heir. This was all very well, but it overlooked two important facts: one, Henry had a son, Edward, whom this Act excluded from the succession; and two, Edward's mother Margaret wasn't the sort of woman who would sit idly by and see her son shoved to one side.

Late in 1460 she was in Scotland and the North of England, rallying support. Richard marched north and arrived at Sandal Castle, now on the fringes of Wakefield, just before Christmas. A Lancastrian army of perhaps 15,000 was at Pontefract, some 10 miles away.

Like most castles, Sandal occupies an excellent strategic position: it's on high ground that enables its inhabitants to spot anyone advancing on it. On the morning of 30 December, that is just what happened – the Yorkists saw the Lancastrians about a mile away, on a patch of rough open land. Rather than defending the castle, Richard made the surprising decision to set forth to confront the enemy. One suggested explanation is that he was running out of supplies and knew he couldn't withstand a siege; another is that the Lancastrians had sent a small part of their army on ahead and fooled Richard into thinking that was all they had. Whatever the reason, the Yorkists suffered heavy casualties and Richard was killed, along with Edmund, Earl of Rutland, the second of his four sons. Their severed heads, Richard's decorated with a mocking paper crown, were displayed in York on Micklegate Bar, the great gate through which many monarchs had entered the city with rather more dignity.

Sandal Castle is a ruin now, but at the time of writing it's being restored and made safer. Visitors can wander round the site, admire the views and imagine what it must have felt like to see 15,000 armed men approaching across the winter landscape. You can also see the remains of a huge oven in the bakehouse and consider the amount of food and

drink that must have been consumed during the Yorkist Christmas celebrations in 1460. Once the current works are finished, you'll be able to explore the keep again. It was said during the 17th century that you could see the keep of Pontefract from the top of Sandal; Pontefract Castle isn't as tall as it used to be, but choose a clear day in a year or so and you never know.

Most of the Wakefield battlefield is built over, but if you follow Manygates Lane away from the castle you reach a remnant of it in Castle Grove Park. Nearby, a Victorian monument to Richard describes him as having fallen 'fighting for the cause of the White Rose'. Nonsense, of course – every description of Richard of York includes the word 'ambitious': he never fought for anything but himself.

As for Margaret, she headed south from Scotland with her own troops and met her victorious army at St Albans, where they swiftly routed a smaller Yorkist force. Margaret marched on towards London but the capital refused to open its gates to her and she was forced to retreat. Henry's days as king were numbered and the new Duke of York, son of the ambitious Richard, was well on the way to becoming Edward IV.

The story continues in the next few entries, but as a footnote for posterity, Margaret shared her husband's interest in education (see page 134) and founded the Queen's College of St Margaret and St Bernard in Cambridge. Apostrophe fiends will like to know that it became Queens' College when Margaret's successor, Elizabeth Woodville, wife of Edward IV, added her name to the list of royal patrons.

41

St George's Chapel, Windsor Castle
Edward IV

We looked at Windsor Castle on page 114, but
St George's Chapel, its own private church – where
Prince Harry married Meghan Markle in 2018 –
deserves special mention. For a start, it is incredibly
tall. You should really take binoculars if you want to
appreciate the fan-vaulting of the nave. The West
Window is over 30ft high and divided into 90 panels of
stained glass; when you turn away from it to face the
altar you realise that the huge area you are in is only half
the story – behind that first altar is an archway, and
beyond that another large space with the choir (or quire,
as it is called here) and the high altar. It goes on and on.
Of all the places in this book, St George's Chapel has
perhaps the greatest – or at least the tallest – wow factor.

Credit for all this belongs to a number of monarchs.
Henry III had a chapel here, and the Galilee Porch,
through which you pass as you leave, was built as his
antechapel in the 1240s. The present nave was built
between 1503 and 1515, having been commissioned
by Henry VII. And the royal memorials are legion.

In the north quire aisle, more stained glass depicts
Richard, Duke of York, and his wife Cecily Neville, the

parents of Edward IV. If you are looking at their images you are very possibly standing on their son's tomb – a dark marble slab on the floor, whose inscription reads simply 'King Edward IIII and his Queen Elizabeth Widvile'. It is Edward IV we must thank for the present incarnation of St George's Chapel. And as he was responsible for a certain amount of bloodshed during the Wars of the Roses (see page 134), it is perhaps only fair to pay tribute to the more peaceable side of his character.

After the death of Henry VI in 1471 (a death in which it is hard to believe Edward was not implicated), Edward's position on the throne was secure. With no apparent irony he took as his motto *Modus et ordo* – 'method and order' – and set about restoring both these qualities to a country that had been ravaged by civil war for over 15 years. Having negotiated an extraordinarily lucrative peace treaty with France, he was able to establish the most sumptuous court in Europe. And he decided to create a grand new spiritual home for the Order of the Garter (see page 116). The Garter was and is highly prestigious and entirely deserving of something as magnificent as St George's Chapel – though the rumour that Edward wanted his project to outshine Eton College Chapel (see page 135), built just across the river by Henry VI, persists. As you go through the arch that leads from St George's Chapel to Windsor Castle's State Apartments, you have, on a clear day, a glorious view across the Thames to Eton. It's impossible not to pause a moment and admire. The unfortunate Henry contributed a bit of wow factor too.

ELTHAM PALACE
Edward IV

THE FIRST SURPRISE ABOUT Eltham Palace is its location: in a leafy southeast London suburb, an easy commute from Charing Cross. The entrance driveway feels like the approach to one of those characterless hotels that host conferences all week and weddings on Saturdays; you pass the shop, the café and the children's play area without realising you are doing anything special. Then you start wandering along a winding path through woods and gardens, across a bridge built in the time of Richard II and rebuilt by Edward IV, towards a lime tree that's obviously been there some time, in the centre of a circular courtyard. And here at last is the house.

The truth is that Eltham Palace is no longer a palace at all. After centuries of neglect its remains were rediscovered and bought in the 1930s by Stephen and Virginia Courtauld, who clearly had money to burn and no qualms about burning it in creating their dream home. The main reason for visiting is to admire the glorious art deco interiors – so clearly designed for lavish entertaining that you feel a little uncomfortable wearing something that isn't evening dress and not carrying a Martini in your hand.

But when you reach the Great Hall, built for Edward IV in the 1470s, visions of Agatha Christie-style

cocktail parties vanish and medieval majesty reappears.
Royal visitors to Eltham go back as far as Edward I, and
in the early 14th century the manor, as it was then
called, was granted to Edward II's queen, Isabella.
From this point on, it was continually extended and
improved, becoming a favourite and a luxurious royal
residence: tournaments and jousts were held here; it was
Henry IV's palace of choice for Christmas festivities;
Henry VIII spent much of his childhood here; and in
Elizabethan times it was larger than Hampton Court.
Then, in the early 17th century, it seems for some
reason to have fallen from favour and been in need of
repair; come the Civil Wars, much of it was ransacked
and destroyed. The deer in the park were killed, the trees
felled for timber to build ships for the navy and the
Parliamentarian who bought it in 1651 went so far as to
strip the lead off the Great Hall roof. Over the next two
and a half centuries it underwent various indignities
(including the Great Hall being used as a barn) before
the Courtaulds and their cheque book came along,
looking for a property within easy reach of London.

The first thing you notice about the Great Hall is
its size – over 100ft long and 55ft high. It's recorded that
Edward IV held a Christmas feast for 2,000 guests here
in 1482 and there would have been plenty of room.
Then there's the roof, an elaborate hammerbeam
confection: it's sort of original, sort of taken apart and
put back together in the early 20th century. Purists may
baulk at some of the hall's features – the guidebook
remarks that the Courtaulds' interventions 'might be
described as "antiquarian revival"' and 'represent

Stephen Courtauld's (and his architects') view of what a medieval hall should look like'. Whatever. It's superb. The tiled floor and the elaborate tapestries that would originally have lined the walls have gone, but there is still a dais where the king would have sat, a minstrels' gallery from which lesser mortals can look down on proceedings, and stained glass designed by one of the foremost designers of his day – even if his day was the 1930s rather than the 1470s. Featured in the glass are roundels bearing the badges of Edward IV: the white rose of York and the 'sun in splendour' that was his personal insignia.

The Great Hall may not be exactly as it was in Edward IV's time, but if you visit on a cold day you're unlikely to cavil at the Courtaulds' underfloor central heating. When you have finished admiring it, it is well worth donning your cocktail frock, slotting a stylishly long cigarette into its stylishly long holder and going in search of that Martini. Today's Eltham Palace has lost a lot of its royal significance, but what the Courtaulds have left behind is magnificent.

43

TEWKESBURY ABBEY
Edward, Prince of Wales/
George, Duke of Clarence

TWO OF THE 15TH CENTURY'S also-rans are buried in
Tewkesbury Abbey. Edward was the son of Henry VI and
would have been his heir had the Wars of the Roses not
intervened (see page 138). George was the brother of
Edward IV and Richard III – drowned, according to
tradition, in a butt of malmsey wine; murdered,
according to Shakespeare, by Richard's connivance.

It's hard not to be impressed by Tewkesbury Abbey.
Founded in the 12th century, it is one of the largest
and finest churches in England; indeed, it's larger than
14 English cathedrals, with a series of chantry chapels
(designated for prayers for the souls of the dead)
radiating out from the choir. The organ has an
extraordinary 4,611 pipes and is said to have been
played by the poet John Milton. The tower used to be
topped by a lead-covered wooden spire 100ft high; this
was destroyed by a gale in 1559 and never rebuilt.
Nevertheless, the 20th-century architectural historian
Nikolaus Pevsner described what remained as 'probably
the largest and finest Romanesque tower in England'.

The highlight – or perhaps the lowlight – of
Tewkesbury's history was the battle fought here in 1471.

The Wars of the Roses had already been waging for 16 years; the Yorkist Edward IV had been on the throne for 10 of them. In 1470 a Lancastrian army led by Richard Neville, Earl of Warwick (known as 'the Kingmaker') had sent Edward into exile in Burgundy and put Henry VI back on the throne. Edward's brother Clarence, who had a well-earned reputation for changing sides whenever it suited him, was by Warwick's side, having been promised the kingdom should Henry's son Edward predecease him. Warwick, it should be said, had two daughters, of whom the elder, Isabel, married Clarence and the younger, Anne, married Edward, Prince of Wales. Warwick wasn't just interested in king-making – he had an eye to making queens, too. (He succeeded, posthumously and briefly, when the widowed Anne married the future Richard III and was Queen Consort for less than two years.)

Edward IV's exile lasted a matter of months. Having drummed up support in Burgundy, he invaded England and won a victory at Barnet in the course of which Warwick was killed. At the same time, Edward, Prince of Wales, now 17, and his mother Margaret of Anjou, returned from their own exile in France and proceeded with an army to Tewkesbury, where they hoped to cross the Severn into Wales, to join other Lancastrian loyalists. That didn't happen. Instead, King Edward's forces defeated the exhausted Lancastrians so thoroughly that the area in which the slaughter took place is still known as the Bloody Meadow. Among the dead was the young Edward, who has the odd distinction of being the only English heir apparent to be killed in battle.

With the Lancastrians routed, Clarence, knowing which side his bread was buttered, contrived to be reconciled with his brother. Briefly. By 1477 he was rebelling against Edward again and was arrested for treason. Imprisoned in the Tower of London, he was tried in his absence, found guilty and 'privately executed'. He had packed an awful lot of trouble into his 28 years.

A GOOD TIME TO VISIT

July is one of the best times to visit Tewkesbury: an annual Medieval Festival includes a re-enactment of the battle and such attractions as 'barber surgeons, preachers and even the odd dragon keeper'.

To revert to Tewkesbury Abbey, many of the defeated Lancastrians sought sanctuary there, but were surrendered to Edward IV, quickly tried for treason and beheaded. In a somewhat belated act of clemency, the King then allowed them to be buried in the abbey's consecrated ground. Edward, Prince of Wales, was buried in the choir: the exact position of his grave is unknown, but a brass plaque in the floor marks the event. As for Clarence and Isabel, behind the abbey's high altar an iron grating in the floor covers stairs leading down to the Clarence Vault, where a glass case containing their bones delights visitors with a taste for the macabre.

The Battle of Tewkesbury marks the end of the second phase of the Wars of the Roses. Edward IV reigned in comparative peace for 12 years, but died leaving a son aged only 12 to succeed him, and, if Shakespeare is to be believed, a wicked brother to serve as Protector of England...

44

THE TOWER OF LONDON
Edward V

SINCE ITS FOUNDING BY William the Conqueror, the Tower of London has been many things: a fortress, an armoury, the home of the Royal Mint and a royal menagerie, with lions, elephants and probably a polar bear as far back as the 13th century. For several centuries, it was a royal palace: Henry III and Edward I both expanded it, and Edward's wife Eleanor of Castile provoked derision when she hung the walls with rich silk cloths and tapestries, and even laid them on the floor, Spanish style.

It's been a prison, with inmates from the Elizabethan courtier Walter Raleigh to the Nazi Rudolf Hess. It's the place where three English queens – Anne Boleyn, Katherine Howard and Lady Jane Grey – were beheaded. And perhaps most notoriously it's where the so-called Princes in the Tower were murdered by their wicked uncle. Or were they?

The princes were the 12-year-old Edward V and his brother Richard, Duke of York, aged nine; they were the sons of Edward IV, who had died of an unknown illness in April 1483. The 'wicked' uncle was their father's only surviving brother, Richard, Duke of

Gloucester, the future Richard III. Edward IV, knowing that he was dying, had named Richard Protector during the new king's minority. Richard ordered the boys to be kept in the Tower, perhaps for their own safety; it was a well-guarded royal residence and young kings were always in danger of being deposed or disposed of, so this was not in itself either odd or sinister.

Within weeks, though, Richard had declared that the young princes were illegitimate, making himself the rightful king. (His elder brother, George, Duke of Clarence – see page 146 – was dead by this time and, because he had been convicted of treason, the Clarence children were barred from the succession.)

There may have been grounds for this claim. Considerable controversy had surrounded Edward IV's marriage to the boys' mother, Elizabeth Woodville. She was the daughter of a mere knight who brought no territory, no great riches and no powerful alliances to the marriage; and she was a widow, five years older than her husband. But she was stunningly beautiful with, according to a contemporary account, 'heavy-lidded eyes like those of a dragon' and Edward was renowned for having an eye for a pretty woman. One rumour had it that she captivated him by the use of witchcraft; certainly the couple were married quickly and secretly, before his advisers at court could put a stop to it.

More importantly, from the point of view of the succession, it was alleged that Edward had had a pre-contract of marriage with a certain Lady Eleanor Butler, which would have invalidated his marriage to Elizabeth and rendered her children illegitimate.

Whatever the rights and wrongs of all this, the two princes disappeared in the summer of 1483. It is known that a doctor had visited Edward a number of times. Did he die of some unknown illness? Was young Richard smuggled away for his own safety? Or were they murdered? If so, was it on the orders of their uncle, so that he could take Edward's place? Or was it later, when Henry VII was anxious to get rid of any Yorkist claimants to the throne? He disposed of a number of other members of the House of York, so it's possible…

What we know for sure is that in 1674 – the better part of 200 years later, during the reign of Charles II – workers demolishing an old staircase in the White Tower found a wooden chest containing the broken bones of two children. It was widely believed that these must be the princes, and Charles ordered that the remains be placed in an urn in Westminster Abbey. A new examination in 1933 confirmed that the bones belonged to children the right age to be Edward and Richard, but there has been no recent DNA test.

Seen from the street or the river, the Tower is disappointingly small these days, dwarfed by the randomly placed skyscrapers of the City of London. But once you're inside, it is still satisfyingly huge and powerful-looking – a symbol of everything that William the Conqueror and generations of his successors wanted it to be. William's original White Tower houses the museum of the Royal Armouries, displaying guns, other weaponry and innumerable suits of armour that make you realise why cavalrymen needed sturdy horses. If you join a guided tour you can visit the Chapel Royal of

St Peter ad Vincula, where those three beheaded queens are buried; you can also revel in the age-old story that the Tower (and the kingdom) will fall if the six resident ravens ever fly away. Today there are seven carefully tended Tower ravens – one spare, just in case. You can shudder at the fate of the numerous prisoners who entered through the Traitors' Gate, most of them never to leave the Tower alive. And, of course, you can gaze on the wonders that are the Crown Jewels (see page 248).

What you can't do is make an informed decision about the fate of the Princes in the Tower. Shakespeare was in no doubt that they were murdered and that their uncle was the villain; he has a shady character in *Richard III* report that the boys were smothered in their bed,

> *girdling one another*
> *Within their innocent alabaster arms:*
> *Their lips were four red roses on a stalk…*

This is very much how later Romantic painters showed them: pictures of innocence, with curly blond ringlets. The Latin inscription on their marble sarcophagus in Westminster Abbey (designed by Sir Christopher Wren) says that they were 'stifled with pillows' and 'privately and meanly buried, by the order of their perfidious uncle Richard the Usurper'. But the truth is we don't know and, until someone authorises a DNA test on those broken bones, we never shall.

45

BOSWORTH
Richard III

A horse! a horse! my kingdom for a horse!
WILLIAM SHAKESPEARE, *KING RICHARD III*

These are the last words Shakespeare has Richard III
speak, but they are to no avail – the next we hear, from
the man who is about to become King Henry VII, is
that 'the day is ours, the bloody dog is dead'. Richard,
like Macbeth (see page 40), has had his reputation
tarnished by Shakespeare, but there is no doubt that
he died at the Battle of Bosworth Field, just outside
Leicester, on 22 August 1485. His death brought the
Wars of the Roses to a close, signalling the end of over
300 years of Plantagenet rule and the beginning of
the Tudor dynasty. A lot of changes just for the want
of a horse.

The people who designed the Battlefield Heritage
Centre and Country Park at Bosworth have done an
excellent job. You could go there on a Sunday afternoon
just to take the dog for a walk, but it would be a shame
to miss the war memorial in the form of a sundial that
details the events of that history-changing day. 'Early
in the morning men prepare their souls and their
equipment for the forthcoming battle,' it tells you, at the
point where the sun would have fallen at 8am. 'Sounds

of stone on blades and murmured Latin prayers are soon drowned out by the din of the drums calling the men to muster.' At noon, 'Bodies strew the field, blood soaks the ground.' Then by three in the afternoon it is all over: 'The last of the Plantagenet kings slung naked across a horse; a victor leads his tired army to Leicester and a day's deeds are recounted.' A thousand men killed in less than seven hours; as you read the words on the sundial you are tempted to bow your head.

Although it was at Agincourt, 70 years earlier and nowhere near Leicester, that English archers really carried the day, the longbow was still a feature at Bosworth. One of the signboards in the country park suggests that you 'look to your right, to the white fence. A good archer could have hit you from there.' There isn't a longbowman in sight and the fence is really quite a long way down the hill, but you instinctively take a step or two away.

Contemporary records describe Richard and Henry's armies as being drawn up on either side of a marsh, with a force led by the Stanleys (the Earl of Derby and his family) between them. The Stanleys, previously loyal to Richard, seem to have turned up on the battlefield without telling anyone whose side they were on and gone over to Henry when it looked as if he was winning, thus hastening Richard's defeat. According to Shakespeare – and there may even be some truth in this one – Lord Stanley plucked the crown from Richard's dead temples and crowned Henry there and then on the battlefield.

Never mind the drama, though; let's focus on the terrain. It was the mention of the marsh that enabled 20th-century historians to estimate where the Battle of Bosworth had taken place and justified the first heritage centre opening here in 1974. Then in 2009 a survey using state-of-the-art technology proved that the battle had indeed been fought not much more than a mile away. A collection of medieval cannonballs and other bits of metal discovered thanks to this survey is now on display in the Bosworth Quest gallery, the highlight being the 'Bosworth Boar', a silver-gilt brooch not much more than an inch long. As the boar was Richard's personal emblem, it is immensely tempting to imagine that he was wearing this endearing little ornament when he was struck down.

Even his enemies acknowledged that Richard fought valiantly to the end, but he was then thrown over a horse and carried into Leicester, where his body was paraded around to convince people that he was dead. Whether he was stripped of his clothing or merely of his armour isn't clear, but either way it was intended to be undignified.

Thanks to the Tudors and Shakespeare, Richard III went down in history as a thorough-going villain. Until, that is, in 1924 a group of friends from Liverpool decided to form a society in an attempt to have him treated more fairly. This evolved into today's Richard III Society, which was instrumental in staging perhaps the most triumphant coup ever in the worlds of archaeology, detective work and rewriting history. Read on...

46

LEICESTER CATHEDRAL
Richard III

THE DISCOVERY OF THE SKELETON of Richard III – 'the king in the car park' – in Leicester in 2012 was one of the most extraordinary events of recent royal history. As one of the archaeologists involved said, going out and digging in a specific place to find a specific famous person is just not the way archaeology works.

Maybe not, but that's what happened in this case. The remains were unearthed just where it had been suggested they would be: in the choir of the medieval Greyfriars Church, spitting distance from today's cathedral. DNA established Richard's identity beyond doubt, and the skeleton showed that he suffered from scoliosis of the spine. He wasn't the deformed monster that Shakespeare portrayed, but he probably had one shoulder higher than the other – a defect that could be exaggerated if you were determined to create a villain.

After his death at the Battle of Bosworth, Richard had been hastily buried in the most appropriate local place. In 2015, after much discussion about where he should be buried again – Westminster Abbey, with a host of other monarchs? York, because, as a member of the House of York, this would have been his own choice? – he was given a grand funeral in Leicester. His cortege, including a hearse drawn by four black horses, processed from Leicester University through the Leicestershire countryside (including Bosworth Field) and back into the city, to the cathedral. The route was lined by tens of thousands of people; the coffin then lay in the cathedral for three days before a ceremony attended by, among others, the Archbishop of Canterbury, the Poet Laureate and the Duke and Duchess of Gloucester. It was quite a tribute to a man who had been dead for over 500 years.

Richard's new memorial in Leicester Cathedral is in a place of honour near the main altar. It's made from fossil stone and sits on a black marble plinth, with Richard's name, dates and motto – *Loyauté me lie* ('Loyalty binds me') – engraved on it. Although you can't see the coffin, buried beneath the monument, it's a nice touch that it was made by a cabinet- and furniture-maker named Michael Ibsen. Descended from Richard's sister Anne of York, he is Richard's 16th great-nephew and the one whose mitochondrial DNA helped to confirm the identity of the skeleton in the car park.

Two minutes' walk from the cathedral, an excellent visitor centre tells you everything you need to know about Richard, his life, death and the discovery of his bones. It even displays the facial reconstruction that, thanks to the wonders of modern science, showed that the skeleton's face looked remarkably like the surviving portraits. It's all fascinating, not least because the whole story is so bizarre. But whether or not you've digested all the information, walking quietly round the elegant memorial in the cathedral is surprisingly moving. Unless you're a Henry VII fan, of course. If you are, please turn the page and keep reading.

The Tudor Era
1485–1603

47

PEMBROKE CASTLE
Henry VII

As we have seen, between 1066 and 1483 there were a number of kings whose claims to the throne were, at best, arguable and had to be established by force. Henry VII probably tops the list of truly dodgy candidates. His paternal grandmother, the French princess Catherine de Valois, had been Henry V's widow; she then married Owen Tudor, whose forebears had been Welsh princes, and produced Henry VII's father Edmund. Through his mother, Margaret Beaufort, Henry VII was descended from Edward III, but only through a bastard son of John of Gaunt. That bit is complicated – the Beauforts had been legitimised after John of Gaunt married their mother, his long-term mistress Katherine Swynford. But by a decree of Henry IV's they had been specifically excluded from the succession. Lots to argue about there, but it means that while Henry VII could stake a plausible claim to the Welsh and French thrones, he was on shakier ground in England. One of his first acts as monarch, therefore, was to declare himself king 'by right of conquest' – he'd defeated Richard III in battle and that was good enough.

Be that as it may, in the wake of all the sympathetic publicity surrounding Richard after his remains were discovered in Leicester (see page 156), the people of

Pembroke – in whose castle Henry was born in 1457
– have made an effort to redress the balance in favour of
their local son. They've erected an elegant bronze statue
of him on Mill Bridge and from that position you get a
clear idea of why Pembroke Castle was so important.
From as early as the 12th century the Earls of Pembroke
were powerful, independent and never out of the
headlines for long. In addition, Pembroke was handily
placed for anyone wanting to invade from France or
Ireland or return from exile there (two things that seem
to have happened a lot over the years). The castle sits on
– almost seems to grow out of – an impressive slab of
sheer rock above a substantial body of water. It wasn't
going to be scaled by anyone less agile than Spider-Man.
Approaching from the road, you'd have come to a very
solid and solidly defended barbican. This was a castle
that meant business. It was and is huge.

It's also enormous fun. There's a lot of it left, and
you can do a surprising amount of unsupervised
exploring – up narrow, winding staircases, out on to
ramparts and up the five-storey keep. Looking down
from there you get a clear impression of what a rabbit
warren the castle must have been – rooms, staircases and
towers appear to sprout all over the place. There's a
dungeon tower where one unfortunate was kept for
seven years in such poor light that he went blind; a huge
map painted on the ground in the outer ward giving the
location of all the (many) major castles in Wales; and
– don't miss this – a vast underground cavern that was
used as a shelter in Palaeolithic times and as a storeroom
once the castle was built on top of it. It's not every

castle that can boast that part of its site has been occupied on and off for the last 12,000 years.

So what was Henry doing here? Well, his father, Edmund Tudor, had died shortly before he was born and his mother was only 13. Henry VI, Edmund's half-brother, was on the throne, but ill; Richard of York (see page 137) was looking after his kingdom. It was a dangerous time to be a prominent member of the House of Lancaster. The Earl of Pembroke at this time was Henry's paternal uncle, Jasper Tudor, and he took his pregnant young sister-in-law into his castle for safety. What is now called the Henry VII Tower is almost certainly where the baby was born.

As a close relation and loyal supporter of Henry VI, Jasper fell out of favour when the Yorkists came to power and escaped to France with his young nephew. Henry Tudor spent most of the next 20 years there, making one failed invasion attempt in 1483 before the successful one that culminated in the Battle of Bosworth in 1485. Within six months of that victory, Jasper had married Katherine Woodville, sister of Edward IV's queen, and Henry had married Elizabeth of York, Edward IV's daughter, uniting the Houses of York and Lancaster and drawing a firm line under the Wars of the Roses.

Sweetness and light did not return overnight, of course, and Henry survived more than one attempt to unthrone him. The most significant rumbled on for much of the 1490s, when a young man of the right age and appearance turned up claiming to be Richard of York, the younger of the Princes in the Tower (see page

149). As Edward IV's son he would have had
a much stronger right to the throne than
Henry. There were still enough Yorkist
supporters around to back him, and when he
invaded Cornwall, promising to put an end
to unfair taxation from London, it looked as
if he might be in with a chance. He got as far as Exeter
before Henry's army stopped him and he was discovered
to be an impostor named Perkin Warbeck. He was
eventually hanged at Tyburn, but as far as Henry was
concerned he had gained a worrying amount of support.

There's a lot to be said that is good about Henry
VII: he restored peace to a country that had been
ravaged by war for decades; he was a great administrator
and, realising that his island kingdom would do well to
have a powerful navy, he instituted a game-changing
programme of ship-building. But even the exhibition at
Pembroke Castle – which is, as you might expect, very
pro him – admits that he had a reputation for
ruthlessness and miserliness. Francis Bacon, writing
a biography in 1621, says that he was 'full of
apprehensions and suspicions [that] were not dangerous,
but troubled himself more than others'. It's just possible
that Henry was bothered by a guilty conscience and a
not entirely unjustified sense of paranoia.

Efforts to rehabilitate him continue, however: one
shop in Pembroke's Main Street even stocks a locally
produced and highly regarded Henry VII cider. Just
don't try it before you tackle all those staircases in
the castle.

48

Ludlow Castle/ Worcester Cathedral
Arthur, Prince of Wales

THERE'S SOMETHING RATHER TRAGIC about the Tudor obsession with establishing a dynasty. Henry VII's claim to the throne may have been ropey (see page 160), but he produced the clichéd 'heir and a spare'; he also had a daughter strategically married to the King of Scotland (and what a complication *that* turned out to be). But although he was succeeded by his son, and that son was succeeded by three of his own children, all those three died childless, and within a century of Henry VII's death the Tudor line too had passed into oblivion.

It's hard not to speculate on what might have happened had Henry's elder son – Arthur, Prince of Wales – not died before he was 16. He had been married six months earlier to Katherine of Aragon, daughter of the powerful 'Catholic Monarchs' Ferdinand and Isabella of Spain, and doubt remains to this day as to whether the marriage was consummated. Katherine said that it wasn't, leaving her free to marry her late husband's brother, the future Henry VIII; Henry, when Katherine had failed to provide him with a male heir and he wanted Anne Boleyn, said that it was and that it had been a sin for him to marry his brother's wife. Out of that came a spate of divorce and beheadings, not to mention the birth of the Church of England. Who would have thought the sexual behaviour of two teenagers could have such a powerful knock-on effect?

Shortly after their marriage, Arthur and Katherine set up home in Ludlow Castle, close to the Welsh border. Anglo-Welsh relations were more cordial than they had been a couple of centuries before and by 1501 Ludlow was more of an administrative centre than a fortress: Arthur was able to rule his principality and the Marches area without its interfering a great deal with his honeymoon. But Ludlow hadn't always been peaceful: there's a story that during the war between Stephen and Matilda (see page 60), Stephen was besieging the castle when one of the defenders threw a grappling hook from the gatehouse tower, snaring a Scottish prince who was fighting on Stephen's side. He would have been pulled up into captivity (and doubtless proved useful for ransom purposes) had Stephen himself not intervened and saved him.

Siege or no siege, the remains of the castle are some of the best in the country. There's a remarkably well-preserved circular Norman chapel in the inner bailey, while the noticeably tall windows in the Great Hall suggest that it would have been a bright and airy – not to mention rich and luxurious – space in its day. The castle was, as most were, sited on high ground, ready to repel any attacks that might come its way; walking round the walls today you can imagine that, from here, you could hold sway over a goodly part of Wales.

Sadly, none of this was any use to young Arthur. After two months of declining strength, this previously healthy prince died – probably of the flu-like 'sweating sickness'. In St Laurence's Church near Ludlow Castle, a plaque says that his 'heart' is buried here. The inverted commas tell you it is a euphemism – it means most of his internal organs, which were removed as part of the embalming process: it took three weeks for news of Arthur's death to reach London and for instructions regarding the funeral to be sent back to Ludlow, so this was a necessary precaution in terms of hygiene.

The body was then carried to Worcester Cathedral. There were all sorts of reasons for this choice, not least a political one: a burial in Westminster Abbey, which might have seemed more fitting for a Prince of Wales, would have drawn too much public attention. Given that Henry VII's new heir – that prudently produced 'spare' son – was only 10 years old, all sorts of unsettling questions about the succession were back on the agenda.

It may have been away from the public eye, but the funeral was as grand as anyone could have wished; the hearse was accompanied by banners representing the kings and queens of both England and Spain, and the monument in Worcester glittered in the light of a thousand candles. Today, Arthur lies in a chantry chapel, in a position of honour near the high altar; the chapel's outer walls are adorned with Tudor and Spanish heraldic symbols, including roses, portcullises and pomegranates. You look around, think of everything you know about Henry VIII and wonder what might – or might not – have been.

49

STIRLING CASTLE
Jameses IV, V & VI of Scotland

YOU COULD ASSOCIATE STIRLING CASTLE with almost any Scottish monarch before 1603 – we've seen that it played an important part in the Wars of Scottish Independence (see page 106). But it was the three 16th-century Jameses who turned it from a fortress into a palace. James IV, coming to the throne in 1488, was the first to latch on to the idea that the King of Scotland could be a cultivated Renaissance man rather than a mere warrior chieftain. He built a Great Hall and a Chapel Royal, and invited poets and scholars to form part of his court. He even had a tame alchemist, but apparently lost interest in him when the poor man failed to turn base metal into gold after five years of trying.

The Great Hall, the largest and finest in Scotland, is the most important survivor of this period. With its cream walls and pale green hangings it isn't perhaps as luxurious as you might expect, but its sheer size is jaw-dropping. It was much restored in the late 20th century: reconstruction of the exquisite hammerbeam roof required the wood of some 400 Perthshire-grown oak trees; five fireplaces stop you worrying too much about how they kept the place warm.

James was killed in 1513 at the Battle of Flodden Field (see page 170), leaving a 17-month-old son to succeed him. Two extremely lucrative marriages allowed that son, James V, to continue his father's plans for Stirling. The first was to a French princess, Madeleine, who died aged only 16 but left him in control of her ample dowry, and the second to a French noblewoman, Mary, from the powerful House of Guise. The Royal Apartments are James and Mary's lasting contribution to the palace: both King and Queen presided over a series of rooms to which access was gained according to strict hierarchical rules. Only the most powerful courtiers and the monarchs' intimates were admitted to the inner sanctums. In a move that would have dire implications for his descendants, the King had placed himself on a metaphorical pedestal, ruling not by his own might but by God's will.

By an odd coincidence, having come to the throne as a baby, James V died six days after the birth of his daughter Mary, the Queen of Scots of whom we shall hear more elsewhere; she was forced to abdicate in 1567, when her son and heir – the future James VI and I – was only a year old. Before that happened, she had had him baptised at Stirling in the last great Catholic Mass to be held in Scotland. There followed three days of celebration, including the country's first ever firework display. But the 'new religion' was taking hold and, a year later, the infant James was crowned in a Protestant ceremony at the Church of the Holy Rude just down the hill.

Lavish – some would say excessive – christening celebrations were something of a feature at Stirling. When James VI's eldest son Henry (see page 236) was

born here in 1594, a new and magnificent Chapel Royal
was built in great haste so that he could be baptised
with appropriate but Protestant splendour. The baby was
wrapped for the occasion in a long robe of purple velvet
studded with pearls. The celebratory banquet afterwards
boasted not only a triumphal
chariot piled high with
pastries, fruits and confections,
but also a ship some 20ft long
and 45ft high, loaded with
lobsters, clams and crabs. As
this entered the Great Hall it
fired a series of volleys from
36 brass guns. It must have
been a hard act to follow.

> **WHILE YOU'RE HERE**
> *Take a moment to visit the Church
> of the Holy Rude. Not only was
> James VI crowned here, but bullet
> marks visible on the tower date from
> the 1651 siege. The name means
> 'Holy Cross', having the same
> derivation as Holyrood Palace in
> Edinburgh (see page 218).*

Stirling was one of many
Scottish royal residences that were neglected after James
VI moved south on becoming King of England, but it
was important enough to play a part in the English Civil
Wars some half-century later. Charles II – exiled from
England after his father's execution (see page 242), but
battling Cromwell's forces in Scotland – left a Royalist
garrison in control of Stirling. The castle, besieged for
several months, was captured by Parliamentarians in
August 1651: the last time in its chequered history that
Stirling was forced to surrender to an English force.

50

FLODDEN FIELD
James IV of Scotland

*The Flooers o' the Forest, that fought aye the
foremost,
The pride o' oor land lie cauld in the clay.*

<small>JEAN ELLIOT *THE FLOWERS OF THE FOREST*, WRITTEN IN 1756 TO
COMMEMORATE THE SCOTS WHO FELL AT FLODDEN</small>

BEING RELATED WAS ABSOLUTELY no guarantee of
friendship among the royals of historic times. James IV
of Scotland was married to Henry VIII's sister Margaret,
the marriage having been one of the provisions of the
Treaty of Perpetual Peace that James had agreed with
his future father-in-law, Henry VII, in 1502. The idea
was to stop the English and the Scots fighting each
other, as they had been doing intermittently for several
hundred years.

It was, obviously, a name whose very optimism was
asking for trouble. The 'perpetual peace' lasted less than
11 years before an English army led by the Earl of
Surrey and a Scottish one led by James himself came
face to face on a battlefield in Northumberland in
1513. The encounter is sometimes known as the Battle
of Branxton Moor, after the nearby village, but more
often as the more romantic-sounding Battle of
Flodden Field.

In addition to being at war with Scotland, England had been in frequent conflict with France over the years. The Norman Conquest had put Normandy under English rule; Henry II's marriage to Eleanor of Aquitaine meant he acquired her substantial territories. There had been other examples, and barely a reign passed without a French king trying to win back parts of his kingdom or an English one feeling the need to put down a French rebellion. The end of the Hundred Years' War in 1453 had left all of France except Calais in French hands, but the young Henry VIII, determined to win back lands that he saw as his, invaded France in 1513.

There was another complication. On the basis that 'my enemy's enemy is my friend', the French and the Scots had entered into what is known as the Auld [old] Alliance as far back as 1294. James IV therefore felt justified in issuing an ultimatum to Henry to withdraw from France; when that was ignored, he invaded England himself. Opinions vary about James's political acumen, but it seems that his usefulness to his Continental allies lay largely in his ability to threaten England's northern border – he had no control over what anyone was up to further south. So although he had sent naval forces to help the French defend themselves against Henry, there was no friendly reciprocal arrangement. And although no one doubts his physical courage, as a military tactician James left a lot to be desired.

In Henry's absence in France, the Earl of Surrey – a 70-year-old veteran of the Wars of the Roses – was

Lieutenant-General (the King's deputy) in northern England. He marched north, accumulating a force of about 26,000 men, and managed to position himself behind the much larger Scottish army, cutting off its lines of retreat across the River Tweed and back into Scotland. The two forces met on uneven ground, with the Scots' advantage of the higher position soon turning into a slippery disaster. It's estimated that anything from 5,000 to 17,000 Scots were killed, as well as perhaps 1,500 English, making it one of the bloodiest battles ever fought on British soil. Many of the Scottish nobility were among the dead, as was, most crucially, King James himself. From the point of view of Scottish prestige, the battle was a humiliation, but in terms of Anglo-Scottish relations, or indeed Anglo-French ones, it had little long-term effect.

> **A GOOD TIME TO VISIT**
> *Coldstream Civic Week in early August includes a day when several hundred people ride out on horseback from the town of Coldstream to Flodden (about 4 miles away) to lay wreaths and, accompanied by a piper, take part in a service to commemorate the dead.*
>
> ❧

Today, you can follow a trail around the battlefield, learn about the importance of the different weapons used by the combatants and pay your respects to the burial pits. There's a monument in the form of a granite cross giving a fine view over the battlefield. On a wind-free day, it's extraordinarily peaceful, thanks in part to the absence of a visitor centre or café. But your overall feeling is one of futility: a *lot* of people killed for no very good reason.

51

PETERBOROUGH CATHEDRAL
Katherine of Aragon

THE IDENTIFYING, UNIQUE FEATURE of Peterborough
Cathedral is its Early English Gothic West Front
– unique in that it is slightly asymmetrical, because one
of the towers was never completed. Having gazed your
fill at this, go into the cathedral, turn left and look up to
see the memorial to 'Old Scarlett' the gravedigger, who
died in 1594, aged 98. In addition to having buried two
generations from every household in Peterborough,
Robert Scarlett had the distinction of having buried
two queens. One of these, Mary, Queen of Scots, was
exhumed in the 17th century on the orders of her son,
by then James I of England; there is still a memorial to
her in Peterborough's south aisle, but her mortal remains
are in Westminster Abbey.

Scarlett's other royal client, Katherine of Aragon,
buried in January 1536, still lies under the north aisle.
Well-wishers leave pomegranates on her grave, a
reference to the fruit that appeared on her coat of arms
(and still appears on the arms of the Spanish city of
Granada, after which it is named). Ironically, given
Katherine's history, the pomegranate with its many rich
and colourful seeds is a symbol of fertility.

Katherine died in Kimbolton, in modern
Cambridgeshire, still maintaining that she was Queen of

England. She'd been married to Henry VIII for 24 years and for a long time the marriage seems to have been at least mutually respectful: Katherine acted as Regent for six months in 1513 while Henry was away in France, unsuccessfully but expensively pursuing his claim to the French throne. But the couple's only surviving child was a girl, the future Mary I, and Henry was desperate for a male heir. He was also desperate for Anne Boleyn, who wouldn't consent to be his mistress. The Pope refused to annul the marriage, so Henry was forced to take drastic measures to divorce Katherine. He declared himself Supreme Head of the Church of England and Defender of the Faith; endured being excommunicated by the Pope; dissolved the country's many hundreds of monasteries and acquired much of their wealth; passed an Act of Succession that made Mary illegitimate; married Anne Boleyn; and banished Katherine from court.

> **A GOOD TIME TO VISIT**
> *Every year, around the anniversary of Katherine's funeral – 29 January – Peterborough holds a weekend-long Katherine of Aragon festival, including a lecture, various Tudor-themed events and special church services.*

Not content with having treated her appallingly towards the end of her life, Henry VIII refused to give Katherine a state funeral in London, on the grounds that it was too expensive. Nearer the truth is that he wanted to avoid embarrassment: Katherine remained immensely popular – much more so than Anne – and her funeral could easily have become a focal point for public protests in the capital. So the honour of burying her was granted to Peterborough because it was the most conveniently situated religious house of suitable status.

Katherine was buried not as Queen but as Dowager Princess of Wales – Arthur's widow rather than Henry's ex. This still entitled her to considerable pomp: having her body conveyed on a wagon covered with black velvet, lots of noble mourners and the light of a thousand candles. One notable absentee was Mary, whom Henry had forbidden to attend: her alleged illegitimacy made the whole business a protocolic nightmare. Not to mention that it might bring people out in support of Katherine's daughter…

The embalming of Katherine's body didn't help Henry's efforts to downplay the occasion: her heart was found to be black, with a black growth on it. Nowadays, this might be recognised as a melanoma; in the 16th century it gave rise to the suspicion of poisoning. Anne Boleyn's hatred of Katherine was no secret: rumours abounded, but we'll never know.

WHILE YOU'RE HERE

Across Cathedral Square is the 17th-century Guildhall. At ground level it looks like the sort of butter cross you find in many market towns – a raised and covered space with rounded arches holding the roof up. And indeed this level was originally used as a poultry and butter market, while the two floors above, with Swiss-chalet-like gables at the top, served as the Guildhall or Town Hall. It was built to celebrate the Restoration of Charles II, whose coat of arms, with the date 1671, adorns the panel below the clock. From here, look back across the square, through the Norman archway to the cathedral itself, doing your best to ignore the rather view-spoiling coffee shop on the left. To be fair, there isn't much of a view to spoil: it's just a flat site on a very flat piece of land. But that slightly off-the-skew façade, framed by the historic arch, is worth another look.

Katherine's tomb was vandalised by Oliver Cromwell's troops in the 17th century; the marble slab we see today dates only from the 1890s, when a woman named Katharine Clayton, wife of one of the cathedral canons, organised a campaign asking every Katharine (or Catherine or any other variation) to contribute a penny to pay for a fitting memorial. The inscription on the slab refers to her as Queen of England and Henry VIII's first wife and spells her name Katharine, presumably because that is how Mrs Clayton spelled hers. Historians tend to prefer Katherine or Catherine, but whichever version you choose, her popularity continues: a tablet marking the 450th anniversary of her death, in 1986, describes her as 'a queen cherished by the English people for her loyalty, piety, courage and compassion'.

A belated one in the eye for Henry and for Anne Boleyn, some would say.

52

DEAL CASTLE
Henry VIII

THE TROUBLE WITH TRYING TO DIVORCE your wife, if she happens to have been born a Spanish princess, is that you may upset her influential relatives. This was the problem Henry VIII had when he wanted to get rid of Katherine of Aragon. Her parents, the powerful Ferdinand and Isabella whose marriage had united much of Spain, were dead by this time. But they had left behind a grandson, Katherine's nephew Charles, who was not only effectively King of Spain but also Holy Roman Emperor, King of Italy, Archduke of Austria and goodness knows what else besides. His domains included colonies in Asia and the Americas and spanned almost 1.5 million square miles.

You didn't want this man for an enemy. But Henry seems to have overlooked that fact. 'The King's Great Matter', as the divorce crisis was known, brought the Catholic powers of Europe – the Emperor Charles, Francis I of France and the Pope – into an alliance against him. So, with every reason to fear that an invasion was imminent, Henry set about fortifying his coastline. His master plan, known as a 'device', provided for over 40 new fortifications stretching from West Wales all the way round to Hull, with the majority concentrated on the Kent and Sussex coast. Of these, one of the most important was at Deal. It was to be one of a trio of artillery castles, linked to the others (Walmer to the south and Sandown to the north) by an earthwork rampart and four further gun forts – all in the space of about 3 miles of coastline. As defensive measures went, this was serious stuff.

A number of things were important about Deal. It overlooked a safe anchorage known as the Downs, which gave shelter to ships of all nationalities when there were storms in the Channel; it was one of the closest points to mainland Europe, giving would-be invaders a minimum of sailing to do; and its shoreline was beach, making it an easier landing place than the cliffs that protected nearby Dover and much of the rest of the coast. All very good reasons for Henry to establish a castle with mighty artillery – and one that could be defended from every angle, be it land or sea.

The plan was for Deal to have 140 guns, but diplomatic relations tend to change more quickly than castles are built. By the time the building works were finished in late 1540, the threat of invasion had abated; within another three years Henry was in an alliance with Charles against the French. Deal had five truly massive outer bastions supporting the gun platforms, and rounded walls designed to deflect enemy fire, but it never had more than 57 guns and 87 longbows, and it wasn't called upon to repel an invasion in Henry's lifetime.

It was re-armed a number of times during the next hundred years when invasions threatened again, but in between whiles it was generally neglected – there was no point in keeping it fully armed when no crisis was looming. It witnessed a battle between the Dutch and the Spanish in the Channel in 1639, but the only role the British fleet played was to drive the combatants out of British waters. Deal was geared up during the Anglo-Dutch Wars of the 1660s, when its strategic position and useful anchorage made it an obvious target, but again it wasn't called upon to defend itself: the Dutch forces stole up the Medway and attacked the naval dockyards at Chatham instead. In fact, that only time Deal was bombarded was during the Civil Wars, when, in 1648, a Parliamentary force attacked it with mortar and the Royalists were forced to surrender.

Deal was never intended to be a palace – there are no state apartments, no Great Hall, and the 18th-century Captain's House that made it a more comfortable place to live was destroyed by a German bomb in 1940. Its location and sheer physical strength made it what it was. Today, you can still see why its position was so important; you can be impressed by the size of its moat, climb over its huge fortifications and explore its underground passageways. You can, if you like, think mockingly that it's a bit of a folly: look at all those invasions it was never called upon to repel. But you can't help wondering what might have happened if it hadn't been there.

53

BLICKLING HALL/
HEVER CASTLE
Anne Boleyn

YOU MAY WONDER WHY a stately home in Norfolk and another in Kent should come under the same heading: it's because both lay claim to being the birthplace of Henry VIII's second wife, Anne Boleyn. The confusion arises because no one is sure precisely *when* she was born. Her parents lived at Blickling from about 1499 to 1505, when her father inherited Hever and moved there. Anne was probably born around 1501, but it might have been as late as 1507, so you see the difficulty.

Even if she was born at Blickling, she wasn't born in the present hall: it is Jacobean, dating from 80 years after her death. Anne's ghost apparently doesn't know or doesn't care about this – she is said to appear each year on the anniversary of her death (19 May), carrying her own severed head, in a coach driven by a headless coachman and drawn by four headless horses.

It isn't only Anne who walks – or rather glides – here: a National Trust poll once voted Blickling the most haunted house in Britain. Anne's father, Thomas Boleyn, also headless, has been seen too. His headlessness seems odd, as he wasn't beheaded: he held the prestigious office of Lord Privy Seal for several years under Henry VIII, was dismissed when Anne fell from grace, but clawed his way back into Henry's favour and died with his head still on his shoulders three years later. It was his son, George, Viscount Rochford, accused of incest with Anne, who was executed. Maybe there was a family likeness and the ghost-watchers have become confused.

If ghosts aren't your thing, the red-brick house is magnificent: it's the work of Robert Lyminge, who also designed Hatfield (see page 212). The grounds – formal parterres and topiary, a walled garden and ancient yew hedges – are a garden-lover's mecca; and at Christmas the 50 Christmas trees and 19,000 lights scattered about the place, inside and out, are, to say the least, eye-catching.

Wherever she was born, Anne Boleyn certainly spent her childhood at Hever; she was living there when Henry VIII was pursuing her and she continued to treat it as home even after she had become a lady-in-waiting at the royal court. Some say she haunts it. But presumably not on 19 May.

If Blickling is a stately home, Hever is quite definitely a castle. Turrets, battlements, moat, the lot, built for defensive purposes in the 13th century: the medieval Council Chamber in the gatehouse survives from that period. It was the Boleyns' family home in the 15th and 16th centuries, and good chunks of the Tudor building, including the Staircase Gallery and Long Gallery, are still intact. But the person to be thanked for much of Hever's splendour today is William Waldorf Astor, the American gazillionaire who bought it in 1903.

He spent a fortune on it, using as far as possible Tudor materials and tools, but quite a bit of it is what a 20th-century American gazillionaire thought a Tudor mansion should be like – including the Tudor-style maze and Tudor-style herb garden.

That doesn't stop it being delightful, though, nor does it detract from the wealth of genuine Tudor memorabilia. There are two illuminated prayer books annotated and signed by Anne herself, and a collection of Tudor portraits said to be the best outside the National Portrait Gallery and including all of Henry's six wives. There's a room called King Henry's Bedchamber containing a lavishly carved 'tester' bed – a four-poster with a wooden canopy. The bed dates from four years after Anne's death, but it's part of Hever tradition that the King visited on several occasions when he was courting her. The chamber is one of the largest in the castle; if Henry stayed here he could well have slept in it, and he would have slept in a bed like this. The decorative wooden ceiling is authentic – 1460s, and a luxury that not every bedchamber would have had. Anne's own sleeping quarters are appreciably less grand.

When Thomas Boleyn died in 1539, Hever passed into Henry VIII's hands and he gave it to Anne of Cleves (as we shall see on page 190, she did *extraordinarily* well out of him); on her death it reverted to the Crown and then passed out of royal hands. But whether Anne Boleyn was born at Hever or not, there is plenty both here and at Blickling to remind us of her. Two possible birthplaces, two possible ghosts – what's not to admire?

54

HAMPTON COURT
Jane Seymour

JANE SEYMOUR WAS THE THIRD of Henry VIII's wives and
is often described as his favourite: this may be, with the
gift of hindsight, because she bore him the legitimate
son for whom he had yearned for so long. Then, poor
woman, she promptly died, aged only 29.

Born into an influential family whose 'seat' was
Wulfhall in Wiltshire (made famous as Wolf Hall in
Hilary Mantel's novels), Jane was maid-of-honour to
both Katherine of Aragon and Anne Boleyn. She seems
to have caught Henry's eye early in 1536, about the
time that Katherine died and Anne suffered a
miscarriage – two events that surely played a part in the
King's looking around for another wife. She seems by
all accounts to have been a nice but rather dull woman,
less educated than her predecessors. Under her regime
the court ceased to be a place of entertainment and
fashion, and became more sober in dress and demeanour.
She was, on the other hand, kind to her stepdaughter
Mary and brought about the Princess's reconciliation
with her father.

Whatever her personal qualities, Jane produced that
much needed heir, the future (and ironically short-lived)
Edward VI – and she did it at Hampton Court, probably
the most famous of Henry's many palaces. Although

Henry was a great builder and commissioner of works,
he wasn't responsible for this one: it had been a farm
estate, acquired by his most trusted adviser, Cardinal
Wolsey, and expanded by him. Wolsey had become both
extremely powerful and extremely rich and there were
those (Henry may have been one of them) who felt that,
by doing up Hampton Court in this palatial way, this
mere butcher's son from Ipswich was getting above
himself. To be fair, Wolsey's intentions seem to have
been, at least in part, to provide accommodation for the
King and the court whenever they chose to visit, and to
have somewhere suitably impressive to receive foreign
dignitaries. But around this time Wolsey was also failing
to arrange Henry's divorce from Katherine of Aragon;
he fell out of royal favour and was – shall we say
encouraged? – to surrender his magnificent property
to the King.

And magnificent is the word. You approach it along
a long driveway, giving you ample opportunity to
admire the rich red Tudor brick of the façade. You
pass through an archway into the Base Court (from
which any self-guided tour you care to take begins),
through another into the Clock Court and thence into
the Fountain Court, where alarmingly lifelike and
life-sized figures loll drunkenly against the elaborate
reconstruction of Henry VIII's wine fountain or sit on
a bench in the sun, waiting for you to be lured into
thinking they are real and going up to pass the time
of day. The faces of Roman emperors carved above
every gateway were commissioned by Wolsey,
apparently to tell the world that he had thrown off

his humble beginnings and acquired a sophisticated Classical education.

Once into the Tudor apartments, you admire the 106ft-long Great Hall with its exquisitely carved hammerbeam roof, but the real joy is the Chapel Royal, still used as a place of worship. It was much revamped in the reign of Queen Anne (and boasts a huge oak reredos from that time, with garlands carved by master woodworker Grinling Gibbons), but thank goodness they left the ceiling intact. And what a ceiling it is: made from oaks specially selected and felled from Windsor Forest, vaulted and painted in the blue of a midnight sky, with the edges of each panel a repeating pattern of stars and the royal motto 'Dieu et Mon Droit' picked out in gold. It is, frankly, dazzling. And if, having been dazzled by looking up, you care to look down, you can contemplate the odd rumour that Jane Seymour's heart and other organs may be buried beneath the floor.

The rest of Jane's body is in St George's Chapel, Windsor (see page 141), where she lies next to her husband, the only one of Henry's wives to be given a queen's funeral. But Jane may not entirely have left Hampton Court: at the time of her death, her tomb in Windsor was not ready for her and it is suggested that the ghostly lady in a long white gown who has been seen carrying a lighted taper down the so-called Silver Stick Staircase and out into the Clock Court may be her. If it is, she isn't alone in her

WHILE YOU'RE HERE
Don't miss Henry VIII's kitchens and wine cellar. The guidebook to Hampton Court tells you that food was very important to Henry's court. The kitchens had to produce 1,200 meals a day and the size of the fireplaces suggests that the roasting of multiple barons of beef was a common occurrence. You can draw your own conclusions from the size of the wine cellar, too.

wanderings. Tradition has it that Katherine Howard (see page 197), learning that she was to be charged with adultery, ran along the processional route that leads from Henry VIII's quarters to the chapel, screaming and begging her husband for mercy. The royal guards seized her and forced her back to her own apartments. She never saw Henry again, but her ghost, still screaming, is regularly seen and heard in what is now called the Haunted Gallery.

Having completed your tour of the Tudor rooms and returned to Base Court, don't imagine that you are done. Hampton Court is two palaces for the price of one. Leave the Tudor one and, through a series of meanderings, you'll emerge almost two centuries later in the time of William and Mary (see page 260).

55

NONSUCH PALACE
Henry VIII

HENRY VIII IS SAID TO HAVE LOVED palaces and to have had 13 of them within a day's ride of London. The grandest – and the only one that he built from scratch – was Nonsuch, on the fringes of the London Borough of Sutton. It was begun in 1538, was unfinished when he died in 1547 and cost the extraordinary sum of £24,000. If you consider that an affluent member of the land-owning gentry might at that time have had an annual income of £500, you can imagine that it was quite something.

Nonsuch or *nonesuch* means a nonpareil, something that cannot be matched or surpassed, and that is precisely what this palace was. Everything about it was in the grand manner: an entire village, including its church and the local mansion, was bought up and destroyed in order to make room for it. The historian William Camden, writing in the 1580s, described Nonsuch as having been built:

> *with so great sumpteousnesse and rare workmanship that it aspire to the very top of ostentation for shew; so as a man may thinke that all the skill of Architecture is in this one peece of worke bestowed and heaped up together.*

Henry, according to Camden, had intended the palace as a 'retiring place…for his own delight and ease'; the surrounding park – covering an area of almost two and a half square miles – was a heavily wooded hunting ground, generously stocked with deer.

But Nonsuch was also a powerful political statement: work on it was begun six months after the birth of the future Edward VI, and on the 30th anniversary of Henry's accession to the throne. With richly adorned turrets and moulded stucco panels, it stood comparison with Francis I's legendary Château de Chambord on the Loire, dating from about 20 years earlier. Henry had a male heir at last and he wanted to show the other European powers that the Tudors were a dynasty to be reckoned with.

Henry may not have lived long enough to revel in his masterpiece, but Elizabeth I and the Stuart Henry, Prince of Wales (see page 236), both spent time here. Perhaps more importantly, European visitors admired it every bit as much as its creator could have wished, and so did local ones. Nonsuch is seen as playing a key role in the development of Tudor architecture, and in the Renaissance style being accepted in England.

Sadly, it was not to last. A mere 150 years after work on the palace had begun, Charles II gave it to his mistress, Lady Castlemaine. Notoriously extravagant, she had it pulled down and sold off the materials to pay her gambling debts. Of all Nonsuch's magnificence, part of the foundations of the Banqueting House – a separate building from which royal owners and distinguished guests could watch the hunting – is all that remains.

A few contemporary depictions of Nonsuch Palace exist, but the best way of seeing what it looked like is to visit the gallery housed in the 18th-century Tudor Gothic mansion that now stands in the park. Here can be found an intricate scale model, adorned with a wealth of architectural detail and featuring 700 stucco panels depicting Roman emperors, gods and goddesses. It is worth marvelling both at the ambition of the original and at the workmanship that went into the 21st-century replica. Today, the house also boasts formal gardens, including rolling lawns and a rose-covered pergola. It's all very charming, but you can't help regretting what used to be.

Hold that thought as you walk away from the house. A path takes you through some trees and up a slope – it is only a slope; you really couldn't call it a hill. But if you turn and look back, you'll find that the house and its formal gardens have completely disappeared from view. It requires no great leap of the imagination to take yourself back 500 years, to a time when this whole area was covered with trees, and deer aplenty were just waiting to be hunted down. Henry VIII, indulging in his 'delight and ease', had no idea that his longed-for but ill-fated dynasty would tumble with the death of his own children, and that this incomparable statement of his own magnificence would perish less than a century later.

56

A Spectacular Divorce Settlement
Anne of Cleves

HERE'S AN IRONY. ANNE OF CLEVES did incredibly well out of the fact that Henry VIII didn't fancy her. Katherine Howard – beheaded before she was 20 (see page 197) – did rather less well out of the fact that he did.

Anne was Henry's fourth wife, the betrothal being engineered by Thomas Cromwell after Jane Seymour's death and boosted by a famously flattering portrait of the bride-to-be by Hans Holbein. Cleves, of which Anne's father was Duke, was an important state within the Holy Roman Empire, in the western part of modern Germany, so for the first time in several marriages Henry was making a political alliance rather than an amorous one. However, ever the romantic (in the first days of a relationship, at least), he went secretly and in disguise to Rochester Castle, where he was to meet his bride. The diplomat Eustace Chapuys recorded that, on New Year's Day 1540, Henry

> ...*went up into the chamber where the said Lady Anne was looking out of a window to see the bull-baiting which was going on in the courtyard, and suddenly he embraced and kissed her, and*

showed her a token which the King had sent her for New Year's gift, and she being abashed and not knowing who it was thanked him, and so he spoke with her. But she regarded him little, but always looked out the window...

Henry seems never to have recovered from this humiliating beginning and maintained that Anne's looks did not live up to the promise of her portrait. Although the marriage took place five days later, it was never consummated and it was not long before Henry's eye was caught by a young lady in Anne's entourage, Katherine Howard. His marriage was annulled, on terms very favourable to Anne. She became known officially as 'the King's Beloved Sister' and, after Henry married Katherine, was second in rank only to the new queen. Outliving not only Henry and his last two wives, but also Edward VI, she survived most of Mary I's reign, dying in 1557, aged 41, and is the only one of Henry's wives to be buried in Westminster Abbey.

So where can you visit sites connected with Anne of Cleves? Well, thanks to that favourable annulment, all over the place. Rochester Castle, where the ill-fated first meeting took place, had been built under the auspices of Henry I and besieged by King John during his war with the barons. In an effort to bring the siege to an end John is said to have poured the fat from the carcasses of 40 pigs on to a fire to help blow up the keep. Even so, the barons held out for another two months and surrendered only when they seemed likely to be starved to death. Rebuilt in subsequent reigns, the castle is currently closed to the public, but seen from the train or the main road, the hilltop Norman tower still looks as if it is guarding the once-strategic Medway river crossing.

As for Anne's own possessions, she was granted an estate near Lewes in Sussex, where the Anne of Cleves House and Museum give an idea of how a wealthy middle-class family would have lived in Tudor times, but make no claim that Anne stayed there. The same is true of her property in Melton Mowbray, Leicestershire. There, a 600-year-old building, once the home of the chantry priests (whose task it was to say prayers for the dead and lessen the time they were doomed to spend in Purgatory), now houses a pub called the Anne of Cleves. There's another irony here: both of these estates had been granted to Thomas Cromwell at the time of the Dissolution of the Monasteries, but Cromwell's role in negotiating Anne's marriage to Henry had brought about his downfall. His estates were thus going begging and available to be handed on to Anne.

Also part of the annulment settlement were Hever Castle (see page 180) and Richmond Palace in Surrey. The latter was largely destroyed under Oliver Cromwell, but the Old Palace Gatehouse survives and still bears the arms of Henry VII, originally Earl of Richmond in Yorkshire, for whom the palace was built. Streets named Old Palace Yard, Old Palace Lane and The Wardrobe, just off Richmond Green, are modern reminders of the place where the King's Beloved Sister spent much of her later – extremely comfortable – life.

57

KING'S MANOR, YORK
Henry VIII

THERE ARE MENTIONS THROUGHOUT this book of the
Dissolution of the Monasteries, which began with an
Act of Parliament in 1536 and ended in 1539 with
hundreds of monasteries and monastic colleges in
England having been broken up, secularised and/or
sold off. Many of these establishments had been
extremely wealthy and their riches were confiscated
for the Crown or, in the case of much of the art and
manuscripts, simply destroyed. Historians continue to
debate Henry VIII's motives: having declared himself
Supreme Head of the Church of England, getting rid
of the trappings of the Catholic Church was part of it.
There was also a financial question: he had spent a
fortune on wars in Europe (see page 177), was flat broke
and desperate to rebuild his exchequer – and he needed
to ensure (that is, buy) the support of the lay nobility
for his religious reforms.

All of this inevitably upset a lot of people (with the
possible exception of the newly enriched lay nobility).
The most vociferous sign of unrest was the so-called
Pilgrimage of Grace, a massive rebellion in the North of
England by people who called themselves 'pilgrims' to
give their demands a religious connotation. Although
the revolt had begun in Lincolnshire, the focus soon

switched to York, which, with its archbishop, its minster and its other religious communities, had strong links to the Church – and until very recently that had meant the Catholic Church. On Henry's instructions, the 'Pilgrimage' was mercilessly suppressed and one of its leaders, a lawyer named Robert Aske, was hanged in chains from the tower in York Castle.

That was in 1536–7; in the summer of 1541, Henry, by this time married to Katherine Howard, took the most sumptuous progress of his reign (and, like his daughter Elizabeth – see page 215 – he was known for the sumptuousness of his progresses). Leaving London at the end of June, the royal party took until mid-September to reach York. Bad weather was part of the reason, but they also stopped off along the way and accepted magnificent presents from those who wanted to assure the King of their loyalty. A deputation of 200 Yorkshire gentlemen, clad in coats of velvet, submitted to him on their knees and – probably more importantly to the purse-pinched Henry – clubbed together to give him the considerable sum of £900.

Henry, Katherine and a substantial entourage – accounts vary, but there were certainly several thousand people – stayed in York for 12 days, during which it is safe to assume that they reduced their hosts to a state of bankruptcy comparable to their own. They took up residence in the King's Manor, built in about 1270 as the abbot's house for St Mary Abbey. Since the dissolution of the abbey, the manor had become the headquarters of the Council of the North, the administrative centre that enabled Henry to keep a

closer eye on what was going on in this incendiary part
of his realm.

Today the ruins of the abbey, in the adjacent
Museum Gardens, display numerous Gothic arches of
what were once beautiful and extravagant windows. The
manor, with the coat of arms
of Charles I above its grand
entranceway, constitutes the
city centre campus for the
University of York: an ideal
setting for the Departments of
Archaeology and Medieval
Studies, both of which are
based here. For the less
academically inclined, the
former Council Chamber
serves as the campus refectory
and retains the magnificent
fireplace that would once have
been necessary to heat such a
vast room. No wonder Henry
VIII brought his own
tapestries from London to hang on the walls, not only
to make the place look more luxurious, but also to
warm it up.

> **WHILE YOU'RE HERE**
> *York Castle was one of the many
> begun by William the Conqueror
> (see page 48). Its former keep – the
> only substantial part that remains
> – dates from the time of Henry III
> and is now known as Clifford's
> Tower, after a family who for several
> generations served as constables of
> the castle, or perhaps specifically after
> a member of the family, Roger de
> Clifford, another unfortunate who
> was hanged in chains from it. That
> was in 1322, after he had rebelled
> against Edward II.*

Extravagant though it was, Henry's progress to York
wasn't entirely successful. In addition to reminding any
remaining insurgents just who was in charge, he had
planned to improve diplomatic relations with Scotland
by meeting with James V and luring him away from his
allegiance to Catholic France. It has been suggested that

While you're here

York Minster, of course, is one of the most magnificent buildings of its kind in Northern Europe – and no one who has visited it will ever again have to ask what a flying buttress is. Inside, the carved and gilded choir screen features statues of all the English kings from William I to Henry VI. There are 15 of them, which means that the doorway is off centre, with seven statues to its left and eight to its right. The story goes that it was designed in 1420, during the reign of Henry V, when only 14 statues would have been needed. Henry's early death required a hasty redesign to include the new king.

James was afraid of being kidnapped: he had no legitimate children (his daughter Mary, the future Queen of Scots, was born the following year) and he was Henry's nephew, so were anything to happen to him Henry could easily claim to be his heir and make a move to take over Scotland. Another explanation is that James may simply have had no intention of kowtowing to Henry. Whatever the reason, he sent a belated message saying he wasn't going to turn up.

Henry had made lavish preparations to receive him, so this was a huge insult. War between England and Scotland broke out – again – and continued for the remaining six years of Henry's life. He, in the meantime, left York and headed south once more. Further humiliation was hard on his heels: the day after he reached Hampton Court he learned that Katherine had been unfaithful to him (see next entry)…

58

Pontefract Castle
Katherine Howard

HENRY VIII'S FIFTH WIFE SEEMS TO have had a complicated love life – remarkably so, given that she died when she was no more than 19. Thanks to the vagaries of her father's career and her mother's early death, she was brought up largely by her step-grandmother, Agnes, Dowager Duchess of Norfolk, and while in her (obviously not very tender or loving) care had two relationships forced on her by older men. The more significant – because it was consummated and because the couple had addressed each other as husband and wife, making it into a binding contract that would invalidate a subsequent marriage – was with Francis Dereham, a gentleman in Agnes's household.

This was before Katherine moved to court when she was about 14, as a maid-in-waiting to Anne of Cleves. Once there, she became involved with a distant cousin, the 20-something Thomas Culpeper, a privileged courtier and close friend of Henry VIII. Then, still only 15, she married the King, who was clearly besotted with her. And not surprisingly: she was, by all accounts, beautiful, vivacious and charming. The royal couple spent about a year on a blissful extended honeymoon, starting with a quiet wedding – in July 1540 – at the idyllic-sounding Oatlands Palace. Sadly, only archaeological remains of Oatlands are left to us, but it boasted a pleasure garden, a deer park and gardens watered by fountains. Much of the rest of the year saw them progressing from one stately home to another; Christmas was a period of banqueting, dancing and masquerades at Hampton Court, during which Henry lavished diamonds, rubies and pearls on his young bride.

But Henry was 50, obese and suffering from an ulcerated leg. By the time of the progress to the North of England in the summer of 1541 (see page 193), he was frequently ill and the idyll was falling apart. While the court was staying at Pontefract Castle two unfortunate events occurred that would bring about Katherine's downfall: Francis Dereham found his way back into her household, giving rise to gossip among those who had known of the previous relationship; and she indulged in clandestine meetings with Thomas Culpeper, including writing an incriminating letter that spoke of how much she was longing to see him and ended 'Yours, as long as life endures'. In a bizarre twist, the lovers' go-between (if they *were* lovers – opinions vary) was Jane, Lady Rochford, whose husband George Boleyn had been beheaded on the charge of incest with his sister Anne.

Katherine's letter found its way into the hands of Archbishop Thomas Cranmer just as the gossip about Dereham was reaching his ears, and he had no choice but to lay it all before the King. The result was inevitable: Dereham was hanged; Katherine, Culpeper and Jane Rochford lost their heads; and Henry VIII, still with only one legitimate male heir – and he only four years old – had to go in search of another wife.

Pontefract Castle is a ruin now. You can no longer see much of the Gascoigne Tower, where Richard II was imprisoned in 1399 and where he probably died of starvation. But the remains of the unusual multi-lobed *donjon* or keep are impressive, and the medieval dungeons are worth a visit, not least to see the graffiti carved into the walls by soldiers held prisoner here during the Civil Wars. Once one of the most powerful fortresses in the North, and a popular place for keeping political prisoners, Pontefract was, like so many, 'slighted' during the Civil Wars. This was apparently a great relief to the locals, who felt that life would be quieter without it. It had been so notorious that Earl Rivers, sent there as a condemned man in Shakespeare's *Richard III*, was able to exclaim:

> *O Pomfret, Pomfret! O thou bloody prison,*
> *Fatal and ominous to noble peers...*

...without the good people of Pontefract deciding to take offence.

Thomas Culpeper wasn't a noble peer, but both he and Katherine had good reason to think that Pontefract was fatal and ominous. It's perfectly probable that they had been no more than indiscreet; it made no difference. Her fall was as quick and as precipitous as her rise had been. She was buried beneath the altar of the Chapel Royal of St Peter ad Vincula in the Tower of London, where a small plaque on the floor is her only memorial. In another twist, Anne Boleyn, Henry's earlier beheaded queen, lies close by.

59

SUDELEY CASTLE
Katherine Parr

THERE WAS A MANOR HOUSE at Sudeley in Saxon times – Ethelred the Unready gave it to his daughter on the occasion of her marriage in about 1024. It became a castle during the civil war between Stephen and Matilda in the 12th century; during the Wars of the Roses the Yorkist Edward IV confiscated it from its Lancastrian owner and passed it on to his brother, the future Richard III. It also changed hands between Royalists and Parliamentarians more than once during the Civil Wars. But for most visitors its historical charms lie in its connections with the Tudors.

When Henry VII came to the throne in 1485, he granted Sudeley to his uncle, Jasper Tudor. Jasper died childless in 1495, the castle reverted to the Crown and in 1547 Edward VI granted it to his own uncle, Thomas Seymour, brother of Jane. Whether he would have done so if he'd known about Thomas's private life is open to question: only months after Henry VIII's death, Thomas secretly married Katherine Parr, who had been the King's sixth wife but with whom he (Thomas) had been involved before the royal marriage. Katherine was a staunch Protestant – her motive in marrying the aging King may have been the hope of providing him with a second Protestant son to secure the succession. She was also a considerable scholar and published three books of prayers and meditations, becoming the first woman – never mind the first queen – to have a book published in English under her own name.

Katherine became pregnant within months of her marriage to Thomas and moved from London to Sudeley. Here, her household included another scholarly young woman – and future queen – Lady Jane Grey (see page 206). Sudeley's roster of Tudor queens is an impressive one: Elizabeth I visited three times, and on one occasion was treated to a three-day party to celebrate the anniversary of the defeat of the Spanish Armada. Her mother Anne Boleyn had also visited for a few days when she was queen and it is perfectly possible that she had her future rival Jane Seymour in her retinue. No wonder the beautiful centrepiece of Sudeley's grounds is known as the Queens' Gardens. Redesigned in the 21st century, it sits on the site of the original Tudor parterre, so visitors admiring the 70 varieties of roses can imagine themselves standing where any one of those four (or perhaps five) queens must have stood.

By Henry VIII's express wish, Katherine retained the privileges of Queen of England after his death, rather than dwindling into a dowager. Already wealthy when she married him, she inherited an income of £7,000 a year, making her one of the richest women in England. Sadly, she didn't live to enjoy these luxuries for long: she died at Sudeley in 1548, a few days after giving birth to her only child. Surprisingly, to those of us who have always thought of her as the matronly wife of

Henry VIII's declining years, she was no more than 36.
She is buried in St Mary's Church in the castle grounds,
giving Sudeley another unique distinction: it is the only
private castle to have a queen buried on the premises.
Her husband didn't survive her for long: involved in all
sorts of inept machinations against Edward VI and his
own elder brother, who was Protector Regent to the
young king, Thomas was executed for treason only six
months after his wife's death. Sudeley then reverted to
royal hands. It is unclear what happened to Katherine
and Thomas's baby daughter Mary, but she never
attempted to claim Sudeley as hers and she almost
certainly died as a child.

There's an odd postscript to Katherine's burial. Due
to years of neglect from the 17th century onwards, the
buildings at Sudeley were reduced to near ruins.
Katherine's tomb was rediscovered by accident in 1782,
almost 250 years after her death. Her coffin was opened
(one is tempted to wonder why) and she was found to
be swaddled both in cloth and in lead. She was also
remarkably intact: a ghoul's delight, she still had her hair,
teeth, nails and soft, moist flesh. Exposure to air soon
put paid to the flesh, but locks of hair and a blackened
tooth survived to be displayed in an exhibition in 2012
marking the 500th anniversary of her birth. Her effigy
now lies in St Mary's, on an elaborate marble tomb that
replaced the original in Victorian times.

60

GREENWICH PALACE
Edward VI

EDWARD VI HAS THE INTRIGUING claim to fame that he
was the first monarch ever to be raised a Protestant. This
is not as remarkable as it might sound – the religion had
only just been invented, so even Edward's father, Henry
VIII, who was responsible for the creation of the
Protestant Church of England, had been brought up a
Catholic. But Edward's education involved a great deal
of the new Protestant theology, and it led him to cast
around for a true Protestant to be his heir. This meant
bypassing both his half-sisters. Mary's Catholicism was
both deep-rooted and outspoken; Elizabeth's
Protestantism was probably more a matter of political
expediency than of devoutness. Instead, Edward settled
on a young cousin-once-removed called Lady Jane Grey.
If this seems surprising in those male-dominated times,
a look at the Tudor family tree will tell you that Henry
VIII wasn't the only one who had difficulty producing
a male heir. Everybody but everybody had daughters.

Like his father before him, Edward divided his time
between the numerous palaces in and around London
– he was born at Hampton Court (see page 183) and
died at Greenwich, where his father and both his sisters
had been born. Edward spent the last few months of his
life there, suffering probably from tuberculosis, and there

is a touching story of his being held up at one of the palace windows to watch three ships setting out down the Thames on a voyage of exploration. This served the double purpose of showing the dying boy-king a sight that excited him, and of attempting to fool the public into thinking he was in good health. But there was really no disguising that he was too weak to stand by himself and too vulnerable to go outside. He was dead, aged only 15, within two months of this incident.

Greenwich had succeeded Eltham (see page 143) as the most popular royal palace; it was known as the Palace of Placentia or of Pleasaunce – the Pleasant Palace. William Camden, writing at the end of the 16th century, remarked on the 'most faire and pleasant prospect open to the river winding in and out, and almost redoubling it selfe, the greene meddowes and marshes underlying, the Citie of London, and the Countrie round about'. Henry VIII married Katherine of Aragon in the nearby church in 1509 and spent a lot of time here. In 1516 he threw a lavish party at Christmas, including what is said to be the first masquerade ever seen in England; according to a contemporary record, there was 'such an abundance of the viands served to all comers of any honest behaviour as hath been few times seen'. There is still an ancient oak in Greenwich Park that Henry is said to have danced around with Anne Boleyn (though it's known as Queen Elizabeth's Oak because Elizabeth I often took refreshment under it).

Like many palaces Greenwich was badly damaged during the Civil Wars and demolished shortly afterwards:

all that remains is a plaque in the pavement. In the 1690s, at the instigation of Mary II, Christopher Wren designed a Royal Hospital for retired sailors on the site; under Queen Anne and George I the artist James Thornhill created for it 'the finest dining hall in Europe', the magnificent baroque Painted Hall. Its richly decorated ceiling celebrates the birth of the United Kingdom, its monarchs and its naval, scientific and cultural achievements in a series of connected paintings that cover over 40,000 sq ft, the area of about 14 tennis courts. Designed as a refectory for the elderly sailors, it was – when it was finally finished, after 20 years of work – deemed far too grand for such a banal purpose and became a tourist attraction from an early stage. At the time of writing it is closed for renovation, but should soon be once again available for weddings, gala dinners and other occasions designed to impress. Young Edward VI was a bit of a Puritan (though the term hadn't been invented in his day) and might not have approved, but you can imagine that Henry VIII would have thrown quite a party here, with whichever wife he had in tow at the time.

Monarchs from Henry VII to Queen Victoria travelled to Greenwich by boat and it's still the best way to do it. If today's Thames ferries lack the gold leaf and the heraldic adornments of royal barges, they still allow you to admire the view that inspired Canaletto in the 1750s, with the Classical symmetry and iconic twin domes of Wren's riverside masterpiece.

61

SYON HOUSE
Lady Jane Grey

IT'S NOT EVERY STATELY HOME that has its own crypt, but
Syon House, the magnificent ducal mansion that has for
centuries been the London home of the Dukes of
Northumberland, was built on the site of the earlier
Syon Abbey, and its crypt remains, housing a mini-
museum of mostly Tudor history. Above it, the house,
redesigned in the 18th century by the great architect
of the day, Robert Adam, retains the general layout of
Tudor times but has adopted Classical and Baroque
styles. The Great Hall, with Doric columns and a black-
and-white marble floor, resembles a Roman basilica –
the author Simon Jenkins describes it as 'the Georgian
ideal of a Roman senate house'; the Red Drawing
Room has wall hangings of crimson silk and serves as
Syon's art gallery, while the Long Gallery, all 136ft of it,
was designed as a promenade for the ladies. Its walls are
lined with alcoves that once housed statues but now
serve as bookcases; these are separated by gilded pilasters
with, above them, roundels depicting the family's
lineage. A tiny segment of the wall (above your head and
to the right as you enter from the Red Drawing Room)
has been cleaned to show the delicate pink and blue of
the original paintwork; much of the decoration, now a
bit grubby, would have been white and the abundant

gold work would have glowed in the dark. With its tall windows overlooking grounds laid out by Capability Brown, it's a gorgeous room; in its heyday it must have been dazzling.

According to tradition, it was here, in the Long Gallery, that the first woman to be proclaimed Queen of England, the teenaged Lady Jane Grey, received the news of her elevation; she is said to have replied, 'This is not for me,' and burst into tears. She knew as well as anyone that Henry VIII's elder daughter Mary should have been next in line to the throne.

She was an interesting girl, Jane Grey. Her parents had no sons, so they had given their eldest daughter the sort of education normally reserved for boys: she spoke several languages and had studied philosophy. She also spent time in the household of another female scholar, Katherine Parr (see page 200). So although it is easy to see her as a pawn in an overwhelming political game, she was no doormat.

Jane was married, probably with very little say in the matter, to Guildford Dudley, the Duke of Northumberland's son. The Percy Earls of Northumberland who featured in the story of Henry IV (see page 129) had forfeited the title during the Wars of the Roses (though they got it back again later); the dukedom had been created as a reward to one of Edward VI's most important ministers. This Duke of Northumberland was a ruthless and unpopular politician who was almost certainly scheming to gain power for himself by replacing one teenaged monarch with another, and having his own son, also a teenager, proclaimed king. When Jane proceeded in pomp from Syon to the Tower of London, eyewitnesses remarked that young Guildford took a position of prominence, in front of his own parents and in front of Jane. But when the question of his kingship arose, Jane flatly refused to make her husband anything grander than Duke of Clarence. However tenuous her claim to the throne might have been, he had none at all.

Jane's moving into the Tower was significant: it was a sign of strength, and also gave her control of the vast quantity of armaments that were stored there, and of the Royal Mint. It was generally believed that whoever controlled the Tower controlled the country. But a very few days showed that this was not always the case.

What happened next we shall see on page 209, but you can see a dramatic depiction of Jane's fate if you care to visit the National Gallery in London. A huge painting by the 19th-century Frenchman Paul Delaroche shows her blindfolded and kneeling before the block. She wears a white under-dress, while a swooning lady-in-waiting looks after the rich outer robes and jewels she has discarded. Another lady-in-waiting has turned her back, unable to watch.

The Lieutenant of the Tower comforts Jane while the executioner, leaning casually on his axe, looks on, waiting for his client to be ready for him. Jane's life, in art as in reality, is about to be over all too soon.

62

FRAMLINGHAM CASTLE
Mary I

AS YOU EXPLORE THE WALL WALK of Framlingham Castle,
one of the signboards tells you that, with a decent
garrison, you could defend it to this day. Hats off,
therefore, to Roger Bigod, the 12th-century Earl of
Norfolk who built the remarkably durable curtain wall.
From it, the view takes in a mere that would once have
supplied the castle kitchen with fish, duck, geese,
pigeons and edible and medicinal plants, and reminds
you that, even in low-lying Suffolk, castle-builders liked
height. In the absence of a decent hill to build on, they
dug a ditch 25ft deep outside the wall to make it both
more impregnable and more impressive-looking.

Over a period of 400 years, Framlingham belonged
to three powerful families – the Bigods, the Mowbrays
and the Howards – who made a habit of falling out with
the king and having their property confiscated, then
having it restored to them when the king needed their
support again. The castle has had its share of moments in
the sun: the Howard who owned it and was Duke of
Norfolk during Henry VIII's reign saw two of his nieces,
Anne Boleyn and Katherine Howard, become Queens
of England – though if you consider what happened to
them you'll realise this was not as happy an achievement
as it might seem. That particular Howard fell from

favour and spent Edward VI's short reign imprisoned in the Tower; he was then pardoned by Mary I and died in his bed. His memorial in St Michael's Church, Framlingham, which combines French and Italian styles with English Late Gothic, is one of the finest of its period to have survived in England. But during his years of disgrace, inevitably, he forfeited his estates, which is why the then Princess Mary owned them at the time of Edward's death.

That happened on 6 July 1553 and, as we have seen (page 203), he had specified that his Protestant cousin Lady Jane Grey should be his heir. Mary, hearing that Jane Grey's father-in-law, the Duke of Northumberland, was plotting to imprison her, took refuge first at Kenninghall in Norfolk – another former Howard property – and then at the more easily defended Framlingham. Here, thousands of people, oblivious to the Catholic/Protestant dispute, flocked to her support; to them she was 'Harry's daughter', a princess they knew, whereas Jane Grey had appeared out of nowhere. Northumberland planned

> **WHILE YOU'RE IN THE AREA**
> *Henry II, having made his peace with the Bigod of the time, restored Framlingham to him but took the precaution of building Orford Castle nearby, so that he could keep an eye on his former enemy. Its main attraction is its well-preserved polygonal keep – a design that would have made it harder than average to undermine. In Henry II's time Orford was closer to the coast than it is now and a busy port and trading centre; a castle here could guard against a possible French attack while maintaining a powerful royal presence in an area where the barons were often up in arms.*

to leave London to confront Mary but for some reason he dithered for a week, missed his chance and never got his forces closer to Framlingham than Bury St Edmunds, some 30 miles away. Mary sent word that she would pardon Jane if she surrendered; otherwise, she threatened war. As Mary's forces grew, those who feared to be on the losing side rallied to her.

On 20 July (and keep an eye on the dates here – it all happened incredibly quickly), Northumberland received word from London that Jane had been deposed and that the Privy Council had proclaimed Mary queen. He promptly surrendered and Mary was able to enter London in triumph on 3 August, with a procession of over 800 nobles and gentlemen. Unsurprisingly, Northumberland was executed before the end of the month. Mary's forces hadn't drawn a sword or fired an arrow in anger, but Framlingham proudly boasts that she issued her first royal commands from the castle and that this is where her reign began.

As for Jane Grey, she was tried and found guilty of high treason. Mary would have spared her life, but the following January Jane's father and uncles were involved in a revolt against Mary's plan to marry King Philip of Spain. There was nothing for it but to get rid of them all; Jane and her husband were beheaded at the Tower of London on 12 February. She'd been a prisoner for six months, having been queen for all of nine days.

63

HATFIELD HOUSE
Elizabeth I

HAVING YOUR MOTHER BEHEADED before you are three years old and being declared illegitimate because your parents' marriage has been annulled doesn't sound like a recipe for a happy childhood, but Elizabeth I seems to have had a reasonably contented time, living mainly at the Palace of Hatfield and at one point having her humiliated elder half-sister Mary as a lady-in-waiting.

It was after Henry VIII died in 1547, when Elizabeth was 13, that things grew more tricky. She went to live with her stepmother, Katherine Parr, and became involved in an inappropriate relationship with Katherine's new husband, Thomas Seymour, uncle to the new king, the nine-year-old Edward VI, and younger brother of the Lord Protector of England. Katherine initially connived at the cuddling and spanking that went on between Thomas and Elizabeth, but eventually decided that enough was enough and sent the young princess away. When she herself died the following year, however, Seymour was accused of plotting to marry Elizabeth, overthrow his own brother and take control of the kingdom. Elizabeth always denied any involvement in such a plot, but Seymour was convicted of treason and beheaded; a certain amount of mud inevitably stuck.

Even muddier waters came after Edward's death in 1553. After speedily disposing of Lady Jane Grey (see page 206), the Catholic Mary came to the throne and recognised Elizabeth, now 19, as a threat. Whether or not Elizabeth was involved in plots to overthrow Mary and put herself on the throne, she was a focal point for the Protestants whose aim this was. Mary imprisoned Elizabeth in the Tower of London for two months, then sent her back to Hatfield, where she lived under virtual house arrest for the next five years; it was here that – while she was sitting under an oak tree in the park, according to legend – she learned that Mary had died and she had become queen. Her first Council of State was held in Hatfield's Banqueting Hall.

The wing containing the Banqueting Hall, with its rich red medieval brick, is the only one of the original four wings of the palace to survive. The house you see today is Jacobean, built by Robert Cecil, first Earl of Salisbury, who succeeded his father William as Elizabeth's chief minister and went on to serve under James I. James didn't care for Hatfield and swapped it for the Cecil family home, Theobalds, 10 miles away. Robert pulled down three-quarters of Hatfield Palace and recycled the bricks to make the present house, which still belongs to his descendants.

It's impossible to mention the Cecils without the word 'spymaster' cropping up: once Elizabeth became queen, the elder Cecil – later first Baron Burghley – instituted the world's first intelligence agency, to keep tabs on the Catholic plots that were a recurring feature of her reign. One of Hatfield's greatest attractions has this as a subtext. Elizabeth was one of the most frequently painted monarchs in history, but the so-called 'Rainbow Portrait', on display in the Marble Hall, is worth a particularly close look. Attributed to either Isaac Oliver or Marcus Gheeraerts the Younger, it dates from about 1601, when Elizabeth was 68, but shows her as a much younger and still powerful woman. Coiled up her left arm a jewelled serpent symbolises subtle wisdom; in her right hand she holds a rainbow, above which is the motto *Non sine sole iris* – 'no rainbow [the sign of peace] without the sun [the glorious light that is the Queen herself]'. But perhaps the most interesting feature of the whole painting is the embroidery on her skirt: a repeating pattern of eyes and ears. As Mary, Queen of Scots, found to her cost, nothing went on in Elizabeth's kingdom that Elizabeth didn't sooner or later hear about.

The black-and-white marble floor that gives the hall its name is arguably the room's least spectacular feature. The richly decorated ceiling, huge tapestries, ornate oak carving and embroidered banners copied from ones presented to the Cecil family by the Duke of Wellington after the Battle of Waterloo all vie rather exhaustingly for the visitor's attention.

Elizabeth obviously never visited the existing house – it was built several years after her death – but a display case in the Long Gallery contains a hat, stockings and gloves said to have belonged to her. The gloves are remarkable for their long, elegant fingers, and all Elizabeth's portraits show her to have had this feature, which was much admired.

64

ROYAL PROGRESSES
Elizabeth I

ELIZABETH WAS NOTORIOUS FOR almost bankrupting anyone she went to stay with: she was also notoriously parsimonious, so her lengthy royal progresses not only took her out of London during the steamy summer months but enabled her to palm the expenses of her household off on to her honoured hosts. She once stayed at Kenilworth (see page 85), with a considerable entourage, for nearly three weeks. To entertain her, her beloved Earl of Leicester put on an extraordinary pageant, likening Kenilworth to Camelot and including a Lady of the Lake who emerged from the waters and declared she had been guarding the castle since Arthurian days. The visit cost Leicester about £1,000 a day – £175,000 in today's money, never mind what he had already spent on improvements. And still it didn't persuade the Queen to marry him.

Kenilworth isn't the only place that owes its past or present magnificence to a promised visit from Her Majesty. Far from it: many wealthy families built so-called 'prodigy houses' – residences of great magnificence (and occasionally dubious taste) – during Elizabeth's reign, often in an E shape in her honour and some of them specifically to provide suitably opulent accommodation for the royal party. Christopher Hatton,

Elizabeth's Lord Chancellor and another of her favourites, built what was then the largest private house in England, at Holdenby in Northamptonshire, and reduced himself from vast wealth to poverty in the process. Designed around two courtyards, the house was larger than Hampton Court and, in a supremely ostentatious display of wealth at a time when glass was prohibitively expensive, contained over 100 large windows. As a sign of his devotion, Hatton refused to sleep in his new home until Elizabeth herself had stayed there: he kept it staffed and ready for eight years. Some accounts say that she never came; others that she finally visited in November 1591, by which time Hatton was in poor health – he died only nine days later.

Holdenby is still a private house, open to the public only by prior arrangement or if you have booked a wedding or function there. You can also be married at Hengrave Hall in Suffolk, another mansion that boasts 'Queen Elizabeth slept here': brides prepare for the day in the Queen Elizabeth Chamber. In Surrey, Loseley House is another popular wedding venue: here the cushions on the 'maid of honour' chairs in the drawing room are said to have been embroidered by Her Majesty.

Burghley House, home of Elizabeth's Lord High Treasurer William Cecil, contains a room known as Queen Elizabeth I's Bedroom, though she never slept in it. She stayed with Cecil at his other houses, but on the one occasion she was due to go to Burghley there was an outbreak of smallpox in the household and the visit was cancelled. The fact that the estate wasn't called upon to entertain the Queen's retinue may explain why a later

Cecil could afford to travel Europe and acquire the astonishing quantity of art that forms the basis of Burghley's magnificent collection.

One of the most spectacular places to boast a Queen Elizabeth Chamber is Knebworth House in Hertfordshire, home since the 15th century of the Lytton family. It no longer looks Elizabethan, though. Rebuilt in Victorian times by the novelist Edward Bulwer-Lytton, its style is predominantly 19th-century Tudor Gothic with odd whimsical touches, such as the oriental cupolas along the façade, the heraldic griffins on pillars above the main entrance and the stained glass at one end of the State Drawing Room depicting the Lytton family's descent from the Tudors. Adding another royal touch, there's a painting by the Pre-Raphaelite Daniel Maclise, showing William Caxton demonstrating his printing press to an intrigued Edward IV, with the Queen and young princes looking on.

Guides to Knebworth House and gardens will take you on a Tudor Treasure Trail, reliving the excitement of the Queen's visit in 1597. Her chamber is hardly restful, with intricate carving on every available inch of wall, and carved figures supporting the equally ornate wooden canopy over the bed. But there is no suggestion that Elizabeth stayed for long, so perhaps the fact that she couldn't sleep didn't matter. She probably just moved on and demanded expensive hospitality from somebody else.

65

THE PALACE OF HOLYROODHOUSE
Mary, Queen of Scots

ENGLAND HAS HAD ITS SHARE of boy kings – those who succeeded to the throne at tender ages because their fathers died young – but nothing to compare with Mary, Queen of Scots. Her father died in December 1542, when she was only six days old; she was crowned nine months later. By this time, she was betrothed to Henry VIII's son Edward, who was a month short of his sixth birthday. The idea was that they would be married when Mary was 10; she would move to England, Henry would oversee her upbringing and the kingdoms of England and Scotland would be united.

It didn't happen – it was never going to, was it? Various wars and changes of diplomatic allegiance got in the way and Mary's French mother took her to France, where she married the short-lived dauphin. A widow at 18, having been Queen of France for 18 months, she was back in Scotland in 1561. There, she married twice more – first her cousin, Henry Stuart, Lord Darnley; then, after his death, the deeply unpopular Earl of Bothwell. Bothwell's unpopularity stemmed from a number of causes, not least that he very probably engineered Darnley's murder. An unexplained explosion

at Darnley's house; his body found in the garden –
it really didn't look like an accident.

A revolt against Bothwell and Mary in 1567, two
months after they were married (and only three after
Darnley's death), led to her abdication and, shortly
afterwards, to her flight into England, of which we shall
read more in the next entry. But during those few years
when Mary was in charge of her kingdom, she made
her home at the Palace of Holyroodhouse.

Holyrood is still the monarch's official residence in
Edinburgh; you can visit the wood-panelled Throne
Room where foreign dignitaries are received, and
admire the Scottish fervour that means the walls are to
this day covered with portraits of Stuart kings. (Pride of
place, over the fireplace, goes to James VI & I, Mary and
Darnley's son, the first Stuart king to rule England as
well as Scotland.) The State Apartments – built, like
most of the rest of the palace, in the 17th century – are
every bit as grand as you could hope. Adjacent to
the palace, the remains of the 12th-century
Holyrood Abbey are particularly splendid:
despite the fact that the nave has lost its roof,
it is not hard to believe that this was once
one of the finest buildings in Scotland. A
number of royals are buried in the choir,
including Mary's father, James V, and her
murdered husband, Darnley.

The beating heart of the palace, though,
is the oldest surviving part – the bit that
houses Mary's apartments. Her bedchamber
and outer chamber, with their richly

WHILE YOU'RE HERE
Climb the hill to Edinburgh Castle to see what may be the original Stone of Scone (see page 91) and the Scottish Crown Jewels. Although both crown and sceptre pre-date Mary, Queen of Scots, it was at her coronation that they were used together for the first time. Unlike the English jewels (see page 248), they avoided destruction by Oliver Cromwell, simply because someone had the sense to hide them. Also here is Mons Meg, the 15th-century cannon capable of firing a 300lb cannonball 2 miles. Meg took part in early sieges all over Scotland, but by 1550 she was defunct and thereafter used only ceremonially. In 1680 her barrel burst when she fired a shot to celebrate a visit by the future James II, who was Lord High Commissioner for Scotland. A bad omen for the future king? Or an English plot to destroy a Scottish icon?

decorated ceilings and wall hangings, are gorgeous, but it is the Supper Room that really captures the imagination. One evening in March 1566, Mary was sitting here with some of her ladies-in-waiting and her private secretary, an Italian called David Rizzio, when Darnley and various other lords burst in. Murderously jealous of Rizzio's relationship with the Queen, they stabbed him no fewer than 56 times. His body was then dragged into the Outer Chamber and left there, where his bloodstains are said still to be visible.

It's just possible that that last bit isn't true, because Mary's chambers are not exactly as she left them: rather, they are as the 18th-century keepers of the palace left them, having seized an opportunity to make Mary's turbulent life into a tourist attraction. They may well have thought that the story about the bloodstains would add a frisson to visitors' enjoyment.

Whatever the truth of that detail, Mary – pregnant at the time – fled from Holyrood and took refuge in Edinburgh Castle, where her son was born three months later. She visited the palace once more, to be married to Bothwell in the Great Gallery in May the following year. Having married Darnley in the chapel, she perhaps wondered if a change of venue would change her luck. If it did, it was only for the worse…

One footnote, to add to the 18th-century romanticising: Bonnie Prince Charlie (see page 277) stayed at Holyrood for six weeks in 1745 and the bed in the Queen's Bedchamber in the State Apartments *is* the one he slept in.

Finally, a brief explanation of the palace's name: 'rood' is an old word for 'cross', so Holyrood simply means 'holy cross'. The story goes that sometime in the 1120s King David I, hunting in the nearby royal forest, was thrown from his horse and pierced in the thigh (probably a euphemism for somewhere more vulnerable) by the antlers of a stag. A 'holy rood' or crucifix appeared in his hand, enabling him to fend off the animal and save his life. In gratitude for this miracle, he decreed that an abbey be built near the spot.

66

ROYAL PRISONS
Mary, Queen of Scots

FORCED IN 1567 TO ABDICATE in favour of her infant son (whom she never saw again), Mary fled to England, where she hoped her cousin Elizabeth would help her regain her throne. Given that Elizabeth, now well into her thirties, remained unmarried, Mary had an eye on the English throne, too. Her paternal grandmother, Margaret Tudor, had been Henry VIII's elder sister, so if you were a Catholic and persisted in believing that Elizabeth was illegitimate, Mary was the rightful queen; even Protestants were forced to acknowledge that, if Elizabeth died childless, Mary was the obvious heir. Except, of course, that she was a Catholic.

To says that things didn't go as Mary hoped is to take understatement to new levels. Wary both of the rebels in Scotland and of the English Catholics who might seek to depose Elizabeth, the English queen kept the Scottish one effectively under house arrest for the rest of her life. Mary spent time in both Carlisle Castle and Bolton Castle, where she lived in some comfort, with suitable furnishings being begged and borrowed from local houses to make her accommodation more fit for a queen. It was at this time – still in 1567 – that the so-called 'casket letters' came to light. These were letters allegedly written by Mary to Bothwell, which, if

genuine, confirmed that she had been complicit in
Darnley's murder. Whether they were genuine is debated
to this day and the whole issue is rife with conspiracy
theories, but it gave Elizabeth an excuse for continuing
to keep a close eye on Mary.

She was moved to Tutbury Castle in Staffordshire,
which had the advantage (from Elizabeth's point of
view) of being remote from both London and Scotland,
the likely centres of any plotting. Mary's health was
always delicate – her personal retinue at Bolton included
an apothecary, a physician and a surgeon – and she
found Tutbury cold and damp, writing that it sat
'squarely on top of a mountain in the middle of a plain'
and subjected her to all the 'winds and injures of
heaven'. She was probably right: a survey conducted
eight years before she arrived describes it as 'an old
stately castle, decayed in many places', and there is no
evidence that anyone tarted it up for Mary's benefit. As
far as the modern visitor is concerned, the location is
glorious, the views across Dovedale equally so and the
ruins (the result, almost inevitably, of a siege during the
Civil Wars) sufficiently substantial that the Great Hall is
hired out for weddings.

Mary's host at Tutbury was George Talbot, the Earl
of Shrewsbury, whose wife was the powerful and
immensely wealthy woman known as Bess of Hardwick.
Between them the couple owned several other grand
homes where Mary spent some time: Chatsworth
House, Sheffield Castle and Wingfield Manor.
Chatsworth is now a prime tourist destination, with the
attractions of the house reinforced by world-famous

gardens and a farmyard full of rare breeds. One feature of the gardens is Queen Mary's Bower, much revamped in the 19th century but originally a raised platform overlooking the water gardens that supplied the household with fish. The name comes from the tradition that it was built as a place where Mary could take exercise, which may or may not be true.

Sheffield Castle, which once occupied a large part of modern Sheffield's city centre, was razed to the ground during the Civil Wars; substantial excavations are currently underway, under the former Castle Market. Wingfield Manor is still palatial – but a palace from which some careless person has removed the roof. The Great Hall and the cellar or undercroft beneath it must once have been vast; now they are both vast and draughty.

One other place where Mary went under the Shrewsburys' auspices was Buxton, known even in those days for its baths and medicinal waters. A small part of the fortified tower in which she was confined survives in the Old Hall Hotel, and the inscription on the window of room 26 is said to be by her:

> *Buxton, whose warm waters have made thy name famous, perchance I shall visit thee no more – Farewell.*

Her last visit to Buxton was in 1584, three years before her death. Perhaps the inscription was inspired by intimations of mortality. Perhaps she realised that her scheming was bringing that mortality ever closer...

67

FOTHERINGHAY CASTLE
Mary, Queen of Scots

THE LAST OF THE MANY GENTEEL prisons in which Mary, Queen of Scots spent her time was Fotheringhay Castle. Genteel it may have been – it had been a royal residence – but it was also remote, surrounded by marshland and difficult to escape or be rescued from. Those were important considerations: Mary was about to be tried for treason, after the discovery of the so-called Babington Plot had finally and firmly implicated her in a conspiracy to murder Elizabeth I.

The outcome of the trial, in October 1586, was a foregone conclusion, but it took Elizabeth several months to agree to sign the death warrant: Mary was not only an anointed queen, but Elizabeth's own cousin: you couldn't chop her head off without giving it a lot of thought. The inevitable happened, however, the following February. Several macabre legends surround Mary's beheading, not least that when the executioner held the severed head up by its hair to show onlookers that the job was done, it became apparent that the Queen had worn a wig – the hair came away in the man's hand and the head rolled away across the floor. Mary was buried in Peterborough Cathedral (see page 173), but later promoted to Westminster Abbey where, as the Fotheringhay Castle website casually tells us, her tomb is slightly larger than Elizabeth's.

There's not a huge amount to see at Fotheringhay Castle today – it was allowed to fall into ruin after Mary's death and only the motte on which it once stood and a small chunk of masonry wall remain. But its history reads like a checklist of medieval royalty. In the 12th century it was the property of David I of Scotland; in 1294 it was forfeited to Edward I of England; in 1377 it belonged to a son of Edward III, who restored the dilapidated keep and turned what had been a fortress into a palace; in 1452 it was comfortable enough for the Duchess of York to be living here when she gave birth to her eighth and last son, the future Richard III; Henry VIII later gave it to Katherine of Aragon (and subsequently though briefly to each of his other five wives). Over the centuries, one generation seems to have spent vast sums doing Fotheringhay up, only to have the next generation neglect it and the next be obliged to repair it again. It was finally dismantled in the 1620s, when one of the huge windows from the Great Hall and the great oak staircase were transferred to the Talbot Inn in Oundle, 4 miles away, where they can still be seen. Mary walked down this staircase at Fotheringhay on her way to her execution and tradition has it that, despite the change of venue, her ghost is sometimes seen on it. (For the record, her executioner, again according to tradition, stayed at the Talbot the night before the deed and dined on pigeon pie.)

However little may remain of Fotheringhay Castle, it's undeniably a pretty spot. A gentle stroll takes you to the top of the motte, where a plaque commemorates Mary's death and another acknowledges Richard III's birth. Royal-watchers should also take in Fotheringhay's 15th-century church. The Duchess of York, Richard's mother, born Cecily Neville, died in 1495 at the age of 80, having outlived all but two of her many children; she's buried alongside the altar, close to her husband and one of her sons.

A FINAL VISIT TO MARY, QUEEN OF SCOTS

During her years in prison, Mary devoted much of her time to embroidery. Both she and Bess of Hardwick, her long-term jailer (see page 223), were accomplished needlewomen and the best surviving results can be seen at Oxburgh Hall in Norfolk. Some of the so-called Marian Hanging there was worked by Mary herself and some of it by Bess. The central panel bears the inscription *virescit vulnere virtus* ('courage grows stronger through wounding'), with the royal arms of Scotland and Mary's monogram; a version of the hanging was sent as a gift to the Duke of Norfolk, a staunch Catholic who may have been planning to marry Mary and overthrow Elizabeth. His grandfather and predecessor was the uncle of Anne Boleyn and Katherine Howard we met earlier (see page 209); this duke had even worse luck and was beheaded on a charge of treason in 1572.

But, while so many plots were revolving round Mary, Elizabeth steadfastly refused to marry. After her death in 1603, with no more violence and no more subterfuge to speak of, it was Mary and Darnley's son who inherited Elizabeth's throne.

The Stuarts 1603–1714

68

CORPUS CHRISTI COLLEGE/ BODLEIAN LIBRARY, OXFORD
James I

IT MUST HAVE BEEN SOMETHING of a relief to the English people to have James I chosen as king: there hadn't been many times over the previous two centuries when the accession wasn't fought over. James was a great-great-grandson of Henry VII on two counts – his parents had been first cousins, and both were the grandchildren of Henry's daughter Margaret. His claim was undeniable: for once there really wasn't anyone else. And – a deep sigh of relief after all the conspiracies concerning his mother, Mary, Queen of Scots – he was a Protestant.

As a king, James was full of contradictions. He believed in the Divine Right of Kings, making him answerable only to God, yet he accepted that he needed Parliament to enforce the law and authorise taxation, and he had favourites (probably lovers) whom he allowed to wield great influence. Extremely popular at the start of his reign, he hadn't been on the throne three years before a group of discontented Catholics tried to blow him up, and the entire Houses of Parliament along with him. He was highly literate, writing, among other things, a treatise on government called *Basilikon Doron* ('royal gift'), intended as a guide to his eldest son on how to be an effective monarch. During his reign a whole genre of drama (now known as Jacobean) flourished and Shakespeare wrote many of his best plays. He was described as 'the wisest fool in Christendom' – wise in small matters and foolish in larger ones.

In amongst all this, he commissioned one of the bestselling books of all time, and one of the greatest works of literature: a translation of the Bible that is sometimes known as the Authorised Version, but more commonly the King James Bible.

The idea was to produce something – Protestant, of course – that satisfied both the Puritans and the 'higher' end of the Church of England. James himself presided over the Hampton Court Conference in 1604 to decide how the task would be approached, and over the next seven years the translation was done by six 'companies' of scholarly churchmen based two each at the universities of Oxford and Cambridge and at Westminster.

The Oxford Companies were drawn from various colleges, but the majority – notably their leading light, John Rainolds – were from Corpus Christi. Today the casual visitor is allowed only into the college's quad, chapel and gardens, but the quad boasts a feature that makes it very much worth the trip: a 16th-century column that is both a sundial and a perennial calendar. It's adorned with various motifs connected with the college and topped by a pelican perched on a globe. The chapel, smaller and less flamboyant than many of its ilk, contains memorials to Rainolds and one of his associates, John Spenser: studious- and serious-looking men, both of them – no careless errors were going to slip into the Book of Jeremiah on their watch.

For more about James himself, a five-minute walk takes you to arguably Oxford's greatest institution, the Bodleian Library. Opened in its present guise just months before James came to the throne, it expanded during his reign from a collection of about 2,000 books to about 16,000. To accommodate this growth its buildings were greatly extended, with wings being built around the present Schools Quadrangle: doors off it still bear Latin signboards indicating that they once led to the School of Moral Philosophy, the School of Divinity and the like. Entrance to the Quadrangle is through the aptly named Great Gate, and opposite that is the resplendent Tower of the Five Orders of Architecture.

In a place of honour in a niche of the tower sits James, equally resplendent. Robed, crowned and carved in stone, he is handing a book to each of the figures to his left and right. One reads, in Latin, 'These things I have written' and the other 'These things I have given'; the recipients are representations of Fame (blowing what one can only assume is her own trumpet) and of the university. The inscription describes him as 'our godlike James, the most learned, generous and excellent of kings'. A bit over the top, perhaps, but there is no denying that he endowed a great library, sponsored a great work of literature and provided the milieu in which Shakespeare wrote *King Lear* and *The Tempest*. Perhaps he wasn't such a fool after all.

69

The Queen's House, Greenwich
Anne of Denmark/Henrietta Maria

THE WIVES OF JAMES I and Charles I are somewhat forgotten queens, and their house at Greenwich is often overlooked by those visiting the *Cutty Sark* or standing with one foot on either side of the prime meridian. That's a shame, because it's a gem.

The story goes that James I commissioned it in 1616 as a present for his wife Anne. It was to serve as an apology for his having sworn at her when she accidentally killed one of his hounds while out hunting. If that is true, she kept him feeling guilty for a long time – she died in 1619, well before the house was completed. Work on it was resuscitated only under Charles I, who gave the manor of Greenwich to *his* wife in 1629.

Greenwich Park was a good hunting ground at the time and the house made a pleasant out-of-town retreat, but Henrietta Maria – French by birth – also filled it with Classical sculpture and other art. Much of this was sold off when Oliver Cromwell was in charge, art being yet another of the accoutrements of royalty of which he disapproved. But today, after recent restoration, the house is more an art gallery than a palace. Its walls are filled with paintings of royalty and their courtiers, and a substantial number of works celebrating Greenwich's maritime history. Pride of place goes to the 'Armada portrait' of Elizabeth I, a fine piece of propaganda intended to reassure anyone who thought that having a female on the throne was a bad idea: richly dressed, dripping with pearls and with her hand placed firmly on a globe, this is not a woman you want to mess with.

Designed by Inigo Jones, who was influenced by his travels to Italy and by the work of the Venetian architect Andrea Palladio, the Queen's House was the first completely Classical building in England, its pale stone a striking contrast to the Tudor red brick that surrounded it. Its most famous feature is the glorious 'Tulip Staircase', so called because of the floral design of its wrought-iron railings. This may be a misnomer: it's likely that they were meant to be lilies, the royal flower of France, as a tribute to Henrietta Maria. No matter: the stairs were the first in England to have no central support; they twirl upwards for three storeys, giving a spectacular, if somewhat dizzying, view towards the cupola above. Sadly, visitors aren't allowed to climb all the way to the top, so it's difficult to assess what the effect of looking down would be – not a happy one for those suffering from vertigo, you might guess.

Upstairs, the Queen's Presence Chamber boasts an extravagantly painted ceiling – coats of arms, gargoyles, heraldic eagles, cherubs, some *trompe l'oeil* effects – every inch is occupied with hectic activity. The ceiling of the King's Presence Chamber has no shortage of gold leaf but, with your head reeling from Henrietta Maria's choice of decor, you're likely to find it elegantly understated.

The Queen's House hasn't been a royal residence since the 1660s, but from Inigo Jones' elegant first-floor loggia you can still look out over Greenwich Park, much as those two hunting-mad queens did nearly four centuries ago.

70

PRINCE HENRY'S ROOM
Henry, Prince of Wales

SADLY, EXCEPT FOR RARE SPECIAL events, the public can no longer gain access to Prince Henry's Room in London: you have to content yourself with gazing at its Tudor glory and its mullioned windows from across Fleet Street.

It's sad for two reasons: first, because the former Prince's Tavern, named to celebrate the investiture in 1610 of Prince Henry as Prince of Wales, is one of the few wooden buildings to survive the Great Fire of London; and second, because Henry himself is worthy of a decent memorial.

All very well, you may be muttering, but who was he?

Well, he was the eldest child of James I, born in 1594 – we mentioned his lavish christening on page 168 – and he died at the age of 18, probably of typhoid fever. It's easy to be cynical and say that dying young makes posterity view anyone kindly, but Henry does seem to have been something special. Perhaps most significantly, he was a staunch Protestant who was going to lead his country to victory against Catholic Spain and – after the religious to-ings and fro-ings of the preceding hundred years – establish once and for all the supremacy of the Church of England.

He was also a great patron of the arts, a scholar and a fine horseman. He amassed a collection of books, paintings and sculpture that formed the basis of today's Royal Collection; he patronised writers, artists, architects and musicians; and he was actively engaged with the navy, exploration and politics. He was interested in the American colony of Virginia, and in the search for the North West Passage some 300 years before Roald Amundsen found it. Not bad for a boy who didn't live to see his 19th birthday.

Once you're tired of standing in Fleet Street, head down the road to the National Portrait Gallery. There, Robert Peake's portrait of Henry, painted when the Prince was about 16, shows him looking every inch the heir apparent: jewels everywhere, from the decorations on his shoes to the hilt of his sword and the brooch on his plumed hat. No shortage of lace, either, and he stands confidently in front of a rich velvet curtain. He has seen the future, it's pretty darned comfortable, and he is in charge of it.

Royal portraits aren't uncommon, of course, but there are a surprising number of the short-lived Henry. He really was the embodiment of the nation's hopes and dreams. This is partly because he was only nine when his father, already King of Scotland, became King of England too and moved south of the border with his elder son and six-year-old daughter. England hadn't had a Royal Family throughout the 45 years of the previous reign – yes, they had had the glorious Elizabeth, but no youthful princes and princesses, and for many years no acknowledged heir. No wonder they took Henry to their hearts. The great artists of the day vied with each other to display his perfections. When he was as young as 10 – in another Robert Peake portrait now in the Scottish National Portrait Gallery – he was portrayed in the robes of the Order of the Garter, and by 13 such was his prowess at jousting or tilting that an admiring French cousin sent him a suit of armour, depicted in two surviving miniatures in the Royal Collection. One anonymous work, housed at Hampton Court, shows him in the hunting field, in the act of drawing an impressively long sword to despatch the stag that lies stunned at his feet; Van Dyck's portrait, at Windsor Castle, also depicts him in armour, ready for the tiltyard. All of this reflects the views expressed in the caption to the National Portrait Gallery image: that Henry was 'reputed to be an ideal warrior prince: athletic, brave, noble, clever, cultured and ardently Protestant'.

And what about his little brother? The boy who became Charles I was six years younger, a sickly child and no match for Henry in athletic prowess. Left behind in Scotland when the rest of the family moved to London, he was in no way prepared to have the kingship thrust upon him. Small wonder that he had no clue about how to handle Parliament and reconcile the religious differences that continued to tear the kingdom apart. Would there have been a civil war if Henry hadn't died so prematurely? Could Charles have stayed in Scotland, keeping the low profile of his childhood, but hanging on to his head? They're among the great unanswered questions of British history.

Newark Castle
Charles I

NEWARK CASTLE'S RUINS ARE among the best preserved in England – you can visit its dungeons (including the intriguingly named 'Debtors' Dungeon') and undercroft and admire the views from the top of the gatehouse. If it's good value now, in its heyday it must have been a sight to see: it was built about 1135 by the then Bishop of Lincoln, with what William Camden called 'most profuse and lavish expense'. Some 80 years later, it was owned by the Crown; King John, having retreated northwards in the course of the First Barons' War, contracted dysentery and died here (you can, if the fancy takes you, visit the room where he spent his last night). Possession of the castle moved back and forth between various kings and bishops over the next centuries, but it was in Royalist hands when civil war broke out in the 1640s.

Armed conflict had been more or less inevitable from early in Charles I's reign. For all his faults, his father James I had had some concept of compromise. Charles, having absorbed the ideas of absolute monarchy that he observed during a trip to Spain as Prince of Wales, didn't know the meaning of the word. Within weeks of coming to the throne, he married a woman who was openly Catholic and stirred up religion-inspired rebellions in both Scotland and Ireland. When Parliament objected to the arbitrary way he chose to rule, he simply dismissed it. Slowly but surely he led the country into civil war. Which is how, in 1645, he ended up in Newark.

By this time the battles of Marston Moor, Naseby and Langport had been fought and proved disastrous for Charles: the Parliamentary forces led by Oliver Cromwell had effectively destroyed the Royalist army; and Charles had argued with and dismissed his most able general, his nephew, Prince Rupert of the Rhine. With the tide of the war turning, control of key towns was proving even more important than pitched battles. Newark sat at the junction of the Great North Road and the Fosse Way (the main road running from southwest to northeast), so it was of great strategic importance – pretty much anyone who was going anywhere needed to pass through it. The castle wasn't massively fortified, but having the River Trent on its doorstep gave it defensive strength.

WHILE YOU'RE HERE

Visit the Newark Town Hall Museum on the Market Square. A Grade I listed building dating from Georgian times (and one of the finest town halls of its kind in the country), it has on display various 'siege coins' minted in Newark in 1645–6. Lozenge-shaped rather than round, many were made from melted-down silver tableware such as platters and trays and still show the beading that would have decorated the original objects. Siege coins were emergency money designed to get the castle and town through a difficult period; the Newark ones are stamped with the initials 'CR' – Carolus Rex or King Charles – showing clearly which side the town was on.

Charles and Rupert converged on Newark in October 1645, attempted a reconciliation and promptly fell out again. Rupert departed in dudgeon, taking a number of senior cavalrymen with him. Charles, hearing that a Parliamentarian army was approaching, withdrew to Oxford, leaving the Newark garrison of about 2,000 men to cope as best it could. Newark had by this time extended its fortifications, building two massive earthworks, known as the King's and Queen's Sconces, at the entrances to the town (the Queen's can be seen today, in Scone and Devon Park, about half a mile along the river from the castle). Siege and counter-raids persisted throughout a harsh winter, with no great breakthrough being made.

In the meantime, negotiations were going on between Charles, the French and the Scots, who formed a large part of the force that was besieging Newark. Hearing that Cromwell's highly disciplined New Model Army was marching towards Oxford, and fearing the worst, Charles deemed it prudent to surrender to the Scots rather than to Parliament. He returned to Newark and gave himself into the hands of the Scottish general there, David Leslie. Leslie wanted to carry the King off to the secure garrison at Newcastle, but was reluctant to abandon the siege. His solution was simple: he 'persuaded' Charles to order his supporters to surrender. Thus the siege whimpered tamely to a finish, and with it ended the First Civil War. Charles was taken away to Newcastle and was never a free man again.

72

WHITEHALL
BANQUETING HOUSE
Charles I

IN TUDOR TIMES, WHITEHALL PALACE was the largest in
Europe, stretching, in modern terms, from Parliament
Square to Trafalgar Square and containing some 1,500
rooms. Monarchs from Henry VIII onwards used it
as their principal residence. Henry had a tilting yard
and tennis courts here; Elizabeth I entertained the
ambassadors of her various noble suitors in a series of
timber banqueting halls, each built for the occasion and
then demolished.

It was James I who had the idea of commissioning a
permanent Banqueting House and in 1622 chose Inigo
Jones as its architect. Still full of the Classical ideas he
had used in Greenwich (see page 233), Jones produced
a room with perfect Classical proportions – a 'double
cube' 110ft long and 55ft wide and high. Built wholly
of stone in a city that was still largely brick and timber,
the Banqueting House stood out from its neighbours in
every possible way.

Its *raison d'être* was lavish entertainment, and
most lavish of all were the masques. These were a
combination of music, dance and drama written by
James's favoured dramatist Ben Jonson, with staging

and costumes by Jones. The more elaborate the better;
expense no object. Although the details of individual
masques varied, the principle was always the same:
a state of chaos was
transformed into peace and
plenty by the timely entrance
of the king and queen. James
loved this form of spectacle;
his son and daughter-in-law
Charles and Henrietta Maria
sometimes even dressed up and
took part in them.

    If the masques were a
none-too-subtle piece of
propaganda, the famous painted
ceiling by the great Flemish
artist Peter Paul Rubens that
Charles commissioned after
his father's death took the
message one step further. It was
all about the fatal Stuart belief
in the Divine Right of Kings.
James and Charles believed that
they had the right to govern as they chose and were
answerable only to God. Parliament wanted the king's
power to be limited by the laws of the land. If you can
sum up the causes of the English Civil Wars in two
sentences, those are they.

    Rubens' ceiling celebrates James's peaceful reign, the
union of England and Scotland and, in case you were in
danger of forgetting, the advantages of a wise monarchy

> **WHILE YOU'RE HERE**
> *Just up Whitehall, on the edge of
> Trafalgar Square, an equestrian
> statue of Charles I looks back
> towards the site of his execution.
> It was made in 1633 for the then
> Lord Treasurer, kept hidden from
> anti-Royalist feeling, bought by
> Charles II after his Restoration and
> installed on the site of the Eleanor
> Cross (see page 98) which had been
> destroyed under Cromwell. Today it
> is rather overshadowed by Nelson's
> Column and its richly carved plinth
> is sadly neglected, but it has been
> there since about 150 years before
> Trafalgar Square was thought of.
> Charles has managed to keep his
> seat if not his head.*

ordained by God. An infant prince (the future Charles II) is shown supported by England and Scotland, while Minerva, Roman goddess of wisdom, holds the crowns of the two kingdoms over him. It is undeniably beautiful but, given that Charles's entire lack of wisdom in his dealings with Parliament led to his having his head cut off less than 20 years later, it is also screamingly ironic.

When, in 1642, Charles's disputes with Parliament made civil war inevitable, he left Whitehall and didn't set foot in the Banqueting House for seven years. After being taken prisoner at Newark (see page 239), he was tried for treason in Westminster Hall – a charge he refused to answer because he didn't recognise the authority of a secular court. He was nevertheless found guilty and condemned to be beheaded outside the very building that he had decorated to display his own and his family's glory.

A scaffold, covered in black, had been set up; it was a cold January day and Charles is said to have worn thick underwear – or, in some accounts, several shirts – so that no one would see him shivering and think he was frightened. The lifelong stammerer made a short, dignified speech in which he recanted not one iota of the views that had brought him to this premature end.

The rest of Whitehall Palace burned down in 1698 and the reigning monarch, William III, removed the court to St James's Palace. The Banqueting House somehow survived unscathed, which is more than can be said for the dynasty to whose misguided revels it was home.

73

THE ROYAL OAK, BOSCOBEL
Charles II

TWO YEARS AFTER CHARLES I was beheaded in Whitehall
(see previous entry), his son, aged only 20, had gathered
sufficient Scottish support to be crowned King Charles
II at Scone (see page 92) and to raise an army to invade
England in an attempt to put himself on the throne
there too. His rather makeshift force was no match for
Oliver Cromwell's New Model Army, however, and
the last battle of the Civil Wars – at Worcester on
3 September 1651 – turned into a rout. Some 3,000
men were killed, 10,000 Royalists were taken prisoner
and Charles was forced to flee.

Riding through the night, he arrived at Boscobel in
Shropshire. Here he took shelter in a loyal supporter's
home, known as White Ladies after the abandoned
priory next door (there are still substantial ruins, said to
be haunted – but presumably not by Charles, who died
34 years later and 150 miles away). He next attempted
to cross into Wales but, finding the Severn too heavily
guarded, famously returned to Boscobel and hid in an
oak tree while Cromwell's men searched for him in
the grounds below. The tree wasn't even in a wood:
according to an account said to be in Charles's own
words, it was 'a great oak, in a pretty plain place, where
we might see round about us; for the enemy would

certainly search at the wood for people that had made their escape'. The tree 'had been lopt some three or four years before, and being grown out again very bushy and thick, could not be seen through'. Charles had with him enough bread, cheese and small beer to last the day; he watched the enemy soldiers 'going up and down, in the thicket of the wood', but remained undetected.

More adventures followed as he tried to reach the coast and escape to France: with a thousand-pound bounty on his head and the threat of execution hanging over anyone found helping him, he dressed as a servant, darkening his skin with walnut juice to disguise the fairness that would betray him as an aristocrat, having his long hair cropped short and riding a horse whenever possible to conceal his great height. There are many tales of how Charles's quick wits stood him in good stead: once when he was staying in the servants' quarters of an inn he nearly betrayed himself by not knowing how to set up a spit over the kitchen fire. 'I am a poor tenant's son,' he said promptly. 'We rarely have roast meat.'

But the story of hiding in the oak tree is the one that remains in the public imagination. Today's Boscobel Oak is a descendant of the original; it stands in the middle of an open field and is surrounded by railings that stop souvenir hunters from despoiling it – you have to content yourself with buying a sapling from the gift shop. The hunting lodge where Charles spent the night of 6 September remains, and you can still marvel at how uncomfortable he must have been in the priest's hole, hiding in case the Roundheads decided to come back and catch him unawares.

Those wanting to follow in the footsteps of the royal escape can take a little over 600 miles to do it: that's the length of the Monarch's Way, a way-marked path that traces Charles's journey north from Worcester to Boscobel, then south towards Bristol, across the Mendips and finally across the South Downs to Shoreham. The less energetic can simply stop for a drink in one of the many Royal Oak inns scattered about – it remains one of most popular pub names in England.

Charles eventually escaped to the Continent, where he spent nine years in exile. Cromwell became effectively head of state, receiving the title Lord Protector of the Commonwealth of England, Scotland and Ireland and retaining it until his death in 1658. Despite his views on a hereditary monarchy, he arranged for his son to succeed him, but Richard Cromwell seems to have had none of his father's authoritative qualities: he held on to power for a mere nine months. Within another year, Charles II was back in London and raring to go.

74

THE JEWEL HOUSE, TOWER OF LONDON
Charles II

IT USED TO BE NOTHING MORE than a barracks, but today the Waterloo Block in the Tower of London is better known as the Jewel House and it houses the largest set of royal regalia in the world. The oldest item in this fabulous collection is the 12th-century spoon, used during the coronation ceremony to anoint the monarch with holy oil, but most of what you see today dates from the coronation of Charles II in 1661. Why? Because in addition to 'slighting' practically every castle mentioned in this book and many more besides, Oliver Cromwell destroyed all the trappings of monarchy he could lay his hands on – an act of anti-royal vandalism that included melting down the 'monuments of superstition and idolatry' that most of us would call the Crown Jewels.

When Charles II was restored to the throne in 1660, he set about bringing back all the pomp, ceremony and ritual that had been abandoned during Cromwell's Commonwealth period. Samuel Pepys, present at Charles's coronation the following April, was so struck by its magnificence that he wrote:

*...besides the pleasure of the sight of these glorious
things, I may now shut my eyes against any other
objects, nor for the future trouble myself to see things
of state and show, as being sure never to see the like
again in this world.*

In order to achieve this splendour, Charles obviously
had to have a whole new set of regalia made, at the
phenomenal cost of over £12,000. The highlight from
1661 is St Edward's Crown, named in honour of Edward
the Confessor. Now set with semi-precious stones
dating from the coronation of George V in 1911, it
weighs a headache-inducing 5lb and is used only for the
act of coronation itself.

But there is much more to Charles II's regalia than
a crown, however splendid it may be. There are two
Sovereign's Sceptres, one of which contains the massive
530.2-carat diamond known as Cullinan I. There's the
orb, there are swords, there are altar candlesticks, an
altar dish, chalices and some 13 maces. Today, three of
these have ceremonial roles in the Houses of Parliament,
but the 10 on display in the Jewel House make an
impressive array. Around 5ft long and weighing over
17lb each, they could cause a lot of damage in the
wrong hands.

Charles II isn't the only monarch represented
here – we seem to update the Crown Jewels at every
opportunity. At the time of his coronation, Charles had
no queen; he married the Portuguese princess Catherine
of Braganza the following year and she was never
crowned. So the Queen Consort's regalia was made for

James II's wife, Mary of Modena, crowned alongside her husband in 1685. Mary's Coronation Crown no longer exists, but her State Crown is still with us and boasts four crosses and four fleurs-de-lis, all made of diamonds, and a circlet of sizeable pearls.

Then there is the Small Diamond Crown created for Queen Victoria after she was widowed, and huge crowns made for the coronation of George V and Queen Mary in 1911. And in case you think all this is a bit tasteful, there is a vast and incredibly showy golden punch bowl commissioned by George IV (who else? – see page 288). Fully 3ft in diameter, it is capable of holding 144 bottles of wine. George was known to give lavish parties, and it's understandable that he would have pulled out all the stops for his own coronation, but goodness knows whose job it was to wield the ladle, which is correspondingly enormous, or to lift the bowl itself, which weighs over 500lb when it's empty.

Can there be a jewel in the crown of the Crown Jewels? If so, it has to be the Imperial State Crown. This dates from the coronation of George VI in 1937, though it replaced several earlier versions. The monarch wears it to leave Westminster Abbey after the coronation, and also for the annual state opening of Parliament. About half the weight of St Edward's Crown, it nevertheless contains the Cullinan II diamond, which weighs over 300 carats. Above this, front and centre, sits the Black Prince's ruby, said to have been worn by Henry V at the Battle of Agincourt, while the sapphire set into the top reputedly belonged to Edward the Confessor. Even Oliver Cromwell didn't manage to get rid of everything.

75

THE NATIONAL HORSERACING MUSEUM, NEWMARKET
Charles II

MOST OF WHAT MOST OF US know about Charles II
is related to his nickname, the Merry Monarch. He
famously had innumerable mistresses (see, for example,
the story of Lady Castlemaine on page 188), enjoyed
music and dancing, and allowed theatres to reopen after
they'd been closed under Cromwell's Puritanical regime.
And, as almost everything about Newmarket is only too
pleased to tell you, he invented horseracing.

Well, not strictly true – Henry VIII had a racing
stables at Greenwich and there was racing in Chester in
his time. Worried about the shortage of cavalry horses,
he also built up a royal stud, importing animals from the
Continent to improve quality. As armour became lighter,
so did the horses, and with reduced size came increased
speed, so that they were suitable for racing.

James I was an enthusiast, too, but it was Charles II
who established the sport as we know it, even riding
in races himself. He held the first race meeting at
Newmarket at Easter 1666 and was so taken with the
area that he rebuilt James's dilapidated palace and moved
his court there twice a year. He thus instituted the idea
of a spring and an autumn 'meeting'. He replaced the

existing Long Course – 8 miles – with a Round Course half the length; it began and ended near the winning post on what is now the July Course.

Today, the July is one of two racecourses in Newmarket; the other's name links it more closely with its royal patron. The Rowley Mile derives from another of Charles's nicknames, Old Rowley, which itself came from the fact that he had a favourite stallion of that name. Near the entrance to the course, a statue of the King elaborately dressed and with a King Charles spaniel at his feet, reinforces the connection: the inscription says that his 'patronage of Newmarket led to the town becoming the home of horseracing'.

On the site of the royal stables today is the National Horseracing Museum, which pays tribute to all the sport's royal enthusiasts, from Henry VIII to Elizabeth II. A slightly surprising inclusion is Queen Anne, who founded Ascot racecourse in 1711: the first race ever run there – for a prize of 100 guineas – was Her Majesty's Plate, and Ascot still has a Queen Anne Enclosure. The Newmarket museum also, of course, pays tribute to the non-regal greats of the sport,

FOR MORE ABOUT
NELL GWYNNE
Another place Charles II liked was Winchester. When he visited the city, protocol suggested he should stay at the Bishop's Palace; the bishop, however, was less keen to welcome Nell. Fortunately, Charles had a loyal courtier who lived a few miles away, at Avington Park, and who spent a considerable sum extending his house to provide suitable accommodation for the King and his mistress. You can still stroll through some of the rooms and grounds where Charles dallied with the woman Samuel Pepys called 'pretty, witty Nell'.

both equine and human, and shows you how to choose your own colours should you ever find yourself the proud possessor of a racehorse.

Across the road is all that remains of Newmarket Palace itself, now called Palace House and the home of the Fred Packard Museum and Galleries of British Sporting Art. Some of its collection is much as you might expect: the works of the 18th-century sporting painter George Stubbs, and Sir Peter Lely's portrait of Charles mounted on a fine grey stallion (could it be Rowley?). But there are also delightful surprises, such as the gold teapot given as a prize for the King's Plate at Leith racecourse in 1736, and a painting by the caricaturist John Leech, who illustrated some of the works of Dickens, showing two ladies in wide hooped skirts in the throes of what is obviously a vicious game of croquet. You can't help thinking that Charles would have approved: he'd have had his arms around the waist of one of them, showing her how to direct her mallet.

Which brings us back to his mistresses. A rumour that an underground tunnel gave discreet access from the palace to the nearby home of Nell Gwynne is unsubstantiated, although a little whitewashed terrace just off the High Street bears a plaque identifying Nell Gwynne's House and another Nell Gwynne's Cottage. Perhaps it is only the 'discreet access' aspect of the story that is in doubt.

76

SEDGEMOOR
The Duke of Monmouth

*The Duke of Monmouth is in so great splendour
at Court, and so dandled by the King, that some
doubt, that, if the King should have no child by the
Queene (which there is yet no appearance of), whether
he would not be acknowledged for a lawful son.*

SAMUEL PEPYS, 1662

AFTER CHARLES II'S DEATH in February 1685, his
brother James II's reign had a shaky start. Charles had
no legitimate children but acknowledged a number
of illegitimate ones of whom the eldest, James, Duke
of Monmouth, was now 35. Born in Rotterdam to a
woman named Lucy Walter, he came to England after
his father's Restoration and was known and popular
there. He claimed (though never proved) that his parents
had been secretly married and that he was therefore the
legitimate heir to the throne. And, most importantly
– unlike his uncle James – he was a Protestant.
Even before Charles died, there had been various plots
to put Monmouth on the throne, with the result that
he had prudently retreated from England and was back
living in the Netherlands. From there, before James had
been on the throne six months, he brought a tiny army

to land in Lyme Regis and make its way north, with a view to capturing England's second city, Bristol, then marching towards London. The idea was that a rebellion in Scotland, led by the Duke of Argyll, would take place at the same time and divide Royalist attention.

But Argyll was badly prepared, James got wind of the plot and the Scottish revolt was suppressed almost before it began. Monmouth was on his own. Although supporters were flocking to him and a proclamation issued in Taunton on 18 June declared him king, he was at the head of what its most ardent admirers would have had to call an undisciplined rabble. James, on the other hand, had a well-trained army, lots of military experience and a very able second-in-command in the form of John Churchill, the future Duke of Marlborough (see page 266). Monmouth's forces were cornered on the bleak and rather featureless lowlands of the Somerset Levels, at a place with the boggy sounding name of Sedgemoor.

The rebels were annihilated. They had planned a surprise night-time attack on the Royalists, but failed to find the stepping stones that would have taken them across one of the deep drainage ditches or rhynes on the moor. A Royalist scout spotted them, the alarm was sounded, the efficient Royalist army was deployed in no time and that was the end of that.

Thanks to modern drainage, Sedgemoor is less gloomy and less treacherous than it was three centuries ago, when a few tiny reed-covered 'islands' stood only a few feet above the surrounding peat. The progress of the battle was recorded in great detail, so interested visitors

(and those who care to read the signboards) can work
out how the armies were deployed and how the action
took place. Those who are happy just to have a look
round can walk to the monument and read the rather
odd – and surely pro-Monmouth – inscription:

> *To the glory of God and in the memory of all those*
> *who doing the right as they gave it fell in the battle*
> *of Sedgemoor 6 July 1685 and lie buried in this*
> *field or who for their share in the fight suffered*
> *death, punishment or transportation. Pro patria*

They can also ponder the rather uncomfortable fact that
1,384 men lie buried in a mass grave beneath their feet.

Those who find the place bleak can take refuge
in the church of St Mary at Westonzoyland, just down
the road, where some 500 prisoners were held after the
battle and where a Battle of Sedgemoor visitor centre
opened in 2017. However you choose to glean your
information, there is no doubt that Monmouth was one
of those who suffered punishment and death. He was
beheaded on Tower Hill only nine days after the battle;
allegedly it took the executioner several blows (perhaps
as many as nine) to do the job. A few months later – at
the 'Bloody Assizes' presided over by the notorious
Judge Jeffreys – almost 150 of his supporters were
sentenced to hang and some 800-plus to be transported
to the West Indies. The remains of those who were
hanged were displayed around the country to discourage
anyone else planning to rebel against the king. You might
have thought James' hold on the throne would be secure now...

77

ST JAMES'S PALACE
James II

ST JAMES'S PALACE IN LONDON isn't open to the public; it is a working palace, the home of various members of the Royal Family and the formal home of the Royal Court – ambassadors and high commissioners from around the world are still accredited to 'the Court of St James's'. You can walk past it, though – it's in Pall Mall, not far from Clarence House (see page 294) and Buckingham Palace (see page 322) – and admire the symmetry of the Tudor brick building, commissioned by Henry VIII as a smaller and less formal palace than nearby Whitehall (see page 242).

St James's was a favoured residence for much of the Stuart period and James II was one of several future monarchs to be born here. In early life, he proved himself an excellent solider and, after Charles II's Restoration, became, as Duke of York, a successful commander of the Royal Navy. Charles put him in charge of the fire-fighting during the Great Fire of London and he earned admiration for his courage – Pepys describes him as riding 'with his guard up and down the City to keep all quiet' and another eye witness wrote that he had 'won the hearts of the people with his continual and indefatigable pains day and night in helping to quench the Fire'.

But this period of popularity didn't last (Pepys speaks disapprovingly of James neglecting his duties in order to go hunting or dally with his mistress); when, in the 1670s, it became known that he had converted to Catholicism some years earlier, anti-Catholic fever reached new peaks.

Nevertheless, when Charles died in early 1685, James succeeded him. We have seen (page 254) that his reign started badly, but there was one ray of hope for the anti-Catholics. James' only surviving children, the future queens Mary II and Anne, had – at the politically astute insistence of Charles II – been raised as Protestants; in addition, Mary, the elder and her father's likely successor, was married to a staunch Protestant, the Dutch Prince William of Orange. But the girls' mother had been dead some years and James had married again, this time to an Italian (and Catholic) princess called Mary of Modena. At the time of his succession, the couple had no surviving children, but in 1688 Mary of Modena gave birth to a boy – who, now that James was king and could raise his children as he chose, was obviously going to be a Catholic.

This child, another James, had an inauspicious start to life: it was rumoured that he was not royal at all. Instead, it was said, he had been smuggled into the Queen's chamber in St James's Palace in a warming-pan, in order to seem to be the desired heir. This was either, depending on which version you prefer, to replace a stillborn child or because the Queen, being past child-bearing age, hadn't been pregnant at all. In fact, although James had turned 50, Mary was not yet 30 and there is no reason to suppose that this far-fetched story is true (though the bed involved can still be seen in Kensington Palace).

The arrival of a Catholic heir brought the various crises of James' reign to a head. Not only had he allowed Catholics freedom of worship; he had given them colleges at which to study and jobs in the service of the Crown. Nowadays we would call this religious tolerance; in the 1680s it was horrific.

Across the Channel, William of Orange thought the same thing. Parliament invited him to come to England and remonstrate with his father-in-law; William arrived with an army. James, despite his considerable military experience and prowess, seems simply to have panicked. Mary of Modena and her baby escaped to France; James quickly followed them, according to tradition throwing the Great Seal of the Realm into the Thames on his way – a symbolic gesture suggesting he thought that affairs of state would grind to a halt without it.

They didn't. What came to be known as the Glorious Revolution was over and no Catholic has sat on the British throne since. Legal discrimination against Catholics continued into the 19th century – they were, among other things, forbidden to hold public office, join the armed forces or purchase land. Perhaps the weirdest of all these restrictions, passed in William III's time – that no Catholic could own a horse worth more than five pounds – was mercifully short-lived.

78

HAMPTON COURT
William III and Mary II

WILLIAM AND MARY WERE FIRST COUSINS (his mother, also Mary, was James II's sister), so William had a substantial dose of Stuart blood – enough to insist that he would be King Regnant, ruling equally with his wife, rather than a mere Prince Consort. With this deal on the table, and with an eye to her Protestant religion once again holding sway in Britain, Mary seems quietly to have overcome any reluctance she may have felt at deposing her own father and ousting her half-brother from the succession. Britain's only diarchy – two rulers of equal status, as opposed to a *monarchy*, which has only one – had begun.

Neither of the royal couple seems to have cared for their palaces at Whitehall or St James's, but they were very taken with the site of Hampton Court and invited star architect of the day Christopher Wren to renovate it for them. What he produced was a Baroque wonder. From the moment you enter it, you are meant to be impressed. The main staircase is adorned with murals by Antonio Verrio, who had also worked at Windsor Castle and Whitehall Palace; it depicts a contest between Julius Caesar and Alexander the Great for favour of the gods. (Julius and Alexander were born over 200 years apart, so you should be aware that this is an allegory, designed to convey that William, too, was a great general.) The Presence Chamber and Privy Chamber, where the King received ordinary members of the court and more privileged visitors respectively, each contain a throne-like chair on a dais, topped by a rich crimson canopy that makes you wonder how it is being held up. In the Withdrawing Room, the tiniest inkling of informality sneaks in – there is still an imposing chair, but no canopy. But throughout the State Apartments, gloriously over-the-top painted ceilings, heavily curtained beds and walls hung with portraits reinforce the message: this is a place fit for a king. And queen. There is only one disarmingly intimate note: tucked away in a tiny side room is a portable 'close stool' – a velvet-padded seat fastened to what looks like an old tea chest, discreetly concealing a chamber pot. The Hampton Court of the 17th century was notoriously lacking in 'facilities', but at least the King was able to make himself comfortable in comfort.

WHILE YOU'RE HERE

Don't miss the Chocolate Kitchens, on a much smaller scale than Henry VIII's vast rooms. In William and Mary's time chocolate was a newly fashionable drink among the privileged classes; Their Majesties had it served to them at their levées, *the audiences they gave to a chosen few while they were dressed ceremonially for the day. Preparing the chocolate was a messy and labour-intensive business, finished off by a specialist who poured it into gilded pots ready to be served.*

Lots of the beauty of Hampton Court is outside. Henry VIII installed real tennis courts and the game is still played on the Stuart replacements; Charles II created the Long Water – a canal/lake that seems to stretch as far as the eye can see and is now embellished with the Jubilee Fountain, installed to mark Elizabeth II's Golden Jubilee in 2002. But the greatest credit must go to William and Mary. Their Privy Garden, its outlines marked by rows and rows of carefully trimmed mini-conifers, is clearly designed to be viewed from the first floor (where Their Majesties lived and held court). Looking at it from ground level you lose the effect, but from above the attention to detail and symmetry are unmissable. Mary was – of all things for a devout 17th-century queen – a keen botanist who collected exotic plants from as far afield as South Africa; some of these (or, let's be honest, more likely some of their descendants) are still on display in her Orangery in the summer. While you're passing, pause to admire the Great Vine – a truly vast specimen, the largest in the world, planted by Capability Brown in 1768 and still bearing tasty Black Hamburg grapes.

Mary died of smallpox in 1694, when she was only 32, and so was unable to enjoy Hampton Court at its most glorious. When she and William took the throne, the arrangement had been that either would continue to reign after the death of the other and it was William who saw their project through to fruition.

> *The Queen [Mary], upon observing the pleasant situation of the palace, proposed a proper improvement with building and gardening, and pleased herself from time to time, in examining and surveying the drawings, contrivances, and whole progress of the works, and to give thereon her own judgment, which was exquisite.*
>
> CHRISTOPHER WREN

79

GLENCOE
William III

THE FIRST IMPRESSION YOU HAVE as you drive through Glencoe is that it is haunted. Even if you don't know what happened here, you have a shivery feeling that it was something bad. And you are right: it was no battle; it was a massacre.

William III, although small of stature, asthmatic and sickly, was a born soldier. And, despite the architectural and landscaping wonders for which he was responsible at Hampton Court (see page 260), he was not a nice man.

Whether he was nice or not, however, it's not to be supposed that the Scots would take kindly to him: he had, after all, supplanted the Royal Family whose lineage – as Kings of Scots – they could trace back to 1371. From the word go, there were plots in both Scotland and Ireland, backed by the Catholic Louis XIV of France, to restore James II. Before he became King of England, Scotland and Ireland, William had been waging war against Louis; he defeated James at the Battle of the Boyne in Ireland in 1690; now it was time to sort out the Scots. The Scottish government – still at this stage separate from the English one – was instructed to get the leaders of the Highland clans to swear allegiance.

The branch of the Clan MacDonald that lived in Glen Coe was a troublesome bunch, known for cattle rustling, raids on their neighbours and general disregard for the law of the land. One man in particular had had enough of them – John Dalrymple, Master of Stair (that's the name of a village in Ayrshire, not a set of steps). A Protestant Scottish Lowlander who in 1691 was joint Secretary of State over Scotland, he was an active promoter of the idea of a union between Scotland and England.

Despite their unruliness, the MacDonalds had every intention of taking the oath – it would have been foolhardy not to – but first they had to free themselves from their sworn allegiance to James II. This wasn't accomplished until late in December 1691 and the deadline for the new oath was 1 January, with severe reprisals threatened against anyone who failed to take it. Dalrymple, aided by the weather, but also employing his own bureaucratic dawdling tactics, engineered that MacLain of Glencoe, leader of that branch of the clan, be delayed; when MacLain arrived late, Dalrymple refused to accept his oath. He then ordered that the MacDonalds be punished for their treason: everyone under the age of 70 was to be put to the sword.

Dalrymple sent members of the Argyll Regiment, commanded by Captain Robert Campbell, a representative of a clan that was the MacDonalds' greatest enemy, to carry out his orders. The instruction to Campbell – signed by a senior officer, Major Robert Duncanson – includes the words 'by the Kings speciall command, for the good & safety of the Country'. There can be little doubt that William knew what was going on.

The soldiers, who, to be fair to them, surely *didn't* know what was going on, were billeted in the homes of the MacDonalds: the pretext for their being there at all was that they were collecting taxes, in which case this wasn't an unusual arrangement. Then, on the night of 13 February, having at last received their true orders and with a blizzard howling outside, they murdered 38 MacDonalds, including MacLain, in their own homes, which they then burned down. Some 40 more escaped onto the freezing mountainside and perished there.

The subsequent investigation resulted in a cover-up of Watergate-like proportions. If Dalrymple had committed an act of 'slaughter under trust', as it was called, then William III must be held responsible too, and that would never do. Dalrymple lost his job as Secretary of State, but not his prominence in government circles. Ten years later, Queen Anne made him an earl. Just don't mention his name – or that of Robert Campbell – to a Scot.

Today, Glen Coe (it's usually spelled as two words, with Glencoe being the name of the village at its mouth) is a part of a designated National Scenic Area that also includes Ben Nevis. A long, steep-sided valley with the River Coe running through it, it's a popular spot with walkers, climbers and tourists generally. It's spectacularly beautiful and the waterfalls are dramatic. You put on solid shoes, pack sandwiches, take the dog and enjoy breathing healthy Highland air. But where it narrows further into the Pass of Glen Coe, you shudder. Those 78 dead MacDonalds are still there somewhere and they aren't happy.

80

BLENHEIM PALACE
Anne

FOR SOME REASON, ANNE is one of our enigmatic monarchs: the things that most people know about her are that she had a huge number of pregnancies but no children who lived beyond the age of 11, and that she became so inordinately fat that she had to be buried in a square coffin. (In fact, she was swollen with dropsy, but the problem for the undertakers was the same.)

The connection between Anne and Blenheim Palace may seem a tenuous one: its construction wasn't finished until after she died, she never visited it and it was never intended that she should live in it. But it was built at her instigation and with some of her money, as the gift of a grateful nation to the Duke of Marlborough after his victories in battle; and it would never have been built at all were it not for her close friendship, even infatuation, with Marlborough's duchess, better known to history as Sarah Churchill.

The battles Marlborough won were part of the War of the Spanish Succession, a complicated business in which England and later Great Britain's concern was to prevent a grandson of Louis XIV of France becoming King of Spain and creating a powerful Catholic alliance in Europe. (I say 'England and later Great Britain' because the great milestone of Anne's

reign was the union between England and Scotland, and
it happened while the war was going on.) England was
in a state of political upheaval, with the predominantly
Protestant Whig party less devoted to the war than the
predominantly Catholic Tories, who accused the Whigs
of prolonging it for their own ends and bankrupting
the country in the process. Anne, who understood
the concept of a constitutional monarchy better than
many of her forebears, refused to ally herself with one
party or the other. That said, the fact that her Catholic
half-brother, the 'Pretender' James Stuart, was living
under Louis' protection and was recognised by him as
the rightful King of England was a further reason for
wanting to limit France's power.

It's the Battle of Blenheim (1704) that is forever
associated with the man who had started life as plain
John Churchill Esquire and ended up owning a palace.
Blenheim is the only palace in Britain that was built
neither for a royal nor for a bishop or archbishop. But
to be fair, briefly, to the Marlboroughs – they're not
easy people to like – that wasn't their idea: when Anne
proposed to Parliament that this gift be made, she
referred to a castle. But a castle tends to be fortified;
when the English nobility built themselves something
grand they called it a house. Both 'house' and 'castle'
were used to describe Blenheim in the early days; the
designation 'palace' – fitting for such a dazzling building
– became established in the 19th century.

Both the Marlboroughs were screamingly ambitious
(comparisons between Sarah and Lady Macbeth are
commonplace), and they employed the foremost

architect of the day, Sir John Vanbrugh – himself a man who liked to think big – and the foremost landscape gardener, Capability Brown. The design of the house is Baroque, monumental, heavily decorated outside and in – love it or hate it, you couldn't call it modest. The Great Hall measures over 40ft each way and a cathedral-like 67ft high, with a lavishly painted ceiling (by James Thornhill of Greenwich fame – see page 205) and richly detailed tapestries, all celebrating the Duke's victories. The library runs the length of one side of the building and contains some 10,000 books. In the park, a 134ft Column of Victory is topped by a statue of Marlborough clad as a Roman general and its inscription takes 23 lines to do justice to his achievements and virtues. You couldn't call that modest either.

It is, of course, in the nature of projects like this that the money runs out. Sarah, having for years been the second most powerful woman in England, interfered in political matters once too often and lost Anne's favour. At the same time, Marlborough's enemies in London accused him of corruption and he too was dismissed from his posts. He and Sarah left the country, state funding of Blenheim was withdrawn and no further work was done until their return, after Anne's death. Delays due to battles over rising costs (Sarah was notorious for her 'thriftiness', too) meant that the building itself wasn't completed until 1722, the year in which Marlborough died, and the chapel wasn't consecrated for another 10 years.

As for the War of the Spanish Succession, Louis XIV's grandson did become King of Spain, but the great Spanish Empire was cut up. For a few decades the skirmishes within Europe went back to being on a smaller scale.

MORE ABOUT ANNE

Elizabeth I wasn't the only monarch who failed to turn up when expensive preparations had been made for her visit (see page 216). Warwick Castle has a Queen Anne Bedroom which Anne never slept in; it earns its name because it contains a bed which, tradition has it, Her Majesty had sent from Windsor in 1704 in advance of her own arrival. For some reason the visit was cancelled but the bed remained and was formally given to the then Earl of Warwick by George III some 70 years later. There are conflicting versions of this story – some say that she died in this bed at Kensington Palace and that it somehow ended up at Warwick Castle after that – but whatever the truth of the matter the bed is a glorious creation, its canopy at ceiling height and hung with crimson velvet.

There's a portrait of Anne above the fireplace in the same room. The work of her court painter Sir Godfrey Kneller, it shows her in coronation regalia – every inch the queen, but very substantially built. Just the sort – and size – of woman who would have been more comfortable in her own bed and might well have sent it to a place she was obliged to visit.

The House of Hanover
1714–1901

81

St George's Church, Bloomsbury

George I

GEORGE I'S CLAIM TO THE BRITISH throne was another
tenuous one. His maternal grandmother Elizabeth was
a daughter of James I, so he was a second cousin of the
Stuart Queens Mary and Anne. Neither of these left
children to succeed them. Many people regarded Mary
and Anne's half-brother James, who had been spirited
away to France as a baby, as the rightful heir, but James
was a Catholic, and the Bill of Rights of 1689 debarred
Catholics from succeeding to the throne. There were all
sorts of things for the English to dislike about George.
He was a foreigner – his mother had married the
Elector of Hanover, a title the German-born George
had inherited in 1698 – and he never bothered to learn
much English. He divorced his wife for adultery and
imprisoned her for the rest of her life. There were also
any number of Catholics with a stronger claim to the
throne. But he was a Protestant, and to many English
politicians that was all that mattered. (Some of the Scots
took a different view, as we'll see on page 277.)

   Mind you, George had his tricky moments. The
South Sea Bubble, when a dubious joint-stock trading
company of which he was a shareholder collapsed

in spectacular fashion, involved him in a damaging corruption scandal; it didn't help his popularity ratings that his mistress had stood to gain substantial sums from the company, too. He was also at permanent loggerheads with his eldest son, the future George II. Without his canny First Lord of the Treasury, Sir Robert Walpole (generally regarded as the first Prime Minister, though he never held that title), things might well have fallen apart.

But for all his unpopularity, George has a fine monument in central London. Some 50 churches had been rebuilt after the Great Fire of 1666; in 1711 Parliament passed an Act allowing for the building of 50 more in or near the expanding Cities of London and Westminster. Several of the resulting churches were designed by the great Nicholas Hawksmoor, and St George's Bloomsbury is widely considered his masterpiece. It was on a difficult site, narrow from east to west (which is traditionally the long dimension of a church, leading up to the altar in the east); some 50 years after its consecration it was revamped, leaving little of Hawksmoor's design intact. But its crowning glory is still there. The steeple resembles a stepped pyramid and is based on a Classical description of the Mausoleum of Halicarnassus, one of the Seven Wonders of the Ancient World. It used to have two life-sized lions and unicorns, representing England and Scotland, fighting over the Crown – perhaps a little tactless, given that Jacobite unrest was still simmering away. The lions and unicorns were taken down in Victorian times on the basis that they were 'very doubtful ornaments' and in imminent danger of falling down; 21st-century replacements now cavort around the base of the steeple.

Above all this stands a statue of George I, dressed as a Roman soldier and posing as his saintly namesake – the patron saint of England to whom the church is dedicated. The statue was not completed until after George's death in 1727, so the idea that he has been lifted up to heaven in saintly guise may have been in someone's head. Opinions vary on the artistic merit of this adornment. The writer Horace Walpole, son of Robert, called it a 'master-stroke of absurdity', and an anonymous wit (or possibly Walpole himself) turned the absurdity into a rhyme:

> *When Henry VIII left the Pope in the lurch,*
> *The Protestants made him the head of the church;*
> *But George's good subjects, the Bloomsbury people,*
> *Instead of the church made him head of the steeple.*

Noble or nonsensical, it quickly became a landmark: William Hogarth's print 'Gin Lane', issued in 1751 and depicting the miseries of gin-sodden life in London's notorious slums, clearly shows George posing regally on his pyramid in the background. Today the area is much more built up than it was in Hogarth's day: to get a decent view you have to stand on the other side of the street and crane your neck a bit. Then you can form your own opinion. Or go into the undercroft, study the informative exhibition there and try to decide what on earth Hawksmoor thought he was doing.

KENSINGTON PALACE
George II

WILLIAM AND MARY ACQUIRED Kensington Palace in
1689, thinking – believe it or not – that its village
location would be good for William's asthma. They
enlarged it and laid out gardens; Queen Anne built
the magnificent Orangery. Victoria spent an unhappy
childhood there. In the 20th and 21st centuries it
has been the official residence of an array of royals,
from Princess Margaret to the Duke and Duchess of
Cambridge. But it had its 10-year heyday from 1727
to 1737, under George II.

George I spent a fortune doing up Kensington
Palace and producing the luxurious King's State
Apartments you see today, with their painted walls,
painted ceilings and bold colour schemes. Then his son,
George II, and daughter-in-law, Caroline of Ansbach,
made the apartments the centre of courtly life, *the*
place to see and be seen, in the early part of their reign.
Although brought up in Hanover, George II was eager
to embrace Britishness; unlike his father, he insisted
that English, not German, be the language of the
court and declared that 'if anyone would make their
court to him, it must be by telling him he was like an
Englishman'. Only the privileged were admitted to the
Privy Chamber and the King's Drawing Room, with its

lovely view over the Round Pond. But when they got there, there were parties, card games for high stakes, and musical entertainments – Caroline in particular was a great patron of the arts.

Moving from the King's Apartments to the Queen's gives an interesting insight into George I's character: estranged from his wife, he saw no need to splash out on rooms that weren't going to be used, so they remain much as they were in the time of the Stuarts. Queen Caroline acquired and arranged paintings and furniture to suit herself, but she didn't have the lavish thrones and richly painted ceilings that adorned her husband's quarters. The most impressive of her rooms is the Queen's Gallery: it's long enough for an energetic stroll, reminding you that delicate aristocratic ladies generally took their exercise indoors, rather than going out for a walk and risking catching cold.

What Caroline did have, however, was the Cupola Room, named for the shape of its uber-decorated ceiling. Centrepiece of the room is the floor-standing clock decorated with allegorical scenes and reputed to have cost £45,000 in the 1730s; it doubles as a musical box, playing the works of Handel, one of the many artists of the day whose career flourished under royal patronage.

Then, in 1737, Caroline died and the court at Kensington was never the same again. George II's grandson and successor George III disliked the place and relocated the court to Buckingham Palace, where it has been ever since. Victoria moved out as soon as she could. But for that brief decade, it sparkled.

83

CULLODEN
Bonnie Prince Charlie

THE NATIONAL TRUST FOR SCOTLAND has been busy lately: not content with providing an immersive experience of the Battle of Bannockburn (see page 106), it has done the same 150 miles further north, at Culloden. Both re-creations are engrossing, loud and rather bloody, the difference being, from the Scots point of view, that Bannockburn was a triumph and Culloden a disaster. On a crucial day in Scottish history – 16 April 1746 – some 1,500 men were killed in the space of an hour, two-thirds of them Jacobites ('followers of James'), and that was the end of any realistic attempt to restore a Scottish king to the throne.

The story began, as we have seen, back in 1688 when James II was deposed. A predominantly Catholic faction would have preferred to restore him, or to put his son, another James, on the throne. But at least the Scottish-bred Stuarts, in the persons of James II's daughters Mary and Anne, continued to rule. The Acts of Union passed during Anne's reign deprived Scotland of its Parliament, causing more resentment north of the border, and then in 1714 Anne died, leaving a German-speaking second cousin to take her place. James II was dead by this time, but supporters pushed the younger James – known by some as King James VIII and III but more familiarly as the Old Pretender – to invade and re-stake his claim to the throne. The timing was unfortunate, for Louis XIV, a staunch Catholic and notorious warmonger, died in 1715, leaving France with a five-year-old king and no immediate enthusiasm for backing a rebellion in Scotland. James was soon forced to retreat and the Rising of 1715 was over.

Fast-forward 30 years: Louis XV is grown up and prepared to support another attempt to restore the Stuarts. James is nearing 60, but he has a 24-year-old son prepared to lead an invasion in his name. At first, this is more successful than the '15 had been: the Young Pretender, Charles Edward, nicknamed 'Bonnie Prince Charlie', captures Edinburgh and advances into England, reaching as far south as Derbyshire before being advised that a powerful government force is marching against him. French support having failed to materialise, he retreats into Scotland, wins an encounter with the English army at Falkirk Muir, but can't capitalise on this victory and finds himself pursued by the Duke of Cumberland as far north as Inverness-shire. Here, marching through the night, he hopes to surprise Cumberland's troops, camped at Nairn. But his men become disorientated in the dark; they are also cold, wet and worn out by tramping 20 miles across rough moorland and through thick woods. The march is abandoned, the government

> **A GOOD TIME TO VISIT**
> *Special tours on 15 and 16 April – the eve and the date of the battle – explain the preparations the night before and the events of the day. Regular Living History presentations also re-enact the battle at other times of the year.*

troops have a good night's sleep and eat a hearty breakfast. By the time the two armies meet at Culloden, a piece of flat moor a few miles outside Inverness, the exhausted and hungry Jacobites have little chance. Charlie's inexperience as a tactician is exposed and his forces are rapidly routed.

Culloden was the last pitched battle on English soil and one of the most brutal. The aftermath was particularly bloody, too – Cumberland's pursuit of Jacobite survivors earned him the nickname 'Butcher' and hundreds were tried for treason, executed or transported. And Bonnie Prince Charlie himself? Turn the page to read what happened to him.

If, today, Bannockburn is tranquil and Glencoe haunted, Culloden, after all these years, remains overwhelmingly sad. It's a bleak place: exposed, windy and – in the middle of nowhere very much – subject to haunting silences that make the hairs rise on the back of your neck. It is also a war grave, where many of those who died here are buried and headstones mark the spots. A 20ft-high cairn honours their memory and coloured flags indicate where battle lines were drawn: red for the red-coated government troops; blue for the Jacobites. It's a place to be treated with respect: without anyone telling you to, you find yourself lowering your voice. Culloden is the place and the moment where a dream – a dream that had perhaps always been foolish and unrealistic, but had inspired many people for several generations – finally came crashing to an end. The Jacobite motto *tandem triumphans* – 'victorious at last' – could not have been more wrong.

84

THE ISLE OF SKYE
Bonnie Prince Charlie

Speed, bonnie boat, like a bird on the wing.
'Onward!' the sailors cry.
Carry the lad that's born to be king
Over the sea to Skye.

SO GOES THE SCOTTISH FOLK BALLAD known as 'The Skye Boat Song'. Unfortunately for his supporters, the lad – Bonnie Prince Charlie – wasn't born to be king at all. He lived more than 40 years after Culloden without bringing his claim to fruition.

If you go to Skye today, you'll find the Royal Hotel in Portree on the site of the old McNab's Inn. Here a young woman called Flora MacDonald said goodbye to the Prince, having brought him secretly to Skye from the Outer Hebrides, where he was hiding after his defeat at Culloden. The Prince, in woman's clothing, was disguised as Flora's maid. Flora then spent several days smuggling him across Skye and saw him off to the island of Raasay, from where he escaped back to France. On the Continent, he lived out his life in clichéd dissoluteness (drink, scandals associated with mistresses, a short-lived and unhappy marriage…). With England at war with France, a final chance for Charlie to take the throne came in 1759. Unfortunately, the French Foreign

Minister, planning to invade England with Jacobite support, met the no-longer-quite-so-bonnie Prince and was so unimpressed that he decided to go it alone. That same year the English defeated the French in two naval battles in quick succession, the invasion never happened and, as far as Charlie and the Jacobites were concerned, that was the end of that.

Keeping the Jacobite spirit alive on Skye is a small collection of Bonnie Prince Charlie memorabilia in Dunvegan Castle. The seat of the Clan Macleod throughout its 800-year history, Dunvegan is an impressive fortress perched on a crag overlooking a sea loch. One rather fun thing you can see in its collection is a Jacobite 'amen' glass. Amen glasses were made only from 1743 to 1749, and fewer than 40 survive. They were engraved with subversive messages proclaiming the owner's desire to see Charlie's father restored to the throne as James VIII of Scotland and ending with the word 'amen' or 'fiat', meaning 'so let it be'. Owners of such glasses, asked to drink a toast to the king, would pass the glass over a container of water, so that although they appeared to be loyal to George II they were in fact drinking to 'the king over the water', meaning James or Charlie, in exile in France.

> **WHILE YOU'RE HERE**
> *Heading back from Skye to Fort William on the mainland will take you past Glenfinnan. Here a monument marks the spot where 1,500 Jacobite troops gathered and Charlie raised his standard to signify the beginning of the 1745 Rising. The 60ft tower is topped by a single and rather poignant kilted Highlander. Nearby, if you feel you've had enough of lost causes, the Jacobite Steam Railway runs over the same spectacular viaduct that the Hogwarts Express used to take Harry Potter to school.*

85

THE STAINED GLASS MUSEUM, ELY CATHEDRAL
George III

IF YOU KNOW WHAT GEORGE III looked like, it's probably
because you've seen the portrait from the studio of
Allan Ramsay that's in the National Portrait Gallery
in London. It shows His Majesty in coronation robes,
flowing ermine cloak over glimmering gold suit, his face
rather expressionless, with prominent eyes and receding
hair covered by a tightly curled powdered wig. Ramsay,
the King's favourite painter, painted him in 1761, the
year of the coronation, and issued many copies – an
18th-century equivalent of the souvenir mugs and tea
towels that celebrate modern royal events.

In Ramsay's version, George is cut off at the knees.
Joshua Reynolds – more fashionable than Ramsay but
not enjoying royal patronage until after the latter's
death – produced a full-length portrait of the same
occasion, apparently based on Ramsay's but with the
addition of white-stockinged legs and shoes with silver
buckles. This portrait is in a private collection, but a
remarkable version of it is to be seen in the diminutive
but fascinating Stained Glass Museum on an upper floor
of Ely Cathedral.

George III in stained glass is the work of James
Pearson, an Irish-born artist who, in partnership with
his wife, enjoyed a considerable vogue in the late 18th
and early 19th centuries, producing work that can
still be seen in Salisbury Cathedral and the chapel of
Brasenose College, Oxford. His George III is remarkable
partly because of its size – at about 8ft x 5ft it's the
same size as Reynolds' original – but more because of
the technique involved. Pearson used coloured enamel
pigments to produce the glowing effect of garments and
backdrop, and he also used enormous pieces of glass, so
that the leads that held them together could be hidden
in the design. There are only about 70 pieces in the
whole thing, which means they average around 80 sq in,
not much smaller than a sheet of A4 paper. The result is
a bit like one of those higgledy-piggledy jigsaws made
for very small children, with pieces that butt up to each
other rather than being linked together, but the detail
is extraordinary.

While you're there, look out for the portrait of
Queen Victoria, produced after her death and showing
the gloomy figure she became in later life; and also one
of her grandson, Albert Victor, Duke of Clarence, which
she commissioned after his death in 1892 at the age
of 28. For some reason he's depicted in the guise of St
George, but with an arrogantly twirly moustache, and
you can see that, had he lived long enough, he would
have ended up looking very like his near relations Tsar
Nicholas II, Kaiser Wilhelm II and King George V. Ely
Cathedral is on the itinerary of every visitor to the area,
but the Stained Glass Museum upstairs is a hidden gem.

MORE ABOUT GEORGE III

Some 200 miles to the southwest, George III has a more conventional memorial, a statue erected in the streets of Weymouth by the town's grateful inhabitants. Known simply as the King's Statue, it stands, surrounded by palm trees, in a little park on a traffic island near the seafront. It shows His Majesty in the robes of the Order of the Garter, in front of a royal coat of arms, a crown and piles of books. Its colours are flamboyant, the plinth on which it is mounted is disproportionately huge and to say it is not to everyone's taste is to gloss over the numerous attempts that have been made over the years to have it removed. But George undeniably put Weymouth on the map. Believing that sea air would improve his health, he visited nearly every year from 1789 to 1805, staying in a house belonging to his brother, the Duke of Gloucester. He even tried the then avant-garde pursuit of sea bathing, after which the Queen announced that he was 'much better and stronger'. The court and the public flocked to follow his example, with the result that Weymouth became England's first seaside resort. Gloucester Lodge is still there, some of it converted into flats, but the pub that occupies part of the building is proud of its royal heritage.

> WHILE YOU'RE IN THE AREA
> *Just outside Weymouth, a white horse cut into the limestone hills of Osmington shows George III on horseback and can be seen for miles around. Measuring about 300ft in both directions and the only such horse in the country to be depicted with a rider, it dates from 1808 and celebrates the prosperity that the King had brought to the area. It's an oddity, certainly, but it's a lot more tasteful than the statue in town.*

86

ROYAL KITCHENS, KEW
George III

THE THING MOST OF US KNOW about George III is that
he 'went mad'. Not all of us would think of going to
Kew to find out more. In fact, that part of southwest
London has royal connections dating back to the
13th century and there were royal residences in Kew
from Tudor times. The merging of the royal estates of
Richmond and Kew in 1772 formed the basis of what
are now Kew Gardens. George III's mother, Augusta, the
Dowager Princess of Wales, spent a lot of time at the
Dutch House (so-called because of its gable-dominated,
Dutch-looking design), which is the most significant
surviving part of the old Kew Palace. With the help
of the architect William Chambers, she created the
Orangery and the Pagoda and substantially remodelled
the gardens themselves.

George III was taken ill at Windsor in the autumn
of 1788, in the first of the numerous bouts of apparent
insanity that would plague him for the rest of his life.
His doctors prescribed a 'change of air', choosing Kew
ostensibly because it had a private garden where the
King could take exercise without being overlooked;
equally likely, the London-based medics didn't want to
have to traipse out to Windsor every time His Majesty
needed them. Whatever the motivation, George was

confined to Kew for the next three months, allowed to see his wife and family only when his doctors thought it appropriate and subjected to such humiliating treatments as being forced to wear a strait-waistcoat, being tied to his bed, being given emetic tartar to relieve stomach cramps and having medication applied to his legs to create blisters and draw 'ill humours' out of the body. During this time – not surprisingly – he suffered periods of uncontrollable rage and others of weeping and low spirits. It didn't help that his doctors were at constant loggerheads over the best way to treat him, with one of them determined to 'break' him as if he were a wild horse. (To be fair, even the other doctors were shocked by this.)

It is now widely believed that George was suffering from porphyria, a rare hereditary disease of the blood, on which none of these treatments would have had any beneficial effect at all. In fact, it is likely that they did actual harm. Although the diagnosis of porphyria has recently been challenged, 21st-century analysis of samples of the King's hair has shown high levels of arsenic, which may well have been present in the emetic tartar and which would have made the attacks of 'madness' longer and more severe.

The newly revamped Georgian Royal Kitchens at Kew show how the building might have been in 1789. They're reached via a charming walled garden planted with the sort of fruit and vegetables that would once have fed the royal household (go at the right time of year and you'll see purple carrots), and you're greeted by liveried footmen and mob-capped kitchen maids.

Placards inside the kitchen complex give details of the foods that were stored in the wet and dry larders (joints of meat hanging from the ceiling and fish in barrels in the former; sugar, spices and wine in the latter) and the activities that went on in the bakehouse and the silver scullery.

Despite the luxuries at his disposal, during his illness George seems to have survived on tea, bread and butter and potatoes, and had frequent altercations with his attendants when he refused to eat; on 18 January 1789 he was allowed meat for the first time since arriving at Kew seven weeks earlier. Perhaps the most chilling snippet of information that you discover in the kitchens is that on 6 February he was allowed to use a knife and fork: presumably he had been literally spoon-fed by his attendants. It was also the first time he had had anything that might be described as a proper dinner. On that night the King and Queen – who were known for their frugality – sat down to a first course of barley soup, roast chickens, minced and broiled pullets, mutton pie, boiled perch, breast of lamb, salmi of duck and loin of veal, followed by a further eight dishes that included various meats and, at the same time, desserts. George was clearly on the mend. At the end of February the *London Gazette* announced that 'by His Majesty's command', the daily physicians' reports on his health were to be discontinued. It was his first official act as king for three months.

BRIGHTON PAVILION
George IV

IT'S BEEN DESCRIBED AS looking as if the Taj Mahal had
produced a litter of puppies, and certainly the Royal
Pavilion's many decorated domes and minarets are
a surprising sight in a seaside town. But they have
a certain symmetry and elegance, as you'd expect
from the work of John Nash (see page 292). It's
inside the Pavilion that Nash's royal patron's taste for
ornamentation has been allowed free rein and can leave
the visitor gasping.

The royal patron in question was the Prince
Regent, later George IV (he came to the throne in
1820, but had been Regent because of the madness of
his father, George III, since 1811).

It's easy to be rude about George IV – very easy
– but he was a dedicated patron of the arts and made
many important acquisitions for the Royal Collection.
We have him to thank for the fact that we (the nation)
own works by Rubens, Rembrandt and van Dyck, as
well as all the major artists, sculptors, furniture-makers
and jewellers of his day. But you always get the feeling
that George's generosity was more to do with a desire to
impress others than with any real kindliness. He wanted
everything to be luxurious, not just for the sake of its
beauty but to show that he had exquisite taste and that

he could afford it. Except that, as it happens, he couldn't. It was all paid for by grants from Parliament – which means, in the end, by the likes of you and me.

The Prince's extravagance – not to mention his scandalous private life – had started long before he became Regent. While he was still in his twenties, Parliament had granted him today's equivalent of over £18 million to pay his debts. He also went through a ceremony of marriage without asking his father's consent. This – let's call it an oversight – automatically invalidated the marriage, although the rigidly respectable George III would never have condoned it if he'd been asked: the bride, Maria Fitzherbert, was not only a commoner six years older than the Prince, she was twice widowed and a Catholic, ticking almost every possible box in terms of unsuitability.

What the Prince actually felt for Mrs Fitzherbert remains unclear – he is alleged to have worn her 'eye miniature' (an uncharacteristically discreet love token, depicting only the loved one's eye) hidden under his lapel; it was buried with him at his request. But he was forced to renounce her publicly in order to make a politically advantageous marriage. He had agreed to marry a cousin, Caroline of Brunswick, because it meant Parliament would increase his allowance, but he found her repugnant and the couple separated as soon as they had produced an heir. Both continued to create scandals wherever they went. Having been very handsome in his youth, the Prince became obese in middle age; this, his extravagance and his unpopular political views were a rich source of inspiration for the satirical cartoonists.

To go back to the Pavilion, George had a passion
for Oriental art: he made full use of hand-painted
Chinese wallpapers, chandeliers in the shape of lotuses
and carvings of flying dragons. All of these can be seen
in the Music Room, where Rossini once performed.
The Long Gallery is intended to resemble a bamboo
grove, although the background colour of the walls is
a more flamingo-like pink. But the *pièce de résistance* is
the Banqueting Room, where the combined effect of a
spectacular chandelier, paintings covering every available
wall space, a huge array of silver gilt tableware and a vast
table laid for a lavish meal frankly makes you want to
burst out laughing.

Although it is less extravagantly decorated, the
kitchen is a worthy support to this panoply of excess.
Two long tables are covered with the preparations
of a meal that includes numerous forms of game
bird, including a swan. Chickens roast on spits in the
enormous fireplace and shelf upon shelf is laden with
shining copper pans and dishes. On display is the menu
for a banquet held here under the auspices of George's
French chef, the great Marie-Antoine Carême; it begins
with five different sorts of soup, presumably to stop
the guests getting peckish waiting for the swan to be
brought in.

Shakespeare wrote about gilding refined gold,
painting the lily and adding another hue unto the
rainbow being 'wasteful and ridiculous excess'. Brighton
Pavilion wasn't built for 200 years after the Bard's death,
otherwise you'd have thought it was exactly what he
had in mind.

88

THE REGENT'S PARK
George IV

GEORGE IV'S LOVE OF LUXURY wasn't confined to
Brighton. As Prince of Wales in 1783 he acquired
what had been his grandfather's home, Carlton
House, between St James's Park and Pall Mall in
London, and Parliament granted him £60,000 to do
it up. Even though that is perhaps £6 or £7 million
in today's parlance, it wasn't enough and he was
granted another £60,000 12 years later. He spent it
on, among many, many other things, a huge Gothic
conservatory, a Gothic dining room and a Chinoiserie
drawing room. Throughout the several decades that
he lived here, he tinkered constantly with the design,
moving chimneypieces from room to room and, on
one occasion, ordering almost 2,000 yards of gold-
coloured satin and 800 yards of matching taffeta lining
for a planned redecoration that never happened. He
entertained lavishly, most famously in 1811 inviting
2,000 people to a grand fete to celebrate his becoming
Regent: not in the best of taste, considering that it had
happened because of his father's illness. That was his
mother's opinion, anyway – she refused to attend and
didn't let his sisters go either.

Carlton House was George's principal home until
he became king in 1820, when he decided he needed

something grander. He began to turn Buckingham House (as it then was), where his parents had lived, into a palace and, in due course, demolished Carlton House, replacing it with two expensive rows of houses now known as Carlton House Terrace. He then used the proceeds from their leases to help fund his continuing improvements to Buckingham Palace. Today, some of the stucco-fronted houses are the headquarters of businesses and learned societies, so you can get in to look at them if you know the right people.

An easier way to appreciate George's contribution to London architecture is to walk up Regent Street to the Regent's Park (its official name includes the definite article, though you rarely hear anyone use it). The land now occupied by the park was once a hunting ground of Henry VIII's; later it was leased by the Crown to tenant farmers. But when George became Prince Regent, he saw an opportunity to make money – by building elegant houses on the land and selling them off – and to make his mark as the future monarch by building himself a summer palace accessed by a processional route from Carlton House.

John Nash, the architect who had already done a lot of work at Carlton House, laid out the route: today's Regent Street follows his plan. The only survivor of the buildings that originally lined it is All Souls Church on Langham Place, but the terraces of houses Nash designed for the fringes of the park remain. Making the park circular was part of Nash's scheme, as was the introduction of the lake and the canal. Sadly, plans for the summer palace never came to fruition – it would have been quite something, if Carlton House and the Brighton Pavilion are anything to go by – but George lost interest and focused on Buckingham Palace instead.

Nash had planned 56 villas inside the park, but only eight were ever built. The unoccupied land was leased to various organisations, among the first being the newly formed Zoological Society, which moved in in 1828 and has been there ever since. One of its objectives was to build up a collection of animals that would 'interest and amuse the public'; in 1831 William IV obligingly presented it with most of the animals from the Royal Menagerie, which had been kept in the Tower of London since the time of King John.

Much of the early landscaping of the park survives, though one important change occurred in the 1930s, when Queen Mary's Gardens were laid out. Named after George V's consort, these contain London's largest collection of roses – some 12,000 plants, including 85 single-variety beds and examples of most of the classic and modern English roses. In the right season there's plenty to excite delphinium and begonia fans, too.

Many of the artefacts George IV acquired for Carlton House are in the Royal Collection and can be seen at Buckingham Palace and Windsor Castle. But if it hadn't been for his short attention span Central London's largest Royal Park would have been his private garden and we'd never have been able to enjoy it.

89

Clarence House
William IV

William, Duke of Clarence, was the third of George III's seven sons and for the first 50 years of his life had no thought of inheriting the throne. Like many royal younger sons, he embarked on a career in the Royal Navy. He took part in the American War of Independence, served under Nelson and attained the rank of rear admiral before retiring from active service at the age of 24. All of this earned him the nickname 'the Sailor King'. He subsequently held various honorary positions, including Lord High Admiral, but never heard a shot fired in anger again. Instead, for the next 20 years or so, he dabbled in politics, ran up enormous debts and unsuccessfully courted heiresses in an effort to redeem his financial position.

Then, in 1817, came a monarchic crisis. Princess Charlotte, the only legitimate child of the Prince Regent (soon to become George IV), died in childbirth and her baby died with her. Given the state of his marriage, George was unlikely to father another heir; the eldest of his brothers, Frederick, Duke of York and Albany (whose statue can be seen in Waterloo Place, just off the Mall in London), was also childless and living apart from his wife. Next in line was William, and at least his fertility was not in doubt: he had lived for 20 years with an actress named Dorothea Jordan, by whom he had 10 children. With Charlotte's death, William, in better health than either of his elder brothers, suddenly stood a good chance of becoming king one day. Producing legitimate heirs became a matter of urgency.

Just eight months later – and only weeks short of his 53rd birthday – he married a German princess, Adelaide of Saxe-Meiningen, who was half his age. Happy and lasting though the marriage was, it didn't serve its primary purpose: neither of its two children survived infancy. George III's fourth son, the Duke of Kent, was more fortunate: he too rushed into marriage when he turned 50, but he sired a daughter, Alexandrina Victoria, known to future generations by her second name.

Securing the succession was not the only reason for William's marriage – he was still heavily in debt and Parliament promised to increase his allowance if he settled down. Once he could afford it, he set about building himself and Adelaide a new home. He employed his eldest brother's favourite architect, John Nash (see page 292) to create a three-storeyed stucco mansion in the Classical style, incorporated into the Tudor buildings of St James's Palace. Although nothing like as extravagant as anything Nash had produced for the Prince Regent, Clarence House obviously suited William's simpler tastes: he opted to stay there, rather than moving across the road to Buckingham Palace, when he became king.

For become king he did, aged 64, when George IV died in 1830 (brother Frederick had gone three years earlier). William's seven-year reign is notable for two hugely important political developments: the Great Reform Act of 1832, which extended the franchise and redrew outmoded constituency boundaries; and the abolition of slavery throughout the British Empire. How much William had to do with either of these measures is unclear: he was not deeply involved in politics and may have been opting for a quiet life.

William died aged 71 in 1837 and Adelaide, never in good health, spent the rest of her life moving from one supposedly salubrious place to another. Since then Clarence House has been occupied by a succession of royals, including Queen Victoria's mother, the Duchess of Kent; the Princess Elizabeth and the Duke of Edinburgh before she became Queen Elizabeth II; Queen Elizabeth the Queen Mother after her daughter's succession; and the Prince of Wales and Duchess of Cornwall. Various extensions and alterations have been made over the years: William IV created a first-floor passage so that he could walk into St James's Palace, where official business was conducted; Princess Elizabeth and her husband, married at a time of post-war austerity, used their wedding presents – including a mahogany sideboard and four side tables given by her grandmother, Queen Mary – to furbish the house; and the Queen Mother built up a considerable art collection which visitors can still admire (as long as they are there in August, the only time the house is open to the public). But as its name suggests, it's a house rather than a palace – a place where a humble sailor with no aspiration to be king could have felt at home.

90

OSBORNE HOUSE
Victoria and Albert

QUEEN VICTORIA'S GERMAN HUSBAND was a busy man.
Not only was he fascinated by the arts and sciences,
he wanted to put them to practical use. He designed
a model farm and dairy at Windsor and established a
kitchen garden that meant the royal household was self-
sufficient in fruit, vegetables and flowers all year round.
When he and Victoria wanted a peaceful retreat where
they could spend the summer with their young family,
he designed it himself. Victoria had fond childhood
memories of the Isle of Wight, so in the mid-1840s they
bought a house there and set about extending it. Having
sold the extravagant Brighton Pavilion to fund the
project, Albert employed Thomas Cubitt, the architect
responsible for the new façade of Buckingham Palace,
and produced an Italian palazzo. Your first impression,
looking at the house from a distance, is that if the
producers of the 1960s television series *The Prisoner*
hadn't chosen to film at whimsical Portmeirion, they
could just as successfully have set it at Osborne.

    Albert's choice of style was influenced by the
pleasant climate and the fact that the view reminded
him of the Bay of Naples; Victoria wrote that it was
'impossible to imagine a prettier spot'. Osborne's
views are perhaps its most appealing feature: there are

WHILE YOU'RE IN THE AREA
A well-preserved Norman keep, dating back to the reign of Henry I, Carisbrooke Castle played a role in the civil war between Stephen and Matilda (see page 60) and in the 14th- and 15th-century Hundred Years' War against France, when it was raided five times in the space of 35 years. But its most important royal 'visitor' was Charles I, imprisoned here for nearly a year in 1647–8. He had been under house arrest in a number of places since the Scots had handed him over to the English Parliament in January 1647. During this time various proposals and negotiations had tried and failed to establish a form of constitutional monarchy that would be acceptable to all concerned; in November, Charles escaped to the Isle of Wight, where he thought the governor was on his side. Instead, he found himself a prisoner yet again. Two attempts at escape failed, the first for the farcical reason that he got stuck trying to climb out the window, the second – more conventionally – because someone betrayed him. You can still see the window through which that second attempt was to have been made.

terraces all over the place, all overlooking the sea. For the same reason, there are huge plate-glass windows in the downstairs reception rooms, making Osborne – unlike so many stately homes – gloriously light. Albert's practicality extended to kitchens, bathrooms and the like: he made sure they were properly equipped and conveniently placed. And he used his own knowledge of landscaping to lay out the grounds, installing a cottage imported from Switzerland where he taught his children the art of market gardening (he taught them the finances, too, and paid them for their produce).

Albert died of typhoid fever at Windsor on 14 December 1861. He was only 42, and Victoria was famously overwhelmed by grief. She went to Osborne for Christmas and stayed there for two months; she wore black for the rest of her life and ordered that Albert's rooms be kept exactly as he had left them, his clothes and books ready for him to return at any moment. She spent time at Balmoral and Windsor, too, earning herself the nickname 'the Widow of Windsor' and causing one disgruntled subject to post a notice on the railings of Buckingham Palace, her official residence, announcing 'these commanding premises to be let or sold in consequence of the late occupant's declining business'. But it was Osborne, where Albert's imprint was stamped on every room and every flowerbed, that drew her most often. William Gladstone, becoming Prime Minister in 1868 and anxious that the Queen should return more openly to her duties, wrote, 'There is no doubt that Osborne during the [Parliamentary] Session is the great enemy.'

He never really succeeded in breaking the spell. Victoria was at Osborne for extended periods during most summers and most Christmases for the rest of her life. Unwell at Christmas in 1900, she died there on 22 January 1901. Her funeral took place at St George's Chapel, Windsor; on the first stage of her journey from the Isle of Wight her body was borne back to the mainland on a royal yacht named, perhaps inevitably, *Alberta*.

91

BALMORAL CASTLE
Victoria and Albert

NOT SIX YEARS AFTER they bought Osborne House (see page 297), Victoria and Albert decided that they needed a Highland retreat as well as an island one. They had fallen in love with the Scottish Highlands when they first visited a few years earlier; when the opportunity to acquire the lease on Balmoral Castle came up, they took it, paying £30,000 – about £4 million in today's terms – for a property they had never seen. They then discovered that the house was too small for their growing family and Albert, as was his wont, set about designing a new one. As a result Balmoral has some 40 rooms, including a vast ballroom, on the ground floor alone. Its architectural style is officially known as Scots Baronial – a sophisticated way of saying it looks like a castle, with a touch of Disney's Fantasyland thrown in.

Ever since Victoria's time, Balmoral has been the place where the Royal Family can 'be themselves'. Long before the advent of paparazzi and the invention of the long lens, Victoria felt the need for a private retreat: she described Balmoral as 'Paradise in the Highlands'. And who can blame her? Having been extended over the years, it is today a 50,000-acre estate of stunning scenery, grouse moors and salmon fishing in the River Dee, and it is still where the Royal Family spends two months every summer.

Victoria and Albert had an idealised view of Scotland, drawn more from the wildly popular (and wildly romanticised) novels of Sir Walter Scott than from any grasp on the hardness of life in a cold climate. Wanting everything to be as Scottish as it possibly could be, they decorated their new home with tartan carpets, tartan cushion covers and tartan tablecloths. They introduced a tradition that has endured ever since of having the bagpipes played outside the Queen's window every morning – not the way everyone would choose to start the day. And Albert – German-born, let's not forget – designed the Balmoral tartan which only privileged members of the Royal Family are entitled to wear. Its mix of red, grey and black reflected the granite of the Aberdeenshire scenery. He may have loved it, but a painting of him dressed in full Highland regalia – plaid socks, sporran, huge cairngorm brooch, you name it – shows him looking rather embarrassed.

When Albert died, the memorial Victoria had erected to him at Balmoral took the form of a cairn. Although cairns are most frequently erected in memory of the dead, the royal couple had already built a purchase cairn to celebrate their acquiring the estate, and one to mark the marriage of their eldest daughter, another Victoria; thereafter, the Queen continued the tradition for another seven of her children. Unsurprisingly, Albert's is the grandest of them all. It's not a mere pile of stones, but a symmetrical, disciplined pyramid, its base 42ft square, one foot for each year of

WHILE YOU'RE HERE

The local parish church – Crathie Kirk – is where the Royal Family attends services. There has been a church on the site for over 1,000 years, but this one, built in the local granite, dates only from 1893, when Queen Victoria laid the foundation stone. She also donated two stained-glass windows and various other features, from the communion table to some of the bells, were also royal gifts.

The best known name in the churchyard is that of the ghillie John Brown, made famous by the film Mrs Brown. *His gravestone describes him as 'the devoted and faithful personal attendant and beloved friend to Queen Victoria'. There is a life-sized statue of John somewhere in the grounds of Balmoral, but you have to look for it: Edward VII disapproved of his mother's friendship with this lowly person and had the statue removed from the prominent position she had given it.*

Albert's life, with a fulsome dedication to the 'great and good Prince Consort' from 'his broken-hearted widow'. There are newer cairns, too, to mark Elizabeth II's Diamond Jubilee in 2012, and a walk round them – permitted when the Royal Family is not in residence – offers glorious views of the estate and gives a good idea of why Victoria and Albert fell in love with both the place and the good, clean Highland air.

It was so calm & so solitary as one gazed around, that it did one good & seemed to breathe freedom & peace making one forget the world & its sad turmoil.

QUEEN VICTORIA'S JOURNAL,
8 SEP 1848, HER FIRST DAY
AT BALMORAL

92

ALBERT'S MEMORIALS
Victoria

WE'VE SEEN (PAGES 297 AND 300) that Victoria's husband
Albert liked a project. Perhaps his most lasting
achievement was to sponsor the Great Exhibition which
took place in Hyde Park in London in 1851, the first of
its kind to be envisioned on an international scale. The
Crystal Palace, built for the occasion (and subsequently
moved to South London, where it burned down in
1936), was nearly 2,000ft long and housed 15,000
exhibitors from all over the world. In just under six
months, over six million visitors paid to see everything
from huge pneumatic lighthouses to the Koh-i-Noor
diamond, lent by the Queen. The result was a profit of
£150,000 – close to £13 million in modern terms.

Albert wanted these vast profits to be used for the
continued enlightenment and edification of the public;
money was ploughed into the area south of Hyde Park
sometimes disparagingly referred to as Albertopolis. The
buildings that resulted include the Victoria and Albert
Museum, the Science Museum and (although they were
built after Albert's death) the Natural History Museum
and the concert hall that bears his name. Few individuals
have contributed more to making knowledge and
culture widely available in Britain than the German-
born Albert.

It's fitting, then, that the memorial built opposite the Albert Hall to commemorate his premature death in 1861 should pay tribute to this. The lead architect was the great Gothic Revivalist Sir George Gilbert Scott, and in a career not noted for its understatement he arguably reached his apotheosis here. Every adornment – and there is no shortage of them – makes reference to science, the arts or the international nature of Albert's interests. At each corner of the ornate gold- and-red railing stands a statue representing one of the continents, its people, their activities and their animals (the American bison is particularly dramatic). The base of the monument is adorned by the so-called Frieze of Parnassus, in which 187 carved figures depict celebrated artists, writers, musicians and architects – Parnassus being the home of the Muses in Greek mythology, the inspirational goddesses of the arts. Above this, a gilded Albert sits on a throne beneath a canopy roof adorned with mosaics and four triangular pediments depicting painting, sculpture, architecture and poetry.

There are further statues representing the cardinal and Christian virtues and other arts and sciences; and topping it all off are pointed turrets, the tallest of which reaches a height of 176ft – 6ft higher than Nelson's Column. The memorial cost the equivalent of about £12 million in today's money and a similar sum was spent to restore it in the 1990s, in one of the most complex restoration projects ever undertaken.

The only way to get inside the railing and see the memorial close up is to take a tour (on the first Sunday of the month from March to December). Failing that, go on a sunny autumn day, when the glinting of the golden statue and the golden railings is matched by the glow of the leaves on the nearby trees. You'll forget what an extraordinary piece of excess this is and, just for a few minutes, be persuaded that it's beautiful.

ANOTHER ALBERT MEMORIAL

The memorial in Kensington Gardens is not the only expensive tribute Victoria had erected to her beloved husband. As you leave St George's Chapel, Windsor (see page 141), you pass the door of the Albert Memorial Chapel and, although you aren't allowed in, it's impossible not to pause and gape. The chapel knocks the London statue for six in terms of High Victorian over-the-top style. Everywhere you look you see gold mosaic and marble, but surprisingly the highlight is not Albert's cenotaph (the word means an empty grave – he is actually buried in Frogmore, in Windsor Great Park, in the mausoleum Victoria had created for the purpose). No, the real eye-catcher is the tomb of the Duke of Clarence and Avondale, Victoria's eldest grandson, who died of influenza in 1892, aged only 28. This is the work of Alfred Gilbert, most famous as the sculptor of the statue known as Eros in Piccadilly Circus, and he has really gone to town here. Mexican onyx, a statue of St George leaning on a sword that is taller than he is and a bronze grille adorned by 12 pairs of pirouetting angels, each supporting a saint. Not to everyone's taste, but undeniably…opulent.

THE 20TH AND 21ST CENTURIES

93

SANDRINGHAM
Edward VII

EDWARD VII DESCRIBED SANDRINGHAM as 'my favourite place to be'. And it is easy to see why. If you visit Buckingham Palace or Windsor Castle as a paying member of the public, you probably think, 'Wow! What a lot of amazing stuff!' At Sandringham, the reaction is more likely to be, 'This is cosy.' You pass through rooms where you can imagine the Royal Family has just had tea, using the china collected by Queen Alexandra or Queen Mary.

In about 1860 Victoria and Albert decided that when their eldest son turned 21 (as he did in November 1862), he should have a country home of his own. The search for a suitable property was halted only briefly when Albert died in 1861; the Queen wanted the purchase to go ahead as he would have wished and in due course the Prince of Wales – Albert Edward, known as Bertie until he came to the throne as Edward VII – inspected and approved Sandringham.

At the same time, Victoria and Albert had been seeking a suitable bride for their playboy son, and found her in Princess Alexandra of Denmark. She and Bertie were married in March 1863 and the so-called 'People's Palace', then being built in North London, was renamed the Alexandra Palace in her honour.

From the word go
Sandringham was the couple's
home whenever royal duties
permitted. Over the next six
years they had five children
(a sixth, born a few years
later, lived only one day); the
Georgian house they had
bought became too small for
their needs, was demolished
and replaced with the existing
one. Bertie continued to
improve it and spend money
on it for the rest of his life;
both his son and grandson, the
future George V and George VI,
wrote that they loved the place,
and Elizabeth II has spent
Christmas there throughout her
reign. It was from Sandringham
that George V broadcast the
first Royal Christmas Message,
in 1932, and Elizabeth the first
televised one in 1957.

If the house is likable, the
gardens are a delight, with
woodland walks, dramatic
rockeries and elegant avenues
of pleached limes. At the end of one tree-lined walk,
a particularly rotund gilded Buddha, flanked by two
attendant lions, can't help but make you smile. In

> WHILE YOU'RE HERE
> *Having seen the house and gardens,
> don't miss the Sandringham
> Museum, housed in the old coach
> house and stable block. There are
> curios of all sorts, but the highlight
> is the collection of vehicles, from a
> 1939 Merryweather fire engine via
> a Rolls-Royce Phantom V used
> by Elizabeth II to an eco-friendly
> taxicab that until early 2017 carried
> the Duke of Edinburgh round
> London.*
> *Then take in the church of St
> Mary Magdalene, where the Royal
> Family attends the Christmas Day
> service. From the outside, it's a
> fine 16th-century example of the
> carrstone workmanship typical of
> this part of the country. But inside,
> it's worth spending a moment to
> take in the full glory of the silver
> altar and reredos and the silver and
> wood pulpit. These were presented
> to Alexandra by an American
> newspaper magnate as a memorial
> to Bertie: clearly no expense had
> been spared.*

another part of the garden and in a very different style, a statue of Old Father Time, with a beard like an Old Testament prophet and the wings of an avenging angel, is decidedly grim.

On the face of it, Bertie spent a long time in the wings: born only four years into his mother's long reign, he was 59 when he finally came to the throne. But when Victoria went into seclusion after Albert's death, he took on an active role as Prince of Wales. With an eye on access to the Suez Canal, under construction in the 1860s, he made an extensive tour of the Middle East, the first royal progress to be recorded by an official photographer. He gave public appearances a new and practical twist, opening the Mersey Tunnel and Tower Bridge, among others. Both as Prince of Wales and as king, he was popular; endearingly jovial to grand and not-so-grand alike, he was also a respected diplomat who worked – and smoked – himself to death, but never lost his love of the lighter side of life. His dying words are said to have been, 'Yes, I have heard of it. I am very glad' – because a horse of his had won at Kempton Park that afternoon.

94

BOGNOR REGIS
George V

NOT MANY PLACES IN ENGLAND are entitled to call themselves 'Royal'. Edward I granted Lyme a Royal Charter in 1284, allowing it to style itself *Regis* – 'of the king' – and there are perhaps 15 lesser known places with a similar privilege. Queen Victoria liked Leamington Spa so much she granted it the honorific 'Royal' in 1838; after her death Edward VII did the same to Tunbridge Wells in recognition of the fact that his parents and grandmother had been among the many who had gone there to drink the medicinal waters. Then in 2011, after a lull of more than a century, Wootton Bassett was recognised because of its proximity to RAF Lyneham and its role in repatriating the war dead from Iraq and Afghanistan.

But what about Bognor? It had become a thriving seaside town by the late 18th century, when sea bathing and taking the sea air were fashionable and said to be 'salubrious'. In the 19th century George IV's daughter Princess Charlotte visited several times and Queen Victoria liked it, calling it 'dear little Bognor'. But it had to wait until 1929 to achieve official recognition. George V had spent several months there the previous year, convalescing after a lung operation, and gave Bognor the title 'Regis' as a token of his gratitude.

Or did he? There are (at least) two explanations for
how he came to utter the oft-quoted words 'Bugger
Bognor'. The first is that, after he had recovered and
returned to London, the town petitioned him to grant
it royal status. When his private secretary delivered
the petition, George is said to have said, 'Oh, bugger
Bognor,' after which the secretary felt able to inform
the dignitaries of Bognor that His Majesty had been
graciously pleased to grant their request. The other is
that the King made the remark on his deathbed, when
he was assured that he would soon be well enough to
return to Bognor. Whether or not either of these tales
is true, they suggest that George's memories of his
convalescence were not entirely happy ones.

He had a gift for the pithy remark, though. During
World War I, the fact that he had a German grandfather,
Albert, and a German surname, Saxe-Coburg and
Gotha, aroused public animosity. He responded by
changing the royal surname to Windsor, and to H G
Wells' criticism of 'the alien and uninspiring court' with
the words, 'I may be uninspiring but I'll be damned
if I'm alien.' He made several visits to the Front and
he and his wife, Queen Mary, were the first royals to
make a habit of visiting hospitals, factories, dockyards
and other places where they came into contact with
'ordinary people'. Presiding also over the General Strike
of 1926, the Great Depression and Britain's first Labour
government, George has been credited with creating
the modern monarchy, making the Royal Family seem
less aloof and more in touch with its subjects. When he
was taken to see some poor homes during the General

Strike and learned with horror how little many people earned, he remarked, 'Is it possible that my people live in such awful conditions?...If I had to live in conditions like that I should be a revolutionary myself.' In 1932, he became the first monarch to deliver a Christmas Message', broadcasting on the radio from Sandringham – against his better judgement, but again accepting what he was assured was the will of the people.

Although he was frequently stigmatised as dull, he had become so popular by the time of his Silver Jubilee in 1935 that the occasion was one of national exultation. As he drove to St Paul's Cathedral amid cheering crowds, he is said to have remarked, 'I can't really understand all this; after all, I am only an ordinary fellow.' For many years afterwards there was a pub in Chatham, Kent, called The Ordinary Fellow, whose inn sign showed a coin bearing George's head.

As for Bognor, the house where the King stayed was pulled down after a fire in the 1930s and has had a housing estate built on its grounds, so the town's name is the only tangible souvenir of the royal visit. The Royal Norfolk Hotel, which has stood on the Esplanade since the 1830s, can apparently claim only one royal guest: Napoleon III stayed for a week in 1872, long enough to encourage the new owner to add 'Royal' to the Norfolk's name when he took over the hotel 14 years later.

95

FORT BELVEDERE
Edward VIII

ANOTHER OF GEORGE V'S many pithy remarks (see
previous entry) was 'After I am dead, the boy will
ruin himself in 12 months.' 'The boy' was his eldest
son, known as David when he was the glamorous
Prince of Wales and later as King Edward VIII. Was his
father right? George died on 20 January 1936; Edward
abdicated on 11 December. As the saying goes, you do
the maths.

The story is too well known to need much retelling:
Edward wanted to marry an American divorcee named
Wallis Simpson and this provoked such a political storm
that he abdicated rather than give her up. As king,
he was ceremonial head of the Church of England,
which at that time did not condone the remarriage
of divorcees if the ex was still alive. More importantly
in certain circles, divorce was considered rather
disgraceful, so – to employ the damning phrase of the
period – Wallis was 'socially unacceptable'. Not an ideal
description of a Queen Consort.

Edward was adamant, however, and his abdication
is the only instance of a British monarch voluntarily
surrendering the throne (although one or two, as we
have seen, have been forcibly removed).

The formal 'Instrument of Abdication' was signed at Fort Belvedere in Windsor Great Park, Edward's home since 1929. It had been built in the 1750s for, of all people, the 'Butcher' Duke of Cumberland of Culloden notoriety (see page 277); it was extended in the 19th century and used as a summer retreat or for informal dinner parties, with the unusual feature of a resident bombardier who fired a cannon to mark royal birthdays. With its crenellated terraces and turret serving no practical purpose, it can only be described as whimsical. The socialite Lady Diana Cooper, a contemporary of Edward VIII, remarked: 'It was a child's idea of a fort. The sentries, one felt, must be of tin.' But Edward loved it and renovated it, adding a swimming pool, a tennis court, a steam room, central heating and – remarkably for the 1930s – ensuring that every bedroom had a bathroom nearby. It became the place where he could spend time with Wallis away from prying eyes.

After his abdication, Edward was given the title Duke of Windsor and he spent much of the rest of his life abroad. He married Wallis in 1937 and, confounding the cynics, the marriage lasted until his death in 1972.

As for Fort Belvedere, it is leased by a Canadian billionaire, who entertains royalty (and royally) and has created a polo stud in the grounds. Sadly, unless you can cadge an invitation, it isn't open to the public. But it is a quirk of fate that Fort Belvedere is today in the Borough of Runnymede, Runnymede being where King John put his seal to Magna Carta (see page 79). True, John wasn't giving up quite as many rights as Edward was, but perhaps there is something in the water…

96

Dartmouth
Royal Naval College
George VI

ALMOST EVER SINCE there has been a Royal Navy – and
that's a long time, over 350 years – young male royals
have served in it. We've seen (page 294) how William
IV earned himself the nickname 'the Sailor King'. A
century later the future George V and his elder brother,
Prince Albert Victor, became cadets at Dartmouth Naval
College at the ages of 12 and 14 respectively, their father
believing that the navy was 'the best possible training for
any boy'. Later generations followed suit: both Edward
VIII and George VI attended Dartmouth, formally
known as the Britannia Royal Naval College – as did
the Duke of Edinburgh and his sons the Prince of Wales
and the Duke of York.

George VI was no scholar, though his boyhood
inability to concentrate may have been worsened by
his being a natural left-hander forced to write with
his right hand; this may also partly explain his famous
stammer. Whatever the reason, he came bottom of his
class at Osborne (the training school for junior cadets,
a sort of preparatory school to Dartmouth), failing
the key subjects of maths and engineering. He did
fractionally better at Dartmouth, reaching a high spot

of 61st place out of 67. Very much in the shadow of his
glamorous elder brother, he achieved the reputation
of being sensible, honest and reliable, though one of
his tutors wrote that it was 'rather like comparing an
ugly duckling with a cock pheasant'. He moved on to
active service at the beginning of World War I and was
mentioned in dispatches for his role at the Battle of
Jutland in 1916, but, suffering from a duodenal ulcer,
he was invalided out of the service shortly afterwards.
Undertaking royal duties as the Duke of York, he
reinforced his reputation for decency with his interest in
the plight of the poor; when he became king, his choice
of the name George (rather than his own first name,
Albert) underlined his reliability, linking him to his
popular grandfather and emphasising the continuity
of the monarchy after the upheaval of the abdication.

Dartmouth is a pretty little town, with steep hills
running down to a deep-water harbour. This offers an
easy and calm approach for ships, making it an ideal
place for novices to have a go at sailing. Its small size
and isolated location also appealed to the powers that
be: Dartmouth's adolescent cadets would not be exposed
to the dangerous temptations of larger ports. The first
students, enrolled in 1859, lived and trained aboard
HMS *Britannia,* a ship of the line launched in 1820
and taken to Dartmouth on her retirement (not to be
confused with the Royal Yacht *Britannia* which served
Elizabeth II for over 40 years and is now open to the
public in Leith).

By the beginning of the 20th century it was
apparent that the naval college needed to be larger and

more permanent; the distinguished architect Aston Webb was commissioned to design a suitable building. Webb's other work included the façade of Buckingham Palace and the Victoria and Albert Museum in London – he had a talent for the large-scale and the ornate, and his work at Dartmouth can best be described as palatial. Curving driveways lead through the parade ground to an entry staircase that any royal would be proud to mount. The main frontage has 37 bays – which means row upon row of mullioned windows, topped by bell towers and navy-themed carvings, including the prows of various historic ships. Under the parapet runs the inscription 'It is on the navy under the good providence of God that our wealth, prosperity and peace depend'. The style is reminiscent of the imposing Palladianism of earlier centuries; the result is dignified and confidence-boosting. A hundred years after the death of Nelson, Webb's building declared that this great island nation could continue to repose complete trust in her navy. At one time the college had about 500 naval cadets; today the figure is more like 300, but in a town with a population of 5,000 the college, from its imposing position on the hill above the harbour, dominates in more ways than one.

George VI's memory lives on, too: his uniform is on display in the Britannia Heritage Museum. It's said that his medals have been borrowed on more than one occasion by a senior officer taking the salute at a parade who has forgotten to put on his own.

97

GLAMIS CASTLE
Elizabeth, the Queen Mother

IF SCONE (SEE PAGE 91) IS A FAIRY-TALE castle, Glamis is more solid and schloss-like, though its many rounded turrets add a touch of Disney's Fantasyland. You approach, via the elegant Queen Mother Memorial Gates, along a mile-long oak-lined avenue, ready to be impressed. Originally an L-shaped hunting lodge, remodelled to its current form in the 17th century, Glamis has been the home the Earls of Strathmore and Kinghorne since 1372, when it was given by Robert II to Sir John Lyon, shortly to become his son-in-law. But its royal associations stretch back further than that.

At the start of Shakespeare's play, Macbeth is Thane of Glamis, so the murder of Duncan would have taken place here. History prefers to tell us that Duncan died in a battle against Macbeth's forces rather further north, near Elgin, but that didn't stop a later generation calling the Glamis guardhouse (built in the 15th century) Duncan's Hall. It was here that visitors to the castle would leave their weapons before being admitted to the castle proper, thus reducing the risk of any further assassination attempts. Modern-day visitors may be confused by the existence of Malcolm's Room, but this is a reference to Malcolm II – grandfather of Duncan and great-grandfather of the Malcolm who features in *Macbeth* – who died here in 1034, in unknown but probably not suspicious circumstances.

Although it doesn't lay claim to the ghosts of Duncan, Macbeth or either of the Malcolms, Glamis is said to be the most haunted castle in Scotland. The spectre with the nearest thing to a royal connection – because she was put to death by a king – is the Lady in Grey, Janet Douglas, who is sometimes seen sitting in the chapel. Guides will make ghoulish mileage out of warning you that she occupies a specific seat, perhaps the one you are sitting in at this very moment...

Janet was married to the sixth Lord Glamis, who died in 1528. The Clan Douglas had a long-running feud with the royal Stuarts, and James V saw the opportunity to be avenged on the family and to claim Glamis for himself. He accused Janet of witchcraft and imprisoned her in Edinburgh Castle, where – even in those superstitious times – popular outrage at the obviously trumped-up claims led to rioting in the streets. Nevertheless, she was tried, convicted and burned at the stake on Edinburgh's Castle Hill. Some 150 years later her ghost first appeared at Glamis, and today she is frequently seen sitting quietly (spoiler alert) at the back of the chapel, praying for eternal peace.

A similar pious hope is expressed in the drawing room, where the enormous fireplace dates from 1605 and commemorates the union of the Crowns of England and Scotland two years before. The decoration above it shows the English rose and the Scottish thistle supported by Hermes, Aphrodite and their offspring, representing the two kingdoms joined in harmony.

Food for discussion there, surely, particularly as the Strathmores of the following century were known Jacobites: they briefly housed James Stuart, the Old Pretender, during his unsuccessful attempt to regain the throne in 1715–16 (see page 278). His watch and sword are on display in the Glamis Gallery, though the guidebook acidly remarks that, if he left them in thanks for the Strathmores' hospitality, they weren't the most generous of gifts.

Despite all this history, visitors to Glamis are left in no doubt of its connection with the present Royal Family, for it is most famous for being the childhood home of Lady Elizabeth Bowes-Lyon, daughter of the 14th earl. In 1923 she married 'Bertie', Duke of York; in 1936 they became King George VI and Queen Elizabeth and, following her husband's early death, for the remaining 50 years of her life she was 'the Queen Mother'. Although she wasn't born at Glamis, the embroidered canopy over the four-poster bed in the royal bedroom records 10 births, the ninth of which is 'Elizabeth 1900'.

She did spend her honeymoon here, however, and seven years later it was here that she gave birth to her second daughter, Margaret, the first royal baby to be born in Scotland since Charles I's younger brother, Robert, in 1602. The set of apartments that were converted for the use of Elizabeth and Bertie can be seen today, with family photographs on display just as they might be in anyone else's living room. After all the haunting that has gone on in the early part of the tour, it's an endearingly homely touch.

98

BUCKINGHAM PALACE
Elizabeth II

THE EAST FRONT OF Buckingham Palace is so iconic,
so universally recognisable, that it is perhaps surprising
to learn that it is barely more than a hundred years
old. Indeed, the palace itself is less than 200 years old,
having previously been an unpretentious family home
that George III acquired for his young bride, Charlotte
of Mecklenburg-Strelitz, shortly after the royal couple's
wedding in 1761. Until then it had been known as
Buckingham House; once Charlotte moved in it became
the Queen's House and remained so until her eldest son,
George IV, coming to the throne in 1820, turned it into
something deserving of the name 'palace'. Although the
improvements his pet architect, John Nash, designed
were not completed until well after George's death,
the Grand Entrance, the Grand Hall and the huge
Picture Gallery were all conceived at this period. Today
Buckingham Palace is the monarch's official residence
and administrative headquarters. As such, it is one of the
few 'working palaces' remaining in the world, with state
banquets, investitures and audiences with visiting heads
of state all taking place here.

Despite the fact that Queen Charlotte gave birth to
14 of her 15 children at the Queen's House, and despite
George IV's improvements, in 1845 Queen Victoria

was complaining of the 'total want of accommodation for our little family' (she had had a mere four of her nine children by this time). She also felt the need for 'a room capable of containing a larger number of those persons whom the Queen has to invite in the course of the season to balls, concerts etc.' Further extensions were undertaken, which meant that one of Nash's most elaborate creations had to go. Work on the triumphal arch he had envisioned for the palace's forecourt had stopped when George IV died in 1830; the version that was eventually built was much less elaborate and lacked the bronze equestrian statue of George with which Nash had planned to crown it. Nevertheless, it was in the way of, and out of keeping with, Victoria's new wing; in 1850 was taken down and re-erected just to the northeast of Hyde Park, where it has given its name – Marble Arch – to the surrounding area.

Subsequent monarchs also added to the palace and its look: Edward VII oversaw the creation of the Queen Victoria Memorial, including the ornately carved gates that lead into Green and St James's Parks. Then in George V's reign came the new façade. The East Wing created for Victoria in soft Caen stone was by this time crumbling and filthy and in 1913 it was replaced by more durable Portland stone blocks, which, once they had been fronted by three pairs of bronze gates, gave the look that we see today.

Although the look belongs to George V, it is thanks to Elizabeth II and her husband, the Duke of Edinburgh – and to a disastrous accident – that the palace has become accessible in a way it never was before.

A devastating fire at Windsor Castle in 1992 inspired
the decision to open Buckingham Palace to the public
during the summer. The idea was to raise money to
help pay for repairs at Windsor; now that that has been
done, the half-million visitors who come every year
are contributing to the upkeep of the Royal Collection
– and taking the opportunity to admire many of the
objects in it. Much of the collection is 'held in trust by
the monarch in right of the Crown'. This may mean that
it actually belongs to us, but the security guards would
doubtless have something to say to anyone who tried to
take a painting or a wine glass home with them.

MORE FROM THE ROYAL COLLECTION

The Queen's Gallery in Buckingham Palace Road,
opened in 1962, is an almost-year-round opportunity
to view further items from the Royal Collection (and
to refrain from stealing them). Just along the road, the
Royal Mews display the many carriages used on state
occasions, along with the horses that draw them and a
number of the palace's motorcars, too. The highlights
are undoubtedly the Diamond Jubilee State Coach, first
used for the state opening of Parliament in 2014, and
the fairy-tale-like Gold State Coach, in which every
monarch since George IV has been driven to his or her
coronation. Jaw-droppingly lavish, these two vehicles
encapsulate all that is most spectacular about Britain's
royal heritage and sum up the reason
why citizens of republics the world
over come in droves to admire it.
Nobody does it better.

99

ALTHORP
Diana, Princess of Wales

NOBODY WHO LIVED THROUGH the days following the
death of Diana, Princess of Wales, in 1997 will ever
forget the unprecedented outpouring of public grief
that swamped the country. So it comes as a pleasant
surprise that the memorial to her at her childhood
home should be understated. Indeed, part of it is
so subtle that you miss it if you haven't done your
homework. You approach the house through an avenue
of oak trees, a parkland so beautifully Olde English that
you feel Charles II might be hiding here. In fact, the
oaks were planted after the Princess died: there are 36
of them, one for each year of her life.

The memorial itself is reached by a meandering
path that runs down from the house to the so-called
Round Oval Lake; it consists of an unpretentious
Classical-style pavilion with the name 'Diana' and her
dates of birth and death, 1961 and 1997, engraved on
its pediment. Inside is a bench on which mourners still
leave flowers, a simple marble silhouette of the Princess,
and two plaques, one alluding to her charity work and
the other bearing an extract from the speech given
at her funeral by her brother, Charles, Earl Spencer,
referring to 'the unique, the complex, the extraordinary
& irreplaceable Diana'.

And that is all there is to it. For some years there was an exhibition – a celebration of the Princess's life and legacy – in the stable block, but that has closed now. The grave itself is on an island in the middle of the lake which is not open to the public, and the rest of a visit to Althorp is concerned more with other, earlier members of the Spencer family (who have lived here for 20 generations).

The Spencers first came to Althorp in 1508, but their royal connections go back a good two and a half centuries before that. They make a motley list. The family is probably descended from Hugh Despenser, one of the barons who rebelled against Henry III (see page 82) – his grandson was the Hugh Despenser who was a favourite of Edward II (see page 101). The first Baroness Spencer was related to Lady Jane Grey and what is believed to be the only portrait of the nine-day queen made during her short lifetime is in the Althorp collection. And in 1647 Charles I was imprisoned at nearby Holdenby House but, because it lacked a bowling green, was a frequent visitor to the superior leisure facilities at Althorp. There is also a connection with the Churchill family: the first Earl Spencer's great-grandmother was Sarah Churchill, the favourite of Queen Anne (see page 266).

As you might expect, therefore, Althorp is a splendid country estate, a handsome Tudor building much revamped by the architect Henry Holland in the late 18th century. The architectural writer Nikolaus Pevsner described the Georgian Grand Hall entrance as one of the noblest in the county; the 115ft-long first-

floor Picture Gallery is both magnificent in itself and
houses a magnificent art collection; and the scarlet-
wallpapered Great Room, now used as a dining room, is
frankly stunning. Diana-watchers will be excited to find
a Princess of Wales bedroom, but it was named after
the future Queen Alexandra, wife of Edward VII, who
visited Althorp in 1863. At the top of the main staircase
is a portrait of Diana by the American painter Nelson
Shanks; in the less formal rooms you'll spot a few family
photos, but credit must be given to whoever decided
not to turn this gorgeous house into a shrine.

ANOTHER DIANA MEMORIAL
...is to be found in Hyde Park in London. It's called
the Memorial Fountain, but it's more a sort of water
feature, with water flowing down two channels in a
sloping oval of granite. On one side the water ripples
gently, on the other it bubbles vigorously, before the
two come together in a calm pool at the bottom – it's
said to symbolise the serene and the tumultuous aspects
of Diana's life. It was also designed to be accessible,
but when it first opened it caused controversy because
people slipped when paddling in the water. Today,
visitors are encouraged to sit on the edge and cool their
feet rather than venture further in, but pick your day
and you will see plenty of children, oblivious to killjoy
health and safety warnings, giggling as they frolic in the
water: a sight (and sound) of which the People's Princess
would surely have approved.

100

HIGHGROVE
Charles, Prince of Wales

Elizabeth II's eldest son – the longest-serving Prince of Wales in history – garnered a certain amount of ridicule in the 1980s for his support for complementary medicine and environmental issues, before either of these was mainstream, and for telling the world that he talked to his plants. He also took an interest in architecture, famously and controversially decrying a proposed extension to the National Gallery in London as being like 'a monstrous carbuncle on the face of a much-loved and elegant friend'. There were many who thought this was none of his business, but the remark served its purpose: that particular design wasn't built.

Posterity is likely to acknowledge that many of Charles's concerns were ahead of his time. He took an early interest in organic farming, founding the grocery brand Duchy Originals in 1990 to provide an outlet for his produce. In 1993 he began work on the experimental 'new town' of Poundbury in Dorset, with the intention of creating integrated communities of shops, businesses and housing in an urban rather than a suburban context: the emphasis was to be on pedestrians rather than cars, with the end result being carbon-neutral. The project has been much mocked, with the words 'Disneyland' and 'Marie Antoinette

at Trianon' recurring frequently and one national
newspaper describing the architecture as 'a merry riot
of porticoes and pilasters, mansards and mouldings'.
But 25 years on there's an increasing recognition that
Poundbury might just have something going for it.

Prince Charles's real achievement, though, is the
glorious organic garden he has established at Highgrove,
his family residence in Gloucestershire. Its wildflower
meadow has inspired imitations around the world
and led those who have the space to plant swathes of
alliums, ox-eye daisies and lady's bedstraw in the hope
of speeding Nature on her way towards creating a mecca
for bees and butterflies.

Like many great gardens, Highgrove is a carefully
planned assemblage of rooms, of which the walled
garden is perhaps the one in which you most want to
sit and let the cares of the world wash over you. You
pass through a door set into a Moorish arch to find a
network of flower and vegetable plots lined with neatly
clipped box. They're surrounded by mellow brick
walls supporting climbing roses and an abundance of
espaliered and fan-trained fruit. Apple trees entwine
above your head to form a tunnel leading to a moss-
covered fountain; at the right time of year sweet peas
and runner beans form archways, too.

The arboretum, with its 60ft larches and its rather
smaller maples, Persian ironwood and katsura, to name
but three, is best seen in autumn, when any shade from
delicate buttery yellow through oranges and scarlets to
purplish bronze is on offer. Then there are woodland
areas and spacious lawns, a cottage garden, a 200-year-

old cedar of Lebanon and a Thyme Walk boasting 20 varieties of thyme and lined with topiary of golden yew. There's the area known as the Stumpery, created from literally tons of old stumps, including gigantic sweet chestnuts whose roots have been described as resembling giant wisdom teeth extractions. Painful dental imagery aside, these have been woven into arches and edging for paths and flowerbeds to create something slightly eerie, slightly haunted, perhaps, but certainly magical.

Everywhere you turn there are elegant gateways, rustic seats, Ali Baba pots, mini temples and a vast range of sculptures, of which perhaps the crowning glory, at the end of an avenue of limes half a mile long, is the splendid Column Bird. Sitting atop a 50ft cast-iron column, this is a vast gilded creature, not quite a heron, not quite a phoenix, that looks as if it's about to take off from its untidy nest of gilded sticks and oak leaves.

For those of a meditative turn of mind there are quotations carved on tablets at the back of the temples:

> *Find tongues in trees, books in running brooks,*
> *Sermons in stone and good in everything*
>
> FROM SHAKESPEARE'S *AS YOU LIKE IT*

and

> *They think that virtue is just a word and a sacred*
> *grove merely sticks*
>
> FROM THE *EPISTLES* OF THE ROMAN POET HORACE

'Good in everything' may be going a bit far, but as you wander round Highgrove it's hard to spot anything you could dismiss as 'merely sticks'.

Bibliography

Barrell, A M D *Medieval Scotland* (Cambridge University Press, 2000)

Batey, Colleen E *Tintagel Castle* (English Heritage, 2016 edition)

Bolitho, Hector *The Reign of Queen Victoria* (Collins, 1949)

Brindle, Steven *Dover Castle* (English Heritage, revised 2015)

Brindle, Steven and Brian Kerr *Windsor Revealed: New Light on the History of the Castle* (English Heritage, 1997)

Buckingham Palace Official Souvenir Guide (Royal Collection Trust, 2012)

Carlton House: The Past Glories of George IV's Palace (The Queen's Gallery, Buckingham Palace, 1991)

Castor, Helen *She-Wolves: The Women Who Ruled England before Elizabeth* (Faber, 2010)

Clark, Jonathan *Clifford's Tower* (English Heritage, revised 2016)

Downes, Kerry *Hawksmoor* (Thames and Hudson, 1970)

Fowler, Marian *Blenheim: Biography of a Palace* (Viking, 1989)

Gardner, Juliet and Neil Wenborn (eds) *The History Today Companion to British History* (Collins & Brown, 1995)

Goodall, John *Richmond Castle and Easby Abbey* (English Heritage, 2016)

Hart, Vaughan *Nicholas Hawksmoor* (Yale, 2002)

Hibbert, Christopher *The Illustrated Story of England* (Phaidon, 2016 edition)

Historic Royal Palaces *Explore Hampton Court Palace* (Historic Royal Palaces, 2016)

Historic Royal Palaces *The Crown Jewels* (Historic Royal Palaces, 2010)

HRH the Prince of Wales and Candida Lycett Green *The Garden at Highgrove* (Weidenfeld & Nicolson, 2000)

Jenkins, Simon *England's Thousand Best Houses* (Allen Lane, 2003)

Longford, Elizabeth *Victoria R I* (Weidenfeld & Nicolson, 1964)

Macalpine, Ida and Richard Hunter *George III and the Mad-Business* (Pimlico, 1991)

Morgan, Kenneth O *The Oxford Illustrated History of Britain* (Oxford University Press, 1984)

Pattison, Paul *Deal Castle* (English Heritage, 2017)

Penn, Thomas *The Winter King* (Penguin, 2012)

Pugh, R B and Elizabeth Crittall (eds) 'House of Benedictine Monks: Abbey of Malmesbury', in *A History of the County of Wiltshire: Volume 3* (Victoria County History, 1956)

Spencer, Charles *The Spencer Family* (Viking, 1999)

Stacey, Nicola *Framlingham Castle* (English Heritage, 2015 edition)

Strong, Roy *Henry, Prince of Wales, and England's Lost Renaissance* (Thames and Hudson, 1986)

Taylor, Arnold *Discover Caernarfon Castle* (CADW, Welsh Government, 2015)

Turner, Michael *Eltham Palace* (English Heritage, 2015 edition)

Wilkinson, Josephine *Katherine Howard: The Tragic Story of Henry VIII's Fifth Queen* (John Murray, 2016)

Wilson, A N *The Elizabethans* (Hutchinson, 2011)

Acknowledgements

It's said of various bars around the world that if you sit in them long enough everyone you know will sooner or later pass by; I'm inclined to think that if you sit long enough in front of BBC4 you'll learn everything you could possibly want to know about anything. While I was researching this book, the BBC screened a number of documentaries that meant watching TV could be classified as work. I'm grateful to Helen Castor's *England's Forgotten Queen*, about Lady Jane Grey; Sam Willis's *Invasion!* and *Castles: Britain's Fortified History*; Dan Snow's *1066: A Year to Conquer England*; Clare Jackson's *The Stuarts*; and Andrew Graham-Dixon's *Art, Passion and Power: The Story of the Royal Collection*.

Most of the places I've written about have excellent websites, though Westminster Abbey's (westminster-abbey.org) stands out, as does the website of the Royal Collection (royalcollection.org.uk). The UK Battlefields Resource Centre (battlefieldstrust.com/resource-centre) is excellent on the subject of battles and how they were fought, and English Heritage in particular produces immensely useful guidebooks. I should also mention Kingston Museum, which is charming, informative and, in the best tradition of British museums, free.

When I was writing a book about cake some years ago, I was overwhelmed with offers to help me with my research. Cynics might wonder why. So I am particularly touched by the help I've received with *Bognor and Other Regises*, when cake was, at best, a sideline. Ann, Carol, Elaine, Gill, Jane, Julia, Lois, Lorraine, Niki, Rosey and Sheena generously acted as chauffeurs and travelling companions, shared their knowledge and their books and put up with my obsessions.

My thanks, as ever, to Rebecca for looking after me; to Helen for commissioning the book; and to Donna and the rest of the team at AA Publishing for seeing it through to publication and beyond.

Index